Dreaming

the Chase

Bobbi Patrick

To B. A. D.

1

Breezy Andrews had never thought about what a men's version of a wet t-shirt contest would be like until *he* walked in. The rain dripped off the dark messy curls from his hair and ran down the side of his cheek as he approached her desk. His soaking white tee stuck to his chest as he walked towards her in what felt like slow motion. She wished she could pause him like a DVR and absorb the brown-eyed specimen who now stood waiting for a hello.

"How can I help you?" she asked, sitting up straight and minimizing a webpage showing her humble bank statement on her computer.

"Are you the one I come to for a problem in my building?" he asked in a voice that sounded masculine, yet desperate for help.

"Sure am. As of June first, all four buildings somehow go through me," she said. Go through me? She was already questioning her word choice. "All four buildings are now owned by the wonderful Stevens Chicago Properties, so you can come through me for anything." She did it again, and even worse this time!

"Okay, well, I'm in the Dogwood Building and the power just went out," he said.

"Yep, ours did too. I think the whole area lost it there for a second. It's back on now, isn't it?" Uh oh, maybe this guy didn't know how to reset all of his clocks. She imagined herself guiding him around his apartment, working on every blinking 12:00 until they were all timed perfectly. She would teach him how the clock on the stove worked and then let him try. His large but tentative hands would need guidance from hers and then, once he finally got the right time, they would find their hands still holding, eyes meeting, lips—

"Well, can you help me with that, then?" he asked. Help him with what? What was he babbling about while she had written the perfect scenario on how to get into his apartment? It was something about laundry. She tried to recall the echoes of what his request was.

"It's just that everything stopped in the middle of the cycle and now I can't get it to start back up again without more quarters. I only have enough for the dryer." Okay, it was making sense. She really had to work on her listening skills while her heart was racing. Maybe it wasn't just her heart that had suddenly shifted into high gear.

"Sure thing, let me find my master keys and we'll head over there to see how to work it." Hormones 1, mouth 0. She reached under her desk for her umbrella, grabbed her purse and the keys, and wished again for the DVR pause button. He was using his shirt to wipe the water from his forehead, revealing one, two, three, and now there's four out of the six-pack. And the line! Good God, he had a line like it was drawn in by . . . her. Perfection. She didn't get to see it on the left side, but they had to be perfectly symmetrical, right? Why did this guy do laundry? Why did he even need clothes? How many years would it take for her to go to law school, run for local office, win, campaign for a bigger position, win, finally get elected to Congress and create a bill that said this guy was free from ever having to wear clothes? She paused as the glorious moment finally ended. Right click and save that to the hard drive.

"I'm Bree by the way, but you can call me Breezy. No, wait, that's backwards," she said. That'll show those hormones why they aren't in charge of talking. Was he not going to give a name? *I've got a few he could try. Sir-Abs-A-Lot would do until he finally showed some personality.* Maybe he was just one of those pieces of meat that she would keep for special occasions and—*oh my God, he almost rushed to open the door!*

"Thank you," she said. "I've got an umbrella we can share." Or he could just get wetter on the walk over and call it even.

"Oh, thanks," he said, awkwardly stepping under her little red umbrella. She only came up to his shoulder. His rather large shoulder. A shoulder that couldn't possibly be contained by his cheap white tee. The rain pounded the umbrella as the two made their way across the parking lot. At one point she jumped over a puddle and almost lost her black heel. He seemed to be in a hurry. Could this count as a date, please? It felt like the most romantic thing she had done in years.

Going on dates just wasn't something she did. There had been several guys she would've asked out over the years, but ever since the cafeteria incident her senior year in high school, she vowed never again to be the asker. The only time she was in a stable relationship was midway through college with Brad. Instead of romantic weekends and holidays, their love life consisted of staying over at each other's apartments and watching movies. It was so comfortably easy that neither of them thought of putting any effort into what they had. Eventually, when the sex became less frequent, it became more of an argument about who had to stay over at whose apartment. Guilt became the pillar for both of them, and by graduation they were in two different places. Instead of becoming Mrs. Brad King (she even loved his last name), she remained Bree Andrews.

Looking back, she had wasted those years on Brad—or rather, Brad had wasted those years on her, if she was honest about it. That relationship was a black hole of emotion. She blamed him during the relationship and then blamed herself afterwards. She wasn't ready to settle down and grow up. He went right into a successful business career with stability while she found herself alone but no longer a carefree college girl.

She glanced sideways and then back to a face and body that Brad's would've never competed with. "So how long have you lived at Dogwood—umm, what was it again?"

"Yeah, I'm in Dogwood," he said. *Your name, say your name!* She wanted to reach her free hand up to his head, move her fingers slowly down the side by his ear, and then guide his face right to hers. They finally reached the door as he once again opened it while she shook the droplets off of the umbrella. Inside, she led him down the hallway to the laundry room. Her company had made her endure a week of orientation training for the newly-acquired buildings. By habit, she opened the laundry room door as if she was giving one of her tours to a prospective renter.

"Your building is lucky. You get the new side-loading machines they just installed. I'm over in Parkview and we're still using washboards." *Maybe you'd be up for lending yours?*

"What?" He laughed. "That's not true." Finally. *Something.*

"Okay, maybe it's not that bad, but ours break down all the time and can't handle big loads like yours." For the love of God, who was supposed to be filtering this stuff? She turned away as the red swept across her cheeks.

"Oh wait." He opened the machine and pulled out a stylish pair of jeans. "Maybe it cycled through after all. I'm so sorry to drag you over here." Still no points in the genius category, but c'mon, who needs to judge? She watched as he carefully took out each article of clothing and threw it into the adjacent dryer. Different colors of short-sleeve shirts, a tank top, another pair of jeans—oh, and here comes the answer to the million dollar question: boxer briefs. Gray. Fairly new. Would she ever get to see them again? She stood there thinking to herself: *We shall meet again, my little gray friends.* Yes, she could've said goodbye and headed back to the office where she had clearly forgotten to leave any sort of sign on the door that said she would be right back. Oh well, who was going to come check out an apartment in the pouring rain right before rush hour on a Friday?

"Got everything? Beware of the stray sock, right?"

"Yeah." He bent down and reached his hand around. Nice. "Oops." He grabbed for one more thing and quickly tossed something small and pink into the dryer with an embarrassed smirk on his face. That was some girl's underwear! Some apparently tiny girl's underwear was in his laundry.

Just then the door opened and the owner of the mystery drawers walked in. "Quinn? What are you doing?"

Well, that answered that.

2

Justin had just set his keys down when a frantic knock began on his door. "Just a sec," he said, hanging up his wet jacket before opening it.

"What's up, sunshine?" he said as Bree made her way in.

"You will not believe this!" she said, gesturing for the right words.

"Did somebody hurt you? If so, I'll kick their ass. You're my number one homegirl and if I gotta put the smack down on a—" he went on as he headed over to his fridge. "Sorry, I've been listening to my old hip-hop albums."

"No. Shut up, seriously this time," she said. This usually meant there was a guy involved. The situations were rarer and rarer, but occasionally Bree needed just a bit of help when she met someone. She'd ramble on for hours about what to do and how to do it, and then it would never materialize to anything because she would chicken out when push came to shove-him-down-and-do-it.

"This guy. This amazing guy. Hell, there could be lots of amazing guys in the new buildings we acquired and I'm just stuck in the one with you," she said.

"Thanks, darling." The two were always cracking on each other.

"Anyway, he lives over in Dogwood. He needed help with his laundry because the power went out or something. So on the way over, we had a moment under my umbrella."

"Wasn't that a song in the sixties?"

"I think. But shut up!"

"So you made out with a resident in the rain?"

"No, listen! I wanted to, of course, but I didn't even know his name."

"Never stopped you in college. Boom!" Justin said, pretending to high five a group of imaginary people.

"Are you done?" She tried not to laugh, but he was so good at busting her chops and she would get even eventually. "So anyway, he's putting his laundry in the dryer and I see these tiny little panties or something." Justin started to open his mouth but she cut him off before he could shoot another insult at her. "Not a word!"

"But—" He had a good one.

"Anyway, in walks this hottest guy in the history of apartment living's girlfriend, and guess what?"

"You all had a three-way?" he asked in a perfectly calm voice.

"No, Jackass, she's butt ugly!" said Bree, finally getting it off her chest. This didn't surprise Justin. The other girl was *always* ugly, according to Bree. If she was taller, she was an Amazon. If she was shorter, she was a Munchkin. Bree was always quick to point out the flaws of other girls. Back in the early years of college, she wasn't bad, but certainly not flawless. As a close friend though, Justin knew his role wasn't to point out things like the extra weight, the teeth that needed braces, or the many what-were-you-thinking outfits. Actually, a few times he pointed out Bree's ridiculous outfits, but only in retrospect while going through old photos—never while she was still rotating them through her current wardrobe. As far as his looks—he would never tell her, but a few girls had asked him what *he* was doing with *her* while out at the bars before. Justin didn't have much trouble picking up women with his confidence. He didn't have any trouble setting them down either.

"Maybe they're just roommates, Bree. I mean, we used to live together, right?"

"Yeah, but there were six of us in a bigger house. This is different, and that building is mostly one bedroom apartments," she said. "I mean, this girl was pale, short, and bitchy."

"Is that it?" Wow, she didn't even say *Munchkin*.

"I mean, she had like reddish brown hair, no makeup and looked like a leprechaun . . . or a Munchkin!" There it was.

"I'd still hit it," Justin said. He had his own issues, opposite of Bree's. He could talk his way into a girl's heart and then laugh her out of her pants. He was a low maintenance kind of guy with a nearly-shaved head and clothes that looked good even wrinkled and dirty. Yep, he had the effortlessly attractive look down perfectly. If he didn't feel like shaving for three days: stylish scruff. If he wanted to go somewhere clean cut, he drew women in like a man in uniform. In their old college house Bree had the misfortune of sharing walls with Justin, and therefore knew his sexual routine as well as the sorority row he plucked his flavors-of-the-week from. Between the two of them there were some close calls on a few drunken nights, naturally, but for them to cross that line, alcohol was always the reason it almost did and then didn't happen. The first time, Bree threw up on Justin's bed and then cried. He returned the favor on New Year's Eve that same year after a midnight kiss led to a blacked-out walk upstairs. She cried again when that fell through. Both forced themselves to try to forget that anything ever happened, plus Bree wouldn't dare let herself go through a repeat of her little secret from high school that had already lost her a friend. Her relationship with Justin was strikingly similar to her teenage best friend Keith's. When she met Justin in college it was like having a bandage to patch up the loss of Keith. That whole cliché, "I don't want to ruin our friendship," might as well have been tattooed across her back. She had learned the hard way and would never take a chance like that again.

"You're gross," she said used to Justin's usual guy ways. "What could he possibly see in her?"

"Maybe she doesn't flake out when she has a chance to make a move?"

"What's that supposed to mean?" She knew what it meant. She could feel a touch of anger starting to replace all of the fantasies she experienced with Quinn less than an hour ago. Why did Justin have to be such a straight shooter? Sometimes she missed not having a close girlfriend who would agree that the other girl was a troll and that she deserved the most amazing man ever, no questions asked. Those were much better conversations than a spoonful of reality and a can of beer to wash down the sad truth.

"Look, you'll forget about this guy anyway. Like you said, there are three other new buildings for you to take care of. Certainly someone will need a break on their lease and you can come through with a manager's special."

"Justin!"

"Oh, I'm kidding. Don't get your panties in a wad," he said, pounding a beer.

"Don't you have to work tonight?" she asked. It was Friday, one of the three nights a week her guy pal actually got off his ass and did something productive.

"Yep, I'm opening for someone you've never heard of in front of a crowd of under a hundred," he said. Justin had landed a low paying gig as the house emcee at the local comedy club. They did shows Friday through Sunday and occasionally on Thursdays, leaving him just enough income to scrape by and pay rent another month.

"Well, then drink up," she said, rolling her eyes. "Go make the people laugh: all the happy couples, bachelorette parties, losers with nothing else to do."

"Ah yes, my fans," he said. "You know, the club is trying to drum up more business this summer. Perhaps you could run a promo by the big wigs sometime this month?"

"Like what? Blow the opener who lives in the Parkview building, get in for half-off?" she asked, letting the beer loosen her tongue.

"Love it! Actually, we have a bunch of free passes for the late shows this month. We need to give them away or no one's going to come in for overpriced beer. Summertime numbers are always a struggle."

"And then Quinn and his Wookie could come in and you could make fun of her from the stage! He would realize that he could do better and look toward the lonely girl sitting at the bar." Bree gazed up at the ceiling fan, picturing the moment.

"Um, yeah. That's how it'll work," Justin said sarcastically. "I shit on two customers for no reason—"

"No, just her," she interrupted.

"I'm not being a dick so that you can pretend you're going to make a move on some guy and then pull your chicken shit it-wasn't-the-right-moment excuse."

"Well, excuse me for getting nervous." *Ouch again.* He knew exactly what to say to make her feel bad without even knowing the pain he was bringing back. Justin had been her wingman and led her to so many guys that she couldn't follow through with, it's no wonder he said these things. "I'll let you get ready for work." She hadn't even gone home yet. She came straight to Justin's all excited about her magical umbrella walk and was now faced with another Friday night of nothing. "I'm taking these," she said, reaching into the fridge for the remaining four beers.

"What?" Justin was in his bathroom, reapplying deodorant.

"It's the only six-pack I'll get to handle tonight," she said to herself. She left Justin's door slightly open just to piss him off and made her way past the elevator to the stairwell at the end of the hall. She only climbed the stairs when she was extremely drunk or feeling down, and she wasn't drunk yet.

3

Monday mornings were usually uneventful but, now that Bree had four buildings and a corporate office in charge of her from a distance, the hours flew by. She was about to head back to her place for lunch when Justin strolled in.

"Uh, can I get some help? I don't know how to work a dryer," he said in a ridiculously raspy voice.

"Shut up, you dork. What do you want?" It was rare for him to visit her at work.

"Here's a few hundred passes for this summer." He dropped a pile of multi-colored free admission tickets across her desk. There were probably enough for each resident to go multiple times.

"Wow, the club's in that much trouble?"

"It's summer; it's slow. Whoever ran these off was dreaming and oops, forgot to mention the two-drink minimum on them. There's also talk of making Thursday an open mic variety thingy where I run the show."

"Talks of that, huh?"

"Well, I'm talking about it," he said. This was the most ambition Justin had shown since he dropped out of college. All of her roommates had graduated in a timely fashion except Justin. Instead of studying, he spent all of his nights at the comedy club and playing poker. For the first two years after college he was grossing the most without a degree, while the rest of them struggled through interviews and internships. Over the last several years most of them, including Bree, had landed jobs with a salary and health insurance. No one knew how much money Justin made and lost gambling, they just knew that it wouldn't be around for long. His vices didn't help him keep the ladies, either. As a college kid those habits were almost cute; as a man in his twenties, they served as relationship red flags. Bree figured eventually he would grow up and make something of himself, and by then, if she was still single, she would let him make the move, not her.

"So can we go drop these off?" he asked.

"What are you planning to do, stick them on windshields like Chinese menus? That would never fly," she said, trying to stack the spilled tickets into neat piles.

"Then how about just putting a few of them on the mail-boxes in the main hallways of each building? We'll just see if anyone says anything. If those old women are allowed to post signs for their yard sales, I should be allowed to give away free shit, right?" he said.

"Fine, but I don't want to waste my whole lunch hour on this," she said. They walked to the furthest building down, Edgewood, and placed a small handful of tickets on the shelf by the mailboxes. From there they headed back through the Springview building, leaving another stack.

"Okay, this is his building," said Bree. She took a deep breath, just *knowing* there was going to be another encounter. Nothing.

"I can't believe we didn't run into him. Her. Them," she said, acting relieved but actually disappointed.

"You want another chance to do nothing, huh?" he asked, resuming his cuts on her from Friday.

"Never mind," she said.

"No, seriously, if you want to run into him, we have to arrange it."

"Arrange it? I'm not Stalker Ted." Stalker Ted was a timid geek who always seemed to be drooling whenever he talked with Bree, or any woman for that matter. He popped up at the most inopportune times and was beyond awkward.

"Fine, just wait until he has another technical difficulty with the laundry room. Tell him Merry Christmas because it'll be another six months before you're that lucky."

"Isn't it best to just let things happen?" At least this way there was no pressure on her. No pressure meant no chance of failure. Complete safety.

"That's the difference between us guys and you ladies. We have to do all of the pursuing, so when it's actually your turn to go after someone, you have no clue how it works. This isn't one of your shit Lifetime movies where coincidence leads to love. You gotta work for it," said Justin, getting excited at the prospect of plotting something.

"Okay then, Jonny Big-Balls, what should I do? Break their new washer and dryer so they have to use the ones in our building?"

"Now you're getting it! You don't even have to break any-thing. You have a printer and the authority to put signs wherever you want. Maybe our laundry room is out of order and we have to go over to Dogwood's. What day is his laun-dry day?"

"It was Friday," she said. "But that doesn't mean I can drop what I'm doing here to go and do my laundry on a Friday in a different building."

"Unplug his shit," he said.

"Unplug it? Like just go in there and sabotage an entire building's laundry?"

"Or just let him keep living happily ever after with what's-her-tits, your call."

"I could get in trouble, though," she said.

"By who? You don't have security cameras there, do you? Does anyone else do their laundry on Friday afternoons? No and no. They have a life. They're at happy hours and . . ." he paused to think of a bigger list, "and other happy hours. And then they go out, pretend to be interested in what the other person is saying, and then whoever doesn't have a DUI on their record gets to take the other home for playtime."

"Wait, you lost me," Bree said. "Take him to happy hour?"

"No, create your own! Laundry room will be empty and he'll need your help again. You take it from there," he said, acting as if he'd just explained the mystery of life.

"Yeah, and what if his girlfriend comes down there again?"

"Bree, you're just going to be talking with him, not filming a porno," he said. "It's not your fault some prankster keeps messing with the outlets. And honestly, if she's as ugly as you say, I still don't think they're together."

"She is, I swear! She's got like, reddish hair—" she started into the same description as before.

"I know, I know, but let's do it this way. Maybe dude's got like, a type. Do you have anything similar to her?"

"How dare you!"

"Fine then, I'll go down the list and you tell me how you compare." Justin and Bree had gone through this routine before once or twice, but she was drunk and confident back then. It was his way of being honest with Bree while letting her admit she wasn't perfect either.

"Is she taller or shorter than you?"

"Shorter."

"Thinner or fatter?"

"I don't know."

"That means thinner."

"Justin!"

"How about her smile?"

"Okay, I hate you," said Bree. He knew how sensitive she was about her teeth. Bree's mother was there for her growing up in most ways, just not always financially. As an only child who wasn't gifted in the incisor department, it was unfortunate that braces just weren't an option. Shaking off insults on the playground in fifth grade was one thing, getting let down gently after most first dates with the ones she was actually attracted to was another. It seemed like only the hot guys cared about her teeth. To this day she was sure that was how she lost Keith to another girl.

"What? What did I say? I just asked if she had a nice smile."

"I know. My teeth suck," she said, covering her face with her hands.

"Teeth? Suck? Then you're doing it wrong," he said, trying to make her laugh.

"No, you're right. I'm fat, ugly, and have fangs. A guy like Quinn would never leave his girlfriend for someone who looks like me, I get it."

"Calm down there, eighties movie character, you're not ugly. Do you have a better rack than her? You do, right?" He couldn't tell if she was crying yet.

"Yes," her hands still covered her face.

"There you go, champ," he said, realizing he should've built her up first. Her chest was one of her strengths. "Yeah. See, you got her on that, right? God gave you a gift, Bree!" She let out a small laugh. Justin sighed in relief. "If I know guys in their twenties, and I do, sometimes they just want something different. It doesn't matter if you're more or less attractive than this girl, you just have to be different." He paced in front of her desk like he was delivering a Super Bowl halftime speech and let his voice crescendo with each point that he made. "And another thing." He was able to improv point after point. "You're not going to wait for him to fall for you. No no, my friend. You're going to take him from her! And I'm going to make it easier!"

"How's that?" She was starting to buy this motivational speech.

Justin stepped up into the chair in front of her desk and extended his hands into the air as if delivering a sermon to thousands. "I'm going to bang his girlfriend for you!"

4

It was a long week of work for Bree. The sudden heat wave had caught all of the old air conditioning units off guard, and she spent the week filling out work orders for numerous residents. Nothing from the Dogwood building, of course. No, she would have to follow Justin's plan and trust that he could make it work. If this plan was for her benefit, what had Justin done in the past to get what *he* wanted? The possibilities were scary. Or maybe his plans were very basic and just relied on trusty ol' alcohol. It had worked on her, almost.

The Thursday night before she had stood in front of her fogged-up mirror after a shower. She smiled her crooked-tooth grin and then shut her mouth, frowning. She pulled her long light brown hair back. She considered cutting it or changing the color. Why couldn't Justin have been a gay friend who cuts hair for a living? Where could she get a friend like that? She made a few funny faces in the mirror and then brushed her teeth begrudgingly. As she leaned down to spit into the sink, her towel almost came undone. She readjusted it tighter, which caused her boobs to push up like an opera singers.

"Wonder-towel," she laughed to herself. "Instant cleavage for that confidence boost right before the bathroom scale brings you back down to earth." She slid the scale away with her toes. "Not tonight," she said and went back to adjusting her towel even lower. She posed at several angles, pushing the towel down farther and farther, admiring herself. "You're weird," she said to the reflection, and then made her way to her walk-in closet. Her casual Friday outfit would have to wait. If Quinn was going to see her, she wanted to make a better impression. Corporate would probably frown on her sporting the "Wonder Towel" all day, so she dug around for something that would show her strengths. After ten minutes she was at a loss. Again, the gay friend with fashion sense would've been perfect right now, but she'd settle for Justin's opinion. She put her phone on speaker and continued her closet inventory.

"Hello?"

"Justin, what looks sexy on me?"

"Well, I'd have to—"

"I don't have time for jokes. What should I wear tomorrow?"

"Lingerie," he said.

"You're really not going to help, are you?"

"Actually, I am. I scouted out the Dogwood laundry room and you can't get to the outlets behind the machines unless you have the strength to move a few hundred pounds, which you don't. So, here's what I'll do—"

"*You'll* do?"

"Yep. All of the machines go through the same circuit breaker. You just have to flip a switch back on once I turn it off.

That way you don't have to get down on your hands and knees . . . ha! Until later."

"Very amusing," she said.

"Actually no, that's bad. He'll feel like a dumbass and perhaps embarrassed if it's something that easy. Hmm."

After a few silent moments Bree was getting impatient. "Are you still there?"

"Yeah, I'm thinking. Actually I like you in a vulnerable position, so maybe first you should act like it's the outlets. Show him a little take-charge side of yourself. Actually, show your backside while you're at it."

"What? Justin, I need to know what to wear, not how to perform a mating dance."

"Bullshit! This whole thing is a mating dance, and you're going to show off those tail feathers," he said in a stern voice to show he was serious. "Find a skirt, woman."

"I can't wear my little black skirt to work. Corporate is coming in tomorrow morning and I don't want to look like a dirty whore," she protested.

"Not for them, no. Just for him." Justin thought for a moment, "How about this? How about you go home and change at lunch?"

She hated when he was right. "I guess that would work. There normally isn't much traffic in the office Friday afternoon. But won't that look like I'm trying too hard?"

"Who cares? First, guys are dumb, so we need a little help. Second, we like it when a girl tries. It shows that she wants us. Do you know how frustrating it is always being the hunter instead of the hunted? To always have to make the first move? To always have to buy the drinks? I've slept with ugly chicks just because they put in a great effort."

"Oh, so now I'm an ugly chick?"

"There you go, changing the subject every time I make a valid point. You always have to find some reason to avoid my wonderful advice." He was yelling over the phone now. "I'm not saying you're an ugly chick. I'm saying if you put in some effort and show him that you like him, it'll make you two-point-seven times hotter."

"Two-point-seven?"

"Want to bump it up to four-point-six?"

"Why are there decimals involved here? And yes, how?"

"Wear some thigh-highs," he said in a conclusive tone.

"You mean pantyhose?"

"Did I say pantyhose? No. Your grandma wears pantyhose. I said thigh-highs."

"What the hell is the difference?" Three seconds later there was a knock on her door. "Oh shit, there's someone here," she said.

"It's me. Hang up your phone and let me in." She put on her bathrobe and scurried over to the door.

"Really? We couldn't do this over the phone?"

"No," he said, helping himself to her box of wine in the fridge.

"You're back early. How was the show tonight?"

"Didn't happen. We had two dozen people in the crowd and only one act for open mic. We canceled the show, assuming the audience wouldn't tolerate an hour of half-ass juggling by the dude who showed up. But onto more important things, your outfit."

"Wait, it's a mess in there." But it was too late. Justin marched right into her room without even taking his shoes off. The floor was littered with magazines, a few dirty towels, two pairs of sneakers, flip-flops, and today's work outfit. The right leg of her pants was turned inside out. Her top two dresser drawers were open so Justin helped himself.

"Whoa, whoa, whoa!" she yelled, trying to catch up. "That's personal!" In a weird way she found herself turned on while Justin dug through her room. She briefly pictured the two of them sharing a giant dresser one day. She assumed whatever he found would have the opposite effect on him.

29

"Ha! Stockings! I knew you had some!" He pulled out a pair of nude-colored thigh-highs that Bree hadn't worn in forever, if at all.

"Why do they have to be stockings?"

"Here's the thing," he said, sitting down on her unmade bed. "I'm going to explain the male perspective on the difference between pantyhose—ugh, just the name—and thigh-highs." He connected his hands at the fingertips and rested his chin on his two middle fingers. "Us men are very simple creatures. We like to be one layer away from your, how shall I put this, naughty parts. With pantyhose that layer of fabric starts down at your feet and goes up and disappears under the skirt. For all we know it might cover everything up to your chin." Bree held her palms up, waiting for any of this to make sense. "However!" he yelled so loudly she jumped.

"Keep it down! I have neighbors, you know."

"However," he repeated quietly as if he was about to share a scary ghost story. "When a man such as me sees a *thigh-high*, well. That's a different message. If we somehow get to see the top of that thigh-high in the forbidden area just above where the skirt hides the leg, that tells us we're almost there. That lacy border at the top screams 'You weren't supposed to see this!' and it drives us crazy. It's like seeing really sexy underwear. Our hands start to wonder, 'What would it be like to peel those off one leg at a time?' Or, 'Maybe everything comes off except these?' So are you starting to understand my point?"

"Whatever." His performance was selling her; she just didn't want to give him the satisfaction. "So what am I supposed to do? Go over to help him turn the dryer back on and ask him if he'd like to play a game of Twister while we're at it?"

"Nope, just find a reason to get down on all fours and oops! My little skirty-skirt has crawled up my leg," he said in a high-pitched girly voice.

Bree bit her lip and looked up, thinking of a reason that would happen. The idea and Justin's logic was starting to make sense. "What if I dropped my pen?"

"Even I know that's too obvious. Maybe you actually will have to plug the outlets back in. Or can at least tell that's why it isn't working. Know anywhere else he can do his laundry?"

"You're, you're . . ."

"Really fucking good at this? Yes, I know," Justin said.

"He'd have to bring his laundry over to our building." Her enthusiasm was doubling.

"Then he's in *your* house," said Justin. "And don't you do your laundry on Friday evenings?"

"I do now! Wait, what?"

"I'm just saying if he's going to be in your dojo, you might as well make the most of it. Now obviously you're still building the foundation here, but if you want to, go for it."

"You've seen too many porno flicks," she said. "By the way, how's your progress coming on sleeping with his girlfriend you've yet to even meet?"

"You worry about your shit and I'll worry about mine," he said. "I figure I'll run into her—them—somewhere. What's their apartment number?"

"I don't know," Bree said, looking up at the ceiling.

"Bullshit! Like you didn't look up everything about this guy the day you got his name."

"One D," she said. "Ground floor."

"That's my girl. Just above that pesky basement where those new washer and dryers are causing more trouble than they're worth. By the way, I'll take care of the electrical problems. I don't need you ruining your little outfit before it's time." Justin had proudly taken on the brains and some of the heavy lifting of this scheme.

"You really need a day gig," she said.

"Like promoting my open mic night to the local residents? Hmm, which apartment should I focus my attention on?" He tapped his index finger on his sealed lips.

"We are truly sad," she said.

5

The meetings with Corporate went fine, for the most part. Only once did the area VP say, "You seem a little distracted" to her. She was. She had daydreamed about the walk under the umbrella over and over like a favorite childhood movie. She made up different versions of how it ended, instead of the other woman coming in and ruining it. In one version he carried her across the lot. In another they only made it halfway, ditched the umbrella, and then made out in the rain for hours. Her favorite version was the one where he led her to his empty apartment even after she said, "But the laundry room is in the basement." He insisted she get out of her wet clothes and then threw her over the edge of the couch in an aggressive, yet sensitive way. First he kissed her back up and down several times and then rolled her over to face him while her body somehow balanced perfectly on the arm of the couch, her back arched so that her feet could barely reach the floor with the rest of her body suspended and vulnerable to his needs. *Dear God, had Justin rigged that outlet yet?*

It wasn't even lunch yet. She was still in her corporate polo, and one o'clock couldn't come soon enough. *What if he comes in while I'm away?* Her sign would say that she wouldn't be back until two, but she'd trim it down to a half hour today. Or would she? The outfit was ready, but what about more makeup? What if he didn't like makeup? His girlfriend certainly didn't seem to have any on during that brief encounter. What if he was sick of his girlfriend and wanted someone who put a little more effort into her look? Should she shave her legs again? Is lipstick out of the question? What's her excuse for dressing like this? As her lunchtime finally arrived, the questions kept coming. What if they were a perfectly loving couple that did nothing but save puppies all day, and she and her friend were trying to break up a beautiful example of love? What if someone else came into the laundry room while they were there? What if his girlfriend did the laundry this week? Hell, what if he didn't even do laundry on Fridays and that was just a one-time thing? What was she going to do if things did work and she had him alone in her laundry room? Would it be wrong to get a drink at lunch? Would it be wrong to have a box of white zinfandel in her bottom desk drawer? Why couldn't she just have straight teeth? Was there a white film under her arm from her deodorant? Who the hell wears a little black dress and stockings to work? Justin was an idiot and she would never forgive him for this. In fact, she wouldn't even go through with it. She reached for her phone to text him about aborting the whole mission when his text arrived first.

Expect a resident with a load of washed but not dried clothes this afternoon.

Shit. She got dressed, stockings and everything, and pondered the box of wine. Instead she reached to the bottle full of rum on top of her fridge. Justin bought it for her during spring break her senior year of college. A group of them had made it down to Florida and one night, while drinking rum, she "finally let her guard down," as Justin put it. Actually she wasn't sure what she did that night. She guessed that she had cheated on Brad, but was never sure. She woke up in an empty hotel room that didn't belong to her with a condom wrapper on the floor. She didn't feel like she had had sex, but then again all she could feel was a pounding headache. Her shirt was on, but that was it. It was truly a mystery-fuck if it had happened. When she finally found her friends at lunch the next day, Justin gave her a standing ovation in front of everyone. "Long live rum!" he said, and bought her a bottle of it at the airport on the way back home. It sat on her fridge unopened for years, even making the move to this apartment a year and a half ago when she took this job. It used to make her feel guilty because she might have—well, probably had—cheated on Brad because of the rum with some stranger. As time passed, she admitted to herself that it wasn't the rum's fault if anything had happened. She sabotaged the relationship in other ways because she just wasn't ready. She had kicked herself for it for years, but then finally gave up on him ever coming back. Had she known it was going to be so long before her next shot at a relationship, she would've made the previous one work. More recently, the guilt was gone and she thought of it more as a symbol for what Justin had been encouraging her to do all along. Take a chance. Be the aggressor. Go after what she wanted. Yes, it was finally time to break the seal off this bitch and do a shot during lunch. Who the hell cared, right? She didn't want to spend another Friday night at home alone or watching Justin do his same six jokes at the comedy club.

Maybe she would finally get the nerve to explain to Justin why she was the way she was. She never talked about it with anyone. Her brain tortured her with another version of the cafeteria incident that was now nearly a decade old. She had coordinated with the custodial staff to dim the lights during lunch on a regular Friday a month before prom. Her theater teacher hid with a spotlight in the far corner and cued up "Be My Baby" by The Ronettes. The entire senior class watched on as Bree sang and danced her way over to Keith. She finished the song, told him how much she loved him "talk show style" as witnesses later described it, and then asked him to the prom. With over two hundred peers looking on, he calmly explained that he had asked someone else who he had feelings for. As she walked away into a swarm of mumbles and then laughs, he yelled that he didn't want to ruin their friendship. Sadly, it even went viral. Making new friends in college was an easy choice.

Do you copy? another text from Justin said. She reached to the top shelf of her cupboard and grabbed a tall shot glass that had never been used, or even washed, for that matter. She continued to move, knowing that if she stopped any of her motions, the voice of reason would halt her immediately. She turned the faucet on, rinsed the dust from the glass, and watched it overflow down into the drain for a moment. Her wet hands struggled to open the sealed rum. She glanced at the clock and saw she had four minutes until the office was supposed to reopen, according to the sign she left on the door. She should've taken the full hour. Squeezing as hard as she could, she heard the seal on the bottle finally give in with a rewarding crack. *Keep going, keep going, don't think, don't think.* She poured the shot glass all the way up past the C in Cancun—she had never even been to Cancun—and plugged her nose to mask the taste of the liquid courage. It stung, burned, and warmed her all at the same time. She coughed a bit as she set the glass down. An aftertaste of coconut lingered in her mouth. Her sinuses opened and, for a moment, she was back in Florida having a carefree time. She glanced at the clock on the stove: three minutes until she was due back. She lifted the bottle and tried to force down one last gulp of the rum before heading back to the office. "What are you doing?" she asked herself, sliding her feet into her black heels. Dressing like this, doing shots of liquor at lunch, and sabotaging a dryer? It must be love.

Roger that and thank you! she texted back to Justin.

Back at her office she could barely sit down. The liquor had helped her nerves, but now she felt like doing anything but working. Getting to two o'clock felt like an eternity; how was she going to survive until the office closed at five? This buzz wasn't going to last all that long, and she felt awkward sporting her best heels at the office. Still, she was an inch or two taller, and it gave her a slightly different perspective on the place in which she spent forty hours a week. She turned the radio off in hopes that time would pass faster if they didn't keep reminding her what time it was. The sun was so bright outside she didn't need the light from the humble chandelier that greeted potential residents as they entered.

The phone rang once, and she explained to a resident that the pool would probably be opening on Sunday. Over the spring they had expanded it to allow for all four buildings to share. Though the water was in, the chemical balances weren't satisfactory yet, so no one could swim until then. *Thank you for your patience.*

But where was hers? Sure, the rum had spiked her hopes, but her body temperature followed. She was sweating a little. Did she smell now? Was any of this worth it?

Just after three-thirty, she heard the door open. Adrenaline pulsed through her heart as she turned away to make it look like she was busy with something else and not planning her entire life on one not-so-chance encounter.

It was Stalker Ted. He had on outdated, stonewashed jeans and a faded Superman t-shirt that hugged his underarms with sweat marks. The lenses in his glasses had gone dark from being outside in the sun, but were slowly fading back to clear. He was either attempting to grow a beard or had just put off shaving for a week. Splotches of dark facial hair rested on the bottom half of his jaw. The Velcro strap on his left sneaker hadn't been fastened, and he had somehow tucked his jeans behind the tongues of both of his shoes.

"Wow Bree, you look nice!" he said in a nasally voice. "I mean, you always look nice, but now you look really nice. Are you going on a date tonight or something?"

"Uh, yep, that's it, Ted. I have a date right after work so I won't have time to change."

"I noticed you're looking really nice. I wish it was a date with me," he went on.

"Well, I'm taken. What can I…" she reconsidered her phrasing and friendly tone. "What do you want, Ted?"

"Oh, it's just that I washed my clothes and now the dryer won't work. None of them will. All three of them don't seem to have any power. It looks like somebody moved them, because usually they're lined up perfectly with the washers. I know this. But now they're all crooked and aren't working. They're brand new dryers. Did you keep the receipt?"

Son. Of. A. Bitch. Why did she even try? The universe hated her. Goodbye to any chance of executing this plan. How was she going to rid herself of this kind nuisance? Maybe this could be a dress rehearsal week? "Well, Ted," she said, and tried to contain her frustration, "you've got two options. You can wait for maintenance to come fix it tomorrow morning, or you can go to another building."

"I don't have a key to the other buildings, though," he said. "Why can't maintenance fix it now?"

She felt like the Grinch lying to Cindy-Lou-Who. "Well, Ted, they get to go home early on Friday and the only ones who are left are busy getting the pool ready. You want the pool to be ready, don't you?"

"I want my jean shorts to be clean, though. I'll use the dryers here, then."

"Are you sure you don't want to explore one of the other buildings and use their dryers?" The residents of those buildings would kill her if they knew what she was suggesting.

"Then I would need a key, and I don't have a key. You have keys to all of them. I would have to come get you to get my clothes out, and then we'd have to walk all the way over to the other side." Good point, not happening in *these* heels. She tried to do the math in her head. What time had heaven visited last week? How long would it take Ted to get his basket full of clothes and his head full of questions out of the way? Bree would have to hurry him through and hope for the best.

"Go get your clothes, Teddy," she said. "We'll dry them in Parkview's dryers. But hurry up, it gets busy in there." Calling him Teddy was all she needed to do to get him to obey. He smiled and nodded and jogged out of the office. A few minutes later he returned with a basket of overflowing whites. Briefs, tube socks, and t-shirts with permanent underarm stains consumed the old gray basket.

"Looks like it's been awhile," she said, trying to keep a polite tone.

"Yeah, I haven't done laundry in over a month," he said.

"So, of course, today was the day to do it. Gotta do it today," she said. Really, universe? She grabbed her keys and led him to the connecting Parkview building.

"Your basement is scarier," Ted said on the walk down.

"Yeah, you better finish up before dark."

"I am. I tried to tell the guy who was putting his wash in about the broken dryers."

"There was a guy there? What did he say? Did you get his name?"

"I don't know his name. He was on the phone with someone and wasn't really listening to me. I've seen him around but I don't know him. Should I go back?"

"No!" she said. "I mean, he'll figure it out. Or I can tell him." Was he still there? This might work after all. What if it wasn't Quinn?

Ted loaded his whites and thumbed through the change in his hand. She wished she had her change jar to just pay the six quarters and move him on. Finally, his load started and he was ready to leave.

"Is my basket safe here?"

"Yes, Ted." Did Justin have a plan that would clear Ted out of her way? No amount of genius could've anticipated his interference today.

Ted made his way back outside as Bree followed behind. Hopefully he wouldn't notice her trailing and just go back his to apartment for the hour until his clothes were dry. As he reached the door to Dogwood, he saw her reflection behind him.

"Hey Bree, are you going to let everyone know about the dryers?"

"I sure am. Why don't you let me take care of it so you can head back to your apartment now, Teddy?"

"I'll go with you." Shit.

6

Sure enough, it was Quinn. He was pouring the fabric softener into his wash. She felt like just standing there and admiring that tight little muscled arm that stuck out from his sleeve just above the elbow. The moment ended as Ted barged in behind her.

"The dryers don't work," he said in a loud voice over the rinse cycle.

"I can handle it from here, Teddy. You can head back upstairs." Why wasn't the *Teddy* command working anymore? That extra syllable used to have him trained, and now, when she needed it most, nothing.

Quinn turned around, holding the dripping cap from the fabric softener. "What's up?"

"What's your name, sir?" Ted butted in. No chance of an awkward silence this time.

"Quinn." It was obviously his first conversation with Ted.

"Quinn, I'm Ted and this is Bree. She's going on a date tonight, but not with me. Hey, that rhymes!" He laughed to himself.

"I'll take it from here, Ted." Was there another suffix? Ted-rick? Tedrow? Tedsifer? She'd have to look up his middle name.

"Do you have a girlfriend, Quinn? If not, Bree is already going on a date so you can't have her. But me neither. Sucks, huh?" He could have her anytime, anywhere. This time Quinn blushed a bit and ran his fingers through his hair. Do your thing, Ted.

"Yeah, I have a girlfriend."

"Is she prettier than Bree, Quinn? 'Cause Bree's extra pretty today," he said. Mother of pearl, Ted was a runaway train! Quinn looked to Bree for some help. "What do you do for a living, Quinn?" Good question.

"Oh, I'm in the wedding business. Music, photography, and that kind of thing."

"Theodore, remember how I told you asking too many questions was rude?" She hadn't, but certainly using his whole first name would amount to something.

"Oh, sorry," he said. "How will I know when my clothes are dry?"

"The machines in Parkview take just as long as these. You've got about forty-five minutes left, Ted. Why don't you go check on the pool and see if it's going to be ready for the weekend?"

With a thumb's up, Ted exited the laundry room, leaving Bree with the situation she had been plotting, planning, all-out scheming for, for days. They both listened as Ted's clumsy footsteps faded away.

"Sorry about him. He can wear on you after a while," she said.

"It's cool, that guy cracks me up," Quinn said as the washing machine kicked into the final spin cycle. "So the dryers are broken?"

"Let me check and see what the deal is. They're brand new so it's gotta be something with the outlets or circuit box." She wondered which method Justin had decided on using for a moment, and then realized Ted was right, the machines were a bit out of line. Justin must have nudged them so that he could reach back and pull the plugs. Okay, time for the mating dance, she thought to herself. Or, she could just let Quinn take his things to her laundry room. Wasn't that the original plan? Of course, the original plan didn't account for Stalker Ted and his somewhat intrusive, yet helpful Q & A session. The dryers were all about a foot and a half from the wall, but she wasn't about to stick her hands back there. The plugs were near the bottom. She maneuvered around to the side and gave a rather feminine tug to the first machine. It wasn't budging. How the hell was Justin able to move these even the few inches? What a ridiculous plan. She hoped none of the rum lingered on her breath from earlier. She had had an entire week and this is all they could come up with? Maybe the plugs were higher up on the wall, and she could just reach them from the top. She would have to hop up on the row of machines and reach down that way. Heels on or off?

"Do you want some help?" Quinn finally asked. "Can you tell what's wrong with them?"

"Yeah, this happened once before, I think. Some prankster probably messed with the plugs. Or else they were checking some of the circuits after that storm last week."

"Yeah, this is two weeks in a row of laundry woes," said Quinn. Was he mad? Had she pushed it too far? The first one wasn't her fault. Any longer and his girlfriend would be down there again to ruin another moment.

"Sorry about that. You can always use the machines over in Parkview." She slipped out of her heels and, with her back to the machines, boosted herself on top of the middle dryer. She swung her legs up and bent her right leg. She felt her skirt slide down and pretended to be oblivious, just as Justin had directed her, that the top of her thigh-high was indeed showing. She quickly leaned over and saw all three plugs barely removed from each outlet. One, two, three, she plugged them all back in and spun back around, letting her legs dangle down in front of the dryer. She looked back up at Quinn. For a split second they had an intense moment of eye contact before he looked away. *That's right, soak it in. You saw what you thought you saw. How's your boring girlfriend of who knows how many years?* The washing machine stopped, but, instead of hopping down and acting like a professional, she remained perched on the middle dryer. And here's the detail that Justin would go crazy about when she told him later. Quinn threw his laundry into the middle dryer that she was sitting on instead of the closest one. She put her hands out in front of her between her legs and leaned while letting her feet swing out to the side as she watched him toss everything from his t-shirts to his girlfriend's blue jeans just beneath her. As he finished, she extended her legs straight out so he could shut the door. He reached behind her to hit the start button after inserting his quarters. The dryer began with a mild vibration underneath her. Game, set, match; she could've gotten off just sitting there looking at him. Instead, she reached her arms out, knowing she wouldn't be able to control herself much longer. Was she still at work? Certainly this guy felt *something* between them. Instead of grabbing her arms, Quinn reached lower and picked her up around the hips like she was a weightless angel. It was the most action she'd had in months and it sent her heart into a higher gear. He even hesitated before setting her down, his fore-arms bulging. She was like a doll being moved from a shelf. How did he do that, and how could she get an encore? Sweet mother of mercy, he was strong!

"All set?" he asked her. She couldn't even speak. Her senses, her limbs were in some sort of post-coital trance that she hadn't experienced, maybe ever. She just nodded and slowly reached for her keys from atop one of the empty washers were she had set them.

"Thanks for fixing the dryer. Have fun on your date tonight," he said as she dazedly walked out of the laundry room and back to the ground floor.

7

"So what did you say after he put you down?" Justin was so proud of himself for having arranged the whole thing. He paraded around his coffee table with an I-told-you-so tone.

"I, I don't know. I don't think I said anything," she said. "I was in complete control on top of the dryer and then he turned it on, turned me on, picked me up, and I lost it. I feel like I owe him dinner or something. I've never experienced anything like it." She was still in a daze, nodding her head back and forth in disbelief. He set a beer near her on the coffee table, but she was still a zombie. "I *must* have him. How do I make that happen? It has to happen."

"Well, what else did you talk about?"

"Talk? Hell, I don't know. Ted was firing questions right and left. He admitted he has a girlfriend but we already knew that. His job has something to do with music and photography. I think he mentioned weddings or something." Bree couldn't recall much more than that.

"So Ted left?"

"Oh shit! He still needs into our laundry room. I completely forgot about him."

"Don't worry, I was on the lookout and took care of him. He thanked me a hundred times for letting him back in and said you promised you'd be there."

"Well, that's what he gets for running all that interference."

"Did you at least finish your shift?"

"Yes. Kind of. I mean, I think I took care of everything. So what's the next step?" She had come down from her high from the interaction, but wasn't content for the day. "I can't just wait until next Friday to see him. This laundry business has run its course."

"You leave that to me. I have to seduce his girlfriend."

"Don't say seduce, especially when it's you," Bree laughed.

"What? I'm a prize, babe." He leaped onto the coffee table and posed like a bodybuilder.

"Yeah, but guys can't *seduce*. We either want you ahead of time or not. It's not up to what you do."

"What do you mean? I can throw on the charm with the best of them. I'm irresistible!"

"I hate to break it to you, but all that talking you do is unnecessary. Us ladies decide if we're going to give you a chance before you finish your first cheesy line. All your talking really does is pass the time. Or it can actually kill your chances a lot more than it can help. So please, I repeat, do *not* tarnish the word *seduce*."

"Oh and I suppose you're the big seductress. Just an expert on getting what she wants. Clearly!" Wars of words never went well against Justin. He could get defensive, and with his comedic wit, she usually didn't stand a chance. "All that babble you ladies do at the bar is just killing time while the alcohol runs its course. In fact the more you talk, the less we listen. You know how quickly we decide if we want to get in your pants?"

"How long?"

"Before we even meet you, so there! You ladies are way behind with your four to six seconds. So yes, seduce us. You have all the power; you win, ladies."

"Tell me why you're single again, Justin?" That ought to shut him up.

"So that I can help you get a guy." Nope, he was right. She could always tell when Justin was actually into a girl. She wouldn't hear from him for several days at a time. His old Chevy pickup would be missing from the lot and then, sure enough, at most three weeks later she'd get a text saying, *Free tonight? Getting drunk*. She stopped asking about what happened. She knew the story and how Justin's love interests felt. He was twenty-five going on nineteen.

"Then what's the plan? What are you going to do, ninja your way into their apartment and *hit it*, as you say, while he's busy brushing his teeth?" She thought about Quinn brushing his teeth every night. He probably looked adorable putting the toothpaste on his toothbrush. She wondered what color his toothbrush was. Did he go electric? Did he use the same kind of toothpaste as her (whatever was on sale)? Then she thought about her teeth. How was she going to seduce him, with fangs? She ran her thumb up against her top row, feeling where her right canine stuck out away from her incisors.

"This can't be rushed. From what you've told me, you had a pretty good moment with the guy. He's got that image of you in your stockings stuck in his head. In fact, we ought to take a picture and put those stems online. Bree, fetch me my camera!"

"Not a chance," she said. Her company was extremely strict on social media. "Stop changing the subject. What are we going to do next?"

"You are going out to the comedy club with me tonight. After all, you do supposedly have a date, right?"

"Do I have to wear this?" she was becoming very self-conscious and the thigh-highs were starting to slip down some.

"Yes," he said, "because I'm sure as hell not paying for your drinks."

Bree spent most of the evening out on the club's patio. Chuck's had built an outdoor bar there last summer and used it all of three times. This summer, they were determined to make it a money maker before and after each inside show. Sipping on rum and Cokes, Bree watched what seemed to be a rather large crowd of well over a hundred for the first show disappear into the showroom. She noticed each couple and silently judged whether they were a good match. There was a man well over six feet with a girl who probably wasn't even five feet. There was an older man with slicked back silver hair holding hands with a girl even younger than she was. The girl's shoes and dress reeked of money, but the over-the-top eyeliner gave her away. You can't buy class.

She took a sip from her thin red straw and then thought about what it would be like holding Quinn's hand in a crowd like that. Every lady would be looking at Quinn and wondering how she got so lucky. Would Quinn realize that he could have any of these other women? Surely he must get hit on all of the time. What would it take to keep him loyal to her? Was he the type that would cheat on a girlfriend? She would make sure his bad habits ended with her, of course.

Justin popped out from the showroom to make sure she was okay. "You sure you don't want to come in and watch the show tonight? The two other comics are hilarious."

"No, I'm fine." He disappeared with the rest of the crowd and she found herself alone at the bar. Even the bartender had to abandon her to help with the service bar inside. So much for free drinks. She couldn't even get the fantasies on her lonely nights to come true.

8

The weekend would be another letdown. When did she stop having a life? She pondered going back to waiting tables on the weekends just to make some money, but couldn't get herself to commit to it. She found every excuse to be outside her apartment building because she certainly couldn't justify one more problem in the laundry room. Daydreaming for a moment, she thought of the lengths Justin would go to.

"Bree, there's a loose python in the first dryer. Can I come use the facilities in your building?"

This would all be funny someday. She and Quinn would sit around and laugh about how hard she had to work to free him from an under-appreciative girlfriend.

By Saturday late afternoon she had cleaned her entire apartment. Normally messy, that was the one thing that could put her to work. She didn't need the man of her dreams stepping over old magazines and sports bras. She looked out into her lot again. Her sad blue Saturn hadn't been anywhere in almost two weeks. Walking to work had its benefits, but her car barely moved from beneath the shade of a nearby oak. It was filthy.

Justin would be so proud of her sexy-time carwash. This would be the stunt that would win Quinn over. Enough waiting, enough of his girlfriend, enough of Justin' peer pressure. She would be a chicken shit no more. Her mind had been playing that moment on the dryer over and over. The look in his eyes. He had to have been aroused by that. She was going to get control of this situation so that she could one day think straight again. Or better yet, not have to think straight again, because love would finally be a part of her life. This excitement, *this* is what all of those people in love had been telling her about all of these years. It was finally happening to her.

She found a plain white t-shirt and dug through her bottom dresser drawer for a pair of shorts. None of them would do. One drawer up was a collection of old blue jeans that dated back to early college. She grabbed her scissors and cut the legs off before forcing her newest article of clothing on. They fit around the waist, but barely. Bree hadn't washed her car by hand, ever, but how hard could it be? No bucket, but a small cooler would work. No scrub brush, but an old wash-cloth would suffice . . . which she was also missing. A hand towel? Check. She finally made it out into the lot, hoping to draw some attention from her future husband.

Justin pulled up in his truck. "What the hell are you doing?"

"Washing my car, duh." He'd catch on in a minute.

"Not looking like that, you're not!"

"I'm not wearing thigh-highs to wash my car."

"No; I don't know what those are, but they're not working," he laughed. What was so funny?

"You don't like my new Daisy Dukes?"

"Daisy Dukes? Those look like jorts you bought at Lilith Fair."

Bree looked down at her homemade shorts. They extended almost down to her knees, although the left side was an inch or so higher than the right. "Oh shit," she said, seeing her mistake. Justin followed her inside as they continued their conversation through her closed bedroom door.

"Do I even need to ask why you're washing your car?"

"No."

"I didn't think so. Hey look, maybe you should just let things happen on their own."

"What? How can you say that after all that planning?"

"Here's the deal, Bree. I know what I'm doing. I know what the guy will like. Those shorts, not one of them. What if he had walked up and saw you out there? You've got a small beer cooler full of water, a hand towel and, well, no soap. You don't even have any fucking soap! Even I can see through this farce."

She opened her bedroom door back up and stood there. Her hair was pulled back into a pony tail with a small pink ribbon. The jean shorts were a fraction of their previous length and the white t-shirt was gone. Only a bright pink sports bra remained. Instead of flip-flops, she had white tube socks with two blue stripes near the top to match her barely used running shoes. "How's this?" she asked devilishly.

"Well, I don't think the absence of soap will be noted," he gulped. "Bree, I don't know if this is your style."

"Holy shit, can I do anything without your approval? You know I've attracted a few men in my day without your help, thank you."

"Did you wear that?"

"I know what I'm doing. I saw the look in his eyes the other day in the laundry room. I saw his bitch-face, ugly-ass girlfriend. I fell for him what feels like forever ago, and the two moments we were together were the best thing I've had in years." Her voice got louder as Justin realized joke time was over. "I'm tired of being lonely. I'm tired of spending my whole life in this stupid apartment complex, and it's frustrating knowing that the only person who could make me happy is right fucking over there in that other building and there's not a damn thing I can do about it." She paused and lowered her voice. "Except dumb shit like this."

He should have let her cool off before proceeding, but he was years away from understanding an upset woman. "Look, I saw this guy the other day, I think."

"So?" she was sobbing now.

"And I don't know if he's your type."

"Not my type? *Not my type*?" Here came her second wind of rage. "When was the last time I was excited about anyone? When was the last time I was open about how attracted I was to a guy in front of you? Not my type? This guy is the most fucking beautiful thing I have ever laid eyes on, let alone touched. Not my type? You can't imagine how much time I've thought about him. Oh, he's my type, asshole. He's definitely my type!" She hadn't called him an asshole while sober ever before. How could he change his mind like this? She was back to screaming and pointing at him whenever she felt she wasn't loud enough. "What, are you afraid that I'm going to be happy for once and be with someone else, and then I'll be just like you and disappear from this friendship? I'm ready to become an adult and have a real relationship and you can't handle that!"

"Look at your outfit. What says adult? The tube socks or the fact that your shorts are so short the pockets are hanging down from the inside?"

"You're jealous! That's it, isn't it? You're fucking jealous because I'm the only girl you've known for more than three seconds who hasn't thrown her panties at you!"

"What? No, that's not it, I promise." He was backing away and trying to quell her with a calm tone of his own.

"How do I know that's not it? Guys like you only want what they can't have."

"Chill out. You know I love you, but not in that way," he said, hoping that would help. "I'd never want to ruin our friendship." The Ronettes echoed in her head.

"Oh? You *love me*, do you? Well, lucky fucking me! Let me pass out so you can dry hump my leg. Better yet, I'll just take this ridiculous outfit off now and we can do it right here."

She started unzipping her shorts; a bluff, right? This was a new one for Justin: piss a girl off so bad she strips?

"I just don't want you to get hurt, and he's not your type." Normally when a girl had her pants down and was standing in front of him in her underwear, Justin would say anything he thought she wanted to hear. Now was not one of those times. "Okay, fine. Honestly, I don't think you're *his* type and you're just going to get shot down." He quickly exited the apartment, where a girl in a pink bow and sports bra stood in tube socks with a ruined pair of jeans shorts around her ankles. Another first.

How dare he? she thought. She stomped into her immaculately clean bathroom and looked at her reflection. Why had she taken her shorts off in front of Justin? She knew the answer but was reluctant to admit it. It was a risk-free way to see if he felt the same, but with that timing, obviously he didn't. She looked deep into her left eye, then to the right. They were wet and bloodshot, and her nose was running. She grabbed some toilet paper and blew her nose. It was her teeth, wasn't it? That's the type that Justin meant. Of course Quinn doesn't like girls with bad teeth, but couldn't he make an exception? She could offer him boobs, hair and all the sex he could ever want if he'd just overlook her teeth. Isn't that all a guy needs to be happy? "I just want to be wanted," she said into the mirror. "From this point on I'm going to make that happen somehow."

9

Sometime around midnight she awoke, very disoriented. Oh yeah, her friend was an ass and it would be days, maybe weeks before she had another chance to see Quinn. She thought back on all of the other crushes she had growing up. They were jokes compared to this one. Boy bands and teen heartthrobs came and went. She remembered the time her mother drove her all the way into downtown Chicago with some classmates for her thirteenth birthday to see some singer at a mall. She couldn't believe how many other screaming girls shared her passion and felt hopeless in a sea of glitter makeup and poorly constructed posters. That was the moment she realized there was nothing she could do about her first crush.

The crush on Quinn was different. He knew her, he had talked to her, he had picked her up by the hips, he lived less than a football field away from her—yet she still felt as hopeless as that day at the mall. Justin's advice had gone from dressing like a tramp, to letting things happen, to pretty much giving up because she wasn't attractive enough. Was he right?

She reached over and turned her small blue lamp on. It was weird seeing her bedroom floor so clean. The gray fuzzy carpet was usually a disaster to walk through during the night. She found a tank top and carried it over to the bathroom, where she brushed her teeth. After brushing, she turned to the mirror on her bathroom door and inspected her reflection. Still wearing her sports bra, she sucked in her stomach as much as she could. Her bottom set of ribs emerged and she swelled into an hourglass figure. She exhaled with a large sigh and reality set back in. "It's no wonder," she said. She changed from her sports bra into just a tank top and let it hang loosely on her shoulders. She tugged and pulled this way and that. Her cleavage always made her feel better about herself. She looked over at her phone, knowing she owed an apology.

I'm dumb. Sorry about that.

Just then a text from Justin came through that read: *That was bad, sorry. U still up? What are you doing?*

Not playing with my boobs in the mirror. Good, he had calmed down too. She would let him off a little and call it a night. He was probably done with the Saturday shows and heading home. Back when she used to wait tables on the weekend, they would meet up with coworkers and drink until close. What happened to her Saturday nights?

She used to visit her mother at least one weekend out of the month, but more and more she dreaded the frustrating drive from the northern outskirts to the southern outskirts of Chicago. Being a late and only child of a mother who was now in her sixties and a father who would've turned eight-one that year, they weren't the closest. Her father had abandoned the family when she was in second grade, but her mother was able to get by on the alimony and a little financial support from the surprisingly sympathetic in-laws. The visits only made her admit to the pale relationship their time together had turned into. Mom didn't want to know about her life as a single; she'd rather name grandbabies that were yet to be had. Her mother didn't use a computer or cellphone and passed her time happily with other widows she had met in support groups.

The year after college she still had a few girlfriends to hang out with, but they were quickly swept off their feet, or knocked up, and ended up in marriages. Surely one of those bitches had to be getting a divorce. Nah, they weren't getting away from their kids anytime soon. When did she become such a loner? Sure, there was Justin, but after today could she keep taking her dilemmas to him? She couldn't believe he played the "I love you" card. She took one last look into her dark reflection and let her lips part ever so slightly. Justin was right.

By one a.m. she was wide awake and restless. She popped her head out of her door to see if anyone else on the fourth floor was awake. Silence in the "penthouse." Even though she knew a lot of the personal details of everyone in the Parkview building, she gave them all nicknames. She tiptoed down the hall, still in her bare feet, towards the stairwell. There was a faint sound of music playing from Old Lady Beatrice's place. As she got closer, the TV blared from the living room of Sherlock Holmes. When she arrived at the stairwell, she hesitated. The steps were probably pretty grimy, and she just knew Stalker Ted would somehow be outside waiting for her. Instead, she headed up the metallic ladder steps to the trapdoor for the roof. She had been up there once before when maintenance discovered a tenant had left an old satellite dish up there. She climbed the steps and gave a light shove to create a small opening. Warm air with some of the day's humidity still lingered above her. Cautiously feeling her way, she took a few steps onto the roof, her bare feet warmed with each step on the smooth black surface. A distant glow to the south polluted some of the starlight, but the moonless black sky above her made her smile.

Though she had technically reached it, tomorrow was another day. The pool opened. She hadn't taken a dip once last year. Stalker Ted was always there, and the few families with kids knew how to ruin a relaxing afternoon. She wondered how chaotic it would be with so many residents there at once. Certainly Quinn and his girlfriend would be there. Though she could handle an afternoon of gawking at him through her sunglasses, she didn't trust herself or her body to say or do the right thing. She would need Justin. A shooting star skipped across the atmosphere. She'd have to forgive him, which would be easier than telling him he was right. She wasn't going to give up on account of an ugly girl who was in the way. A light warm breeze blew through her shirt. She would be okay. This was just the beginning, good things come to those who wait... all those other clichés would ring true for her. She went back down and retrieved a few blankets and a pillow. Drifting in and out of consciousness, she imagined Quinn wrestling with her in the pool. Her hands could slide over each individual muscle on his shoulders, inspect the definition of his back, and she would finally wrap her legs around him as they kissed passionately in the deep end. Over and over she saw the scenario in her mind and fell asleep with a smile on her face for the first time in a week. Asleep she stayed until the birds woke her up just before dawn.

10

By Sunday she had made up with Justin and sent him past the pool enough times to earn himself a nickname like Stalker Ted's. Part of her was happy because it meant she wouldn't have to make a decision about what her next move would be. Still, Quinn *would* have his shirt off, and that would be fucking amazing. She didn't even have a bikini that fit right anymore, meaning even if he was there, she would have to run to the mall, try five things on, cry, pay way too much for one that looked right in the dressing room and then looked awful at home, cry, return it for another one that cost even more, and then march her pale ass over to the pool while containing her jealousy in order to deal with the inevitability that his girlfriend would be there rubbing lotion all over his muscular back. Still, he *would* have his shirt off.

After countless casual strolls and texts, Justin finally gave up around four and paid her a visit. "You owe me some beers for this shit," he said. Sweat soaked his blue shirt and he barely broke stride on his way to her fridge.

"You're sure he—they weren't there?" Bree said, cringing because she knew she was out of beer.

"Unless they're an old Indian couple with two kids, they weren't there."

"That's it?" she couldn't believe no one was at the grand opening.

"Well, Stalker Ted stopped by once, but that's a given. Hey, you finally opened the rum!" Justin had spotted the bottle on her fridge. It wasn't in its usual spot, hiding towards the back, so he grabbed it and had the lid off before she could stop him. "When did this get opened? Wow, how mad were you?"

"I opened it Friday, for your information."

"No you didn't, you were out at the club with me Friday."

"At lunch," she said, shamefully. "You know, before the whole encounter in the laundry room."

"I won't judge. I take a beer with me on stage every night while I work," he said.

"We should talk about yesterday," she said, reaching for a two-liter of Coke. "You know how I get when I'm embarrassed. And sexually frustrated."

"You mean when—" he was going to say, "I'm right," but that wasn't the proper way to start peace talks. "When, umm…" He didn't mean to, but he glanced down at the jean shorts that were still a few feet away on the floor.

"Yeah, not sure why I flipped out so bad. I know, it's my teeth, and I'm not hot enough and whatever, but what about the girl he's with?"

"Maybe they've been together since high school or something. You know how sometimes people don't know any better, so they just stick with what's comfortable. One of two things happens. They either eventually get married and then

66

divorced by the time they're in their late twenties, or they break up when one of them finally has an opportunity to move away."

"How do you know this stuff?" She guessed that would've been her and Keith.

"I'm on Facebook. You're really missing out there. And before you ask, I don't know if he's on there. What's his last name?"

Bree's eyes lit up. "Tomorrow!" she yelled. "Tomorrow the new system goes in so I'll have the information for the other three buildings. First names, last names, middle names, dates of birth, credit scores, employer, vehicle information, everything!"

"You know, quality stalkers from the old school like Ted have worked for years to get their information, and you're just going to find it the lazy way."

"I sure am." She held out her hand to high-five Justin. "Don't act like you're above this."

"Why would I care?" he asked. "Oh. I guess I need to follow through with my end of things. I promised I'd have sex with his girlfriend, who I still haven't seen. That information doesn't happen to include weight, does it? I want to know how much I'll have to drink ahead of time. Speaking of, are you ever going to pour these?"

Five drinks in, Justin finally had to ask, "So seriously, why did you take your shorts off in front of me yesterday?"

"I don't know. It's not like you haven't seen me in my underwear before."

"No, seriously, I was aroused and scared at the same time!"

The two laughed simultaneously.

"I guess I just thought it would give me some sort of upper hand in the fight."

"You'll make a great wife someday," he laughed again, and then took a sip. "But seriously, what if I called your bluff?"

"And tried to have sex with me right then and there?"

"Yeah."

"I would've tried to beat your ass."

"And then what? Seriously, what would've happened? You would've yelled for me to get off. I would've made some joke about it. You would've kept pretending to resist me."

"Pretending?"

"And then you would've given in," he said with a cocky tilt to his head.

"And forever wanted that eight seconds of my life back. Boom, bitch!" She stood up dizzily and bowed to an imaginary crowd that was always present during their insult contests.

"Okay, you win." The Tori Amos CD finished its last track and the room was silent.

"Do you remember the times we almost did?"

"No," she lied. She remembered both close calls like a faint dream, but the time he threw up he probably had no recollection of. "Don't get weird on me. There was rolling and puking and more puking." She ruined the mood before she could even dare herself to see where things went.

Was he really doing this now, or was it just the rum? Maybe she needed him to restore some sanity. The hormones had been on full speed ahead since Quinn entered her office, but Justin wasn't Quinn. Still, he was hot and obviously knew what he was doing in the bedroom. But if she lost Justin the same way she lost Keith, she didn't know how she would ever recover.

"Look," she said. "If you have sex with his girlfriend, they break up, and I still strike out?" She jingled the ice in her empty glass. "You get me for . . . a week."

"Get you? You mean unconditional sex whenever?"

"Call me the cable girl because I'm on demand," she said.

"You couldn't handle me for a week. Besides, if you strike out you're not going to be in the mood," he said, shaking his head back and forth. "Plus, I don't want you to fall in love with me, too," he said, arms folded and eyes closed.

She needed to rethink this. Yes, he was right. She wouldn't be in the mood, things would be bad enough. But then again, for her to officially "strike out" she would have to give up, and that wasn't an option. The bigger surprise to her was that she could use the possibility of sex with her as motivation for Justin. He couldn't have been in a slump too. It was all just drunken talk anyway. He knew better than to take her seriously, she hoped. It sure was nice to be wanted, even if it was just pretend.

"Okay, so it's off the table?"

"Wait now, I didn't say that. I just think you'll renege on it if it happens. You'll be crying on my shoulder and I'll be all, hey, cheer up, and while you're at it, let's do it on your kitchen table. You owe me."

The drunken talk continued and the subject finally changed as they approached the double-figures total on drinks. "Tell me how your open mic night is coming."

"It's okay. We have a few comics, a few guitarists, a couple poets and a homeless guy who just rants for his full seven minutes."

"Really? What's your dad so upset about?"

"Good one," he said sarcastically. Justin was never close to his father either. Though he was still alive, his father had been estranged for over a decade.

"You should come out next Thursday. You've got to have something else in your life, right?"

"That's the point, Justin. I've already done everything else. I've been on trips, I've seen movies, I've read books, I've gone to concerts, and I go to bars all the time. And, no offense against you or the few other people we hang out with, but it's not the same. I want—no, I *need* someone else there with me because everything else …" She looked up to the ceiling and then over to the bottle of rum. "Everything else is just boring now. I want to experience life with someone I care about, not just my friends or my mother."

"Did you rehearse that monologue, Ophelia?"

"Shut it!"

"Well, what's your passion?"

"My *passion*?"

"Yeah, what's your passion in life? It can't be someone else, especially if you barely know that person. Is it music? Dancing? Exercising?"

"I know, I need to work out more. I'm well aware that I'm getting—"

"No, that's not what I'm saying. I'm telling you, you have to have a passion in life. Mine are performing, poker, lifting weights, golf. Hell, even video games and sports get me passionate. You've seen me while I'm watching a Bears game, right? So what makes you that passionate?"

"I don't know. I mean, I used to care about volleyball in high school."

"Did you cry when you lost?"

"No! Just because I'm a girl doesn't mean I cried," she snapped back.

"I wish you had. It would've meant that you had passion for it. I like to have a good time when I go out drinking with people, but that can't be my only source of happiness." She wondered where all of Justin's wisdom and sensitivity had suddenly bloomed from. Normally the drunken talks devolved into action movies, boobs, and what happened at poker last week. The little voice in her head told her to put her guard up; he might be trying something.

"I'm passionate about my work. There. Happy?"

"Bullshit. You trudge in and out of there every Monday through Friday. Is that your career? No. You hate it half the time, or it's too easy. Sure, it works now and you make good money, but is that what you pictured yourself doing when you were growing up?"

"No." This hurt. It may have been truth, it *was* truth, but it hurt. He was right. The reason she was so wrapped up in Quinn was because nothing else was going on in her life. She was going to wake up one day at the age of thirty, thirty-five, maybe even forty and still be coasting through this monotone life. Alone. And her apartment buildings didn't even allow pets, so giving up and turning into a cat lady wasn't an option.

"Look, I'm not trying to hurt your feelings again. I just want you to be happy," he paused, "again." They both knew the last time she was really happy was with Brad.

"I know," she said, trying not to cry yet again. *Too late.* The teeter-totter of a night of rum had tipped the other way. Happy time was over and everything was collapsing. "I'm not good at *anything*." Feeling sorry for herself was easy now. "You're talented at comedy and playing poker, and I answer the phone and collect people's rent checks. Why did I even go to college? This wasn't how it was supposed to be. I'm twenty-six, I should be planning my wedding and buying a home."

"What? No one does that shit at our age," he said.

"Yeah they do. Look at the people we used to hang out with in college. Mellissa's got a house and a family. Kelly lives in New York City with her doctor husband. Even Brad bought a home and lives more than an hour from where he grew up."

"They all have rich parents, though. Remember how they didn't even pay rent in college? Who do you think bought their homes? Stop beating yourself up. You've got plenty going for you. Honestly, at this age it's not about achieving hopes and dreams. It's about not making some huge-ass mistake so that you still have a chance at your hopes and dreams when the right time comes."

"But—"

"No buts, young lady! I'm serious. Chill. You've got a great job in an expanding company. You've got me." There was a small pause after those words. "You've got a crush that will eventually stop dominating your life. You don't have any debt, kids, or diseases. That's a win in my book."

She looked up at him, wiping the tears, and forced out a smile. "I guess I just have to find something," she said.

"You know what? First thing tomorrow you can worry about that. For now, let's get you to bed so you make it to work on time tomorrow."

She stumbled her way through her bedroom door as Justin spotted her from behind like a gymnastics coach. "There ya go, find that pillow." She lay down on her tangled sheets, trying unsuccessfully to get underneath them. Justin turned off the light with the best intentions of her not puking. "Is your alarm set on your phone?" She nodded. "Okay, I'm going to get some water and put it on your night stand."

"I need my jammies," she said.

"Not tonight, whatever you have on will be fine. It's pretty early so you'll get plenty of sleep tonight."

"Jammies!" she pouted like a child demanding her blanky.

"Water for now," he said, exiting the room and talking to himself as he filled a clean glass. "Five drinks, deep conversation. Six drinks, completely hammered and depressed." He walked back into her room, leaving the kitchen light on so he could see what he was doing. "A dozen drinks and—naked and asleep?"

Her pale body lay on its side in a rather sophisticated pose, considering the circumstance. He set the water down on the night stand and hesitated before pulling the sheets over her. "Huh," he said to himself. He took a few steps back just in case she woke up. Her shirt was next to her face with a sleeve still hanging on to her at the wrist. Her shorts and panties had evidently been kicked off the foot of the bed. He followed her legs up to the curve of her hip and onto her left breast, which was slightly larger than her right—at this angle, at least. He took two steps toward the door and then paused. "She'd kill me if she woke up naked in front of me in the morning," he whispered. "She'd fuck me if she woke up in five minutes." He tip-toed back over, kissed her forehead twice. The first kiss a peck, but for the second he let his lips stay there a few extra moments. Her skin was warm, she still smelled good, and he could hear her breathing softly. "You've got me and you have no idea," he said, and then quietly exited her apartment.

11

Two minutes after the Monday morning alarm went off, Bree was staring down into her toilet. *Just get it over with*, she thought. She did. Twice. Stupid Justin, what the hell happened last night? She remembered waking up cold, naked, confused, and luckily alone at some point in the night. They were talking about how she didn't have anything worthwhile in her life. Something about passion, and basically she hadn't shown enough emotion on her high school volleyball team. Close enough, she was running behind as it was. Breakfast was not even being considered by her stomach, so she made up a few minutes there and got to the office at two minutes before eight.

"There you are," a man said, getting out of a gray Lexus. "I'm George Simmons, North Central Vice President of Stevens Chicago Properties." Good lord, today? "I'm here to help you with the new system." He popped his trunk and pulled out a new computer tower. "You get the upgrade today."

"Oh, that's today?"

"Yeah, I understand you've been running one of our top potential properties, so you're first on the priorities list. You got my email, didn't you?"

No. "Yes," Bree said, looking down and to the left for a memory. He probably sent it Friday during that whole fiasco.

"So how did the pool opening go?" He walked up, set the large computer box down, and shook her hand.

"Oh yesterday? I don't think many people knew it was open yet. We only had a couple of people there," she said. Her stomach was doing back flips and it looked like she wasn't going to get around to putting her makeup on.

"Well, how many signs did you put out?"

"Signs?"

"Dammit, Bree," he said, looking up as they entered her office. "Did you just ignore the whole email? I specifically asked you to promote the pool opening and to get here a little early today so we could get this out of the way."

She moved the mouse to wake up her current computer. Right there in the inbox was an email from George Simmons titled "Saturday/Monday" still unopened. Busted.

"Did you check out early or something? Are you one of those people who thinks the work day ends an hour early because it's Friday?"

"No," she said thinking of how to defend herself. "There was some trouble with one the dryers in the Dogwood building." There, that was legit.

"Did you fill out a work order for the maintenance crew to take care of it?"

"They were all busy working on the final touches for the landscaping at the pool, so I just went over and fixed it my-self."

"That's not what we pay you for." He was still angry despite her reasons. "I don't want you leaving this desk unless you're showing an apartment to someone. We've got such a high percentage of un-rented property sitting here and you're fixing a washing machine."

"Dryer."

"Whatever the hell it was, it wasn't your job. What happens if a potential resident swings by here on a Friday afternoon, ready to rent?" That never happened. Why couldn't he just go away? Her head was pounding with every angry syllable that came from his coffee-breath mouth. If he got any closer she was going to make the hat trick visit to the toilet.

"I'm sorry," she said, giving up on salvaging any method to defend herself.

"This is the business world. Properties are a real business. Whatever rinky-dink system you had before Stevens took over is long gone. We don't tolerate any bullshit from our employees." Invading her personal space, he turned her computer off, unplugged it, and replaced it with the new one. She slid back on her chair and looked up towards the ceiling fan. It was spinning just fast enough for her eyes to follow each blade. Spinning, dizzy, then she lost it.

"Aw fuck!" George yelled as she vomited on his left shoe. "What the hell is wrong with you?" Bree ran to the bathroom and finished with George still cussing at her desk. "Get me some towels in there or something!" Oh sure, she'd get right on that. As soon as her body stopped trying to kill her she would get down on her hands and knees and wipe off his precious shoe. What an ass.

"Is this morning sickness? Are you pregnant?" *Can he ask that?*

"I'll be fine. Just some food poisoning from last night, I think." His cellphone rang a blaring electronic tune. He looked at the number and hesitated. She would've paid a week's salary to smash his phone through the window. Finally he answered.

"Yeah? . . . It's a mess over here right now, but I'll fix it. We should be up and running by early afternoon." Early afternoon? He was going to be here all morning?

"Can I at least run back to my place to clean up?"

"I don't know, can you?" Wow, really? Grammar lessons now? She wished she could yack on him again.

"I'll be back in a few minutes," she said, pushing the door open without looking back. There was no way she was using the steps today. The elevator took its time but she finally got back to her place. After a splash of water on her face and an encore with her toothbrush she was feeling much better. *Hangover shmangover,* she thought. This guy wasn't going to make her feel inferior. She had already punished his wingtips and felt pretty good about it. She took her sweet time getting back to the office where an impatient George awaited.

"I don't know who you think you are, but my time is very important to me and this company. Get your notepad out and learn this shit the first time I say it," he barked.

Without a word Bree sat near him to absorb more coffee breath and receive her lesson on the official "Stevens Chicago Properties Management System 2.0." It was actually very basic and simple. She picked it up right away, as any twenty-something who had ever used computers before would. A few times George even got stuck, but she let him figure it out rather than correcting him and risking more fury. Each apartment was given an account with a list of residents and their information (bingo). Also included were their credit scores and record of how they paid their last six months of rent. There were other parts to the program that could write up new leases, order more brochures, and communicate with other offices in the corporation, but those weren't difficult either.

"Now you try it," George finally said. "Look up a resident and tell me how and when they paid their rent four months ago." He stood up and folded his arms, thinking he would have an excuse to yell at her again.

"No problem. Justin Hart," she said. This would be interesting. Some months Justin had his rent in a week ahead of time, while other times it was a struggle. It all depended on poker tournaments and football pools.

"February second, money order," she said, expecting the first compliment of the day.

"A day late! Did he include the twenty-five dollar late fee?" Shit. Dammit Justin. His slacking four months ago was getting her yelled at today. "Is he your friend or something? Are you giving special treatment to your friends? I should have you fired right now for costing our company money!" His voice echoed in the office. No one had ever been that loud in all of her time there. She scrolled down a bit.

"Here it is. It came a couple weeks later, but it is in fact turned in." That's right, Just had nailed the Super Bowl pick and was living large through the rest of the winter. "I can find you a copy of the money order if you'd like," she said calmly to juxtapose his crazy mood.

He ignored it and asked, "Are there any more questions?" Any more? She didn't have any the entire morning, Professor Asshole.

"I've got it," she said. He was going to leave early. She could breathe. She could put on her makeup. She could look up Quinn's account. She could get the dirt on his girlfriend. Occupation, credit score, emergency contacts, it was all hers! George was going to leave and be gone for months, or forever. She had met and worked with some of the higher-ups before who seemed respectful, but this guy had it out for her just for not promoting a pool opening. Well, and puking on him. Her stomach was feeling much better and her appetite had returned with a vengeance. Her empty stomach growled and she hadn't gone to the bathroom all morning other than that first messy visit.

"Okay then, I'll see you after lunch hour then," he said. She made a fist, waited until the door closed, and then pounded her desk three times.

"What could there be left to show me? I get it, you dinosaur," she hissed and dug up her "out for lunch" sign for the door. She was about to text Justin with the good news about finding Quinn's info before she thought about what he said last night.

"He's going to think I'm even crazier," she said, putting her phone back in her purse while she headed back to her apartment. She finally ate some three-day-old pizza and washed it down with tap water. Still impressed by how clean her apartment was, she sat down on the couch and watched the news at noon. She wished she had Quinn's number so they could play the game of random texts. She would ask him how he's doing, he would say something adorable back with a smiley face which she normally hated, but his would be different. She wouldn't need a hobby, or female friends, or Justin getting her drunk on a Sunday when she had Quinn at her side, or better yet, on top of her. She stuffed the last bit of crust in her mouth while ignoring something about a triple-homicide somewhere in Chicago. She continued to daydream about him for the rest of the lunch hour, and then finally made her way back down to the office where George was waiting with a frown.

"You're late. It's ten after one, for god's sakes," he said.

"You said you'd see me in an hour. We left at ten after noon, didn't we?"

"Oh, so you're one of those minute counters? Are you union? Did you need that extra ten minutes to watch your stories?"

"My contract says I get an hour, so that's what I took!" She finally raised her voice at him and glared right into his eyes before opening the door to the office. Wow, it worked. He stopped bitching at last.

"Okay, we'll do a final walkthrough of the four buildings and I'll somehow turn everything back over to you." Great, one more thing to make her nervous about. Maybe he could yell at her in front of all of the residents. She could make a fool of herself in front of Quinn. Perhaps Stalker Ted would be out and about and give George a first-hand account of how "pretty" she looked on Friday, and then ask her how her date went right in front of her boss. Then he could lay into her one more time about that email she ignored.

They bypassed Dogwood and started at the far end of the property. "Keep on landscaping about these flowers here. They're the first thing people see from the west entrance."

"Yes, sir," she said obediently.

"Are all of these lights in the lot working properly at night?"

"I think so," she said. Who the hell cared? It was nearly ninety degrees out and she was feeling her hangover get its second wind in this heat.

"You think? I need you to know, not think. If someone gets attacked in the darkness, we can't *think* we did everything we did to keep it safe. We must know." On and on he went about every little detail. One of the tennis court nets wasn't tight enough, the other was too high. Did she have a contractor ready to repaint the lines in the parking lots by next winter? When was her last face-to-face meeting with Carl, the head of maintenance? Why were the numbers so far down in the Dogwood building? For all she cared, as long as one apartment there was occupied, her life still had hope. She tolerated close to an hour of browsing around all four buildings from the outside. Somehow George didn't even break a sweat. He must be accustomed to the heat, seeing as how he was clearly from hell. She endured his final line of questions, showed him a sample of her sales skills by showing an apartment, and then sat down for one last chat back in her office.

"Here's the problem, Bree," he said. "We lose money for every month that these buildings aren't a certain percentage full. You've got to be on the top of your game when showing them."

"I do my best, it's just that some of them don't always look the most inviting. They're a bit pale and undecorated. Should we set one up that's already furnished and show it to interested renters?"

"Can't," he cut her off. "We just can't. Our buildings vary too much and we're not going to put one in each building. I want Dogwood filled first. It's our biggest building but has at least a dozen or so units out of thirty just sitting there."

"So do you want me to just set up a demo for that specific building so we can—?"

"You're not listening," he snapped again. This guy was awful. "Have you happened to actually read the leases our residents sign? They clearly state that we have access to the apartments and have the right to give a twenty-four hour notice to show their place to potential residents. God, what do you do all day?"

Tears welled up in her eyes. George could die. He could die, burn in hell and kiss her ass. She fantasized about Quinn running up and landing a left hook right on George's gray temple. His glasses would fly off and shatter on the ground. Once he fell, Bree would be free to kick him in the ribs and then jump into Quinn's arms and—wait, what was that last part?

"I just randomly choose a Dogwood resident and put a note on their door saying we'll be showing their place to people?"

"Congratulations, you understand basic English!" George looked to the sky. "She *does* have a brain. It's a miracle!"

"Are we done?" Bree asked with her hands on her hips.

"Yes, I can't take any more of this," he said, as if it was all her fault. They exchanged sarcastic goodbyes and she was finally able to sit in peace at her desk, but just for a moment.

"Hey Bree Andrews." Ted entered her office, soaked in sweat with a smell that matched.

"Hello Ted, what's the problem?"

"No problem. Who was that guy? How was your date? Is the pool open for good now?"

"My boss, fine, and yes," she said. He stared at her for a moment while the answers rattled around and then made sense. "Anything else, or can I get back to all this work my boss gave me?"

"Oh, I'm sorry. That's all I need," he said, turning to leave. "Wait," he turned back. "Is that guy who let me into the laundry room the other day your boyfriend?"

"Ted, what have I told you about personal questions?" There was no right answer or lie that would get Ted to leave her alone.

"Sor-ry," he said again, holding on to the last syllable like a child. "Come swimming with me later," he said as he finally left. No thanks, she had so much to learn.

She cracked her knuckles and got into the database of residents. Only one Quinn—was there ever!—in the system. Her hands shook as she hit enter and her eyes couldn't read the page fast enough. Quinn Robertson. She sighed, "Bree Robertson. That works." *He's only twenty-four, he's only been here for two and a half months, he drives a silver Accord with Wisconsin plates. Did he just move from there? He pays his rent on time with a check. He's self-employed. Well, that could be anything.* Technically Justin was self-employed. She wished it had been more specific. He had mentioned something about the wedding business or photography or something in front of Ted. "A fucking webpage!" she yelled, then quickly covered her mouth, hoping no one was walking in. Quickly she did a web search for Quinn Robertson photography. "Thank you!" she praised to the ceiling. "Chitown photo dot com, bitches," she said, clicking the mouse. The phone rang right as a rather high-tech homepage appeared on her screen. It was George.

"Did I leave my mug there at your office?"

"I don't see it," she said, rolling her eyes.

"Did you look?"

"Yes, that's what I do when I see things," she said. It was sitting on a chair near the entrance. Oh well, screw it.

"Well, if you find it, please make sure it's clean and in good shape for when I come back next time." *You fucking pig.*

"Will do." She hung up before he could get in her way anymore. Again her eyes couldn't scan through the page fast enough. Rates, past weddings, testimonials from customers all saying nice things. *"Mr. Robertson covered every inch of our wedding without us even noticing he was there, amazing work!"* How could someone not notice he was there? If she was the bride, she'd be leaving her hubby at the altar for the young photographer. She pictured herself in a wedding dress making a mad dash for him at the exit to some church. She would jump on his perfect shoulders and ride him off into the sunset. "Enjoy the cake!" is all she would yell back to her confused guests.

Next was the contact page. It had a page to send a message asking for rates and availability, as well as a phone number she memorized within moments. She wondered if it was his cell or a business line. Was he one of those people who had to leave a professional outgoing message on their cellphone? Again, her imagination took over.

His sexy voice would say, "Hi, you've reach Quinn Robertson of Chi-town Photography, please leave a message after the beep."

She held her hand up to the side of her face to make an imaginary phone and whispered, "Quinn, it's me. Let's meet at our favorite spot and do it all night again. Don't forget the fabric softener."

Where the hell was the "About Me" page? She clicked back through each option. Finally at the very bottom of the frequently asked questions page, she found what she had been looking for. It wasn't much, but it was a picture of his beautiful face looking back at her. Click and save. She immediately tried to enlarge the picture but it became grainy. "No!" she pouted. "This can't be all I get." If this guy wanted to get business, all he had to do was showcase himself in the photos and wait for the barrage of horny bridesmaids to insist their BFF use Chi-Town Photography for the big day.

She saved the picture to her hard drive and emailed it to her phone. Then she put in his number to her contacts under the name QR and saved the picture to the contact. Someday he would call her or she would call him and that picture would pop up. Someday there would be a point where her heart would slow down when he was around. No, impossible. She would be the happiest woman alive. He could just pick her up and carry her everywhere while she stayed wrapped around his torso.

Daydreaming was interrupted by multiple couples coming in to look at apartments. She hadn't given any notice to the Dogwood residents, so she continued to show the empty units and one set of newlyweds even signed a lease to move in at the middle of the month.

Bree felt much better physically and mentally about everything. Sure, her new boss was the worst person in the world, but he was long gone and she had his favorite mug. She had saved the last hour of the workday to look up all of the information about the girl who interrupted their first magical moment in the laundry room. That would be tomorrow's task to get her through the day. For tonight, she would pretend that girl didn't exist. Her cellphone was cradled in her arms when she finally got home and relaxed on her couch. She stared into the picture, waiting for it to come alive. It was just her and picture Quinn. No rum, no boss, no Justin, no Stalker Ted. Just the two of them.

She started Tuesday morning with a fierce motive. It was time to answer more questions about the obstacles to her destiny. Using the database, Bree glared at the screen to see the name of the evil mistress, Jill Herman. "Her last name is a fucking pun!" she said to an empty office. "The whole universe is a big joke and the gods are all laughing at me." She scrolled down the page. Jill was twenty-seven and also self-employed. Bree assumed the worst about her. *She probably takes advantage of him and takes him for granted at the same time. No doubt she embezzles all of his money from his own business* (just thinking that made her flutter a little). She drove a red Focus and also had Wisconsin plates. Maybe they just moved in together. That never goes well for young couples. She had witnessed a few leases going sour and exes trying to coexist just to fulfill the lease. They were already on their third month, so it wouldn't take that much longer.

It would be the first chilly night of the autumn, the leaves beginning to fall and the sun setting earlier. She would be sitting on her couch with a glass of red wine when a knock on the door would come. She would know exactly who it was and what he wanted. She would open the door and ask, "What took you so long?" and he would be on her like that. She would rip his cashmere sweater off—but without hurting it—and they would tumble to her couch, then the floor, the kitchen counter, the bedroom, the floor again, and then up to her new favorite getaway on the rooftop. She would cry out "Oh Quinn!" so loud that it would echo through Jill's skull as leaves softly fell on their flesh.

She just needed another encounter. Something, *anything* to make the week go by. Justin had been rather distant for some reason, and unless it was to follow through on his end of the plan, she wasn't happy about it. She had forgotten to ask George about promoting the open mic, but she figured it didn't matter. He was already accusing her of favoritism with Justin; the flyers wouldn't have helped. Most of them were still in her bottom drawer, though. Maybe that's what Justin was acting weird about. She didn't mean to blow off his idea, but he just didn't understand the professional world. She couldn't just throw a bunch of passes everywhere without complaints. Thankfully, none of them were still out during the walkthrough. Were people actually taking them?

Wednesday was another marathon, only *nothing* happened. Even a visit from Stalker Ted would've been okay at this point. By midday she decided she finally understood the true meaning of the word *longing*. A guy had used that word on her years ago and she had laughed at him. "Guys don't *long* for things, silly. Only us girls can long correctly," she had told him. This was karma for every guy she had turned down.

Jacob Minster in fourth grade, Eric Martin in seventh, the list went on. Was this what it was like for all of those boys when they had a crush on her? No, that's an unfair comparison. They didn't know what they wanted back then, it was only about looks. They didn't know what sex was, or true love for that matter. She didn't dangle herself in front of them and show off her abs within seconds of meeting. Well, maybe once or twice in college, but that was playful.

Thursday just hurt. She texted back and forth with Justin, but he was just trying to get her to support his open mic show. Stalker Ted came in for a short chat about sunburns, but that was the highlight of the workday. Just before eight, Justin sent her another text saying, *I think you should come to my show tonight.*

She casually waited another fifteen minutes to text back. Stupid Justin and his stupid show. *Why?* she asked.

They're here.

12

She parked in the back of the lot to the club and hesitated before removing the keys from the ignition. The giant orange sign for Chuck's seemed to blend in with the early stages of the sunset. Maybe she should just go home and wait until next week. She didn't have a game plan and had thought of nothing except how to look unintentionally attractive while getting ready in less than twenty minutes. The show had started close to an hour ago, but she could show up fashionably late. That was a good start. She wasn't there for any particular reason, just hanging out and supporting her buddy. Nothing to do with laying the groundwork for the most important relationship of her life. No sir, she was just there for a drink, maybe two because tomorrow was Friday. Would she approach him? Would he approach her? But shit, he said *they're here* instead of *he's here.* Step one would be to just get a drink from the bar and find a seat.

The same back patio that she had sat alone at a week before was now packed with all kinds of people. Groups of college-aged kids, some older folks who were probably supporting a younger family member, and random thirty-somethings filled the tables. There was only one seat left at the bar which Bree darted towards as if she was in the world championship of musical chairs. "Rum and Coke," she whispered to the bartender as a boy who couldn't even be old enough to drink recited some poetry into the microphone. A portable spotlight was aimed to the corner to designate where the stage was. The tables and chairs had been adjusted to face the performance area, and Justin was off to the left sitting next to a group of comics she had seen several times. She scanned the tables for Quinn and his girlfriend but didn't see him. Was this all just a lie to get her out here? She wasn't going to talk to Justin for a week if that was the case. She should be able to spot him right away. He probably has a nice glow in a darker setting. She looked back into the club but only saw a few people stocking coolers behind the main bar. No Quinn.

The younger guy finished his poem to rather noticeably generous applause and Justin came back to the microphone. "Keep it going for Mark," he said as the applause finally died down. "Your next performer is fairly new to the area, but definitely not a rookie. Put your hands together for Jill Herman."

Bree's head snapped to face the stage. The same girl from the laundry room calmly emerged with a large, light-brown acoustic guitar. She gently put the strap around her neck and pulled the stool close to the microphone, which she lowered to her mouth. Her reddish-brown hair was styled perfectly with just the right amount of volume. Her makeup gave her a completely different face than the one Bree had remembered from their first encounter. She wore a white summer dress with green flowers. As much as Bree wanted to label her ugly, she was intimidated by Jill's show-like appearance and casual vibe in front of so many people.

"Hi," she leaned in and said into the microphone. She quickly tuned a string on her guitar and began strumming chords in a slow rhythm. Not bad. She could play guitar, so what? Then the lyrics began. "Something in your eyes tonight, that stole my thoughts away . . ." Pitch perfect. "But I think it's what's inside your heart that steals them every day . . ." And the crowd was hooked. Every table was focused on the pure melody that she sweetly belted out with each passionately phrased lyric. This explained it. No wonder he was living with her. No wonder she didn't have to look good all of the time. She sounded like an angel, no, a mythical siren that lured men to her every note.

"Fuck," Bree whispered to herself, and then accidentally swallowed an ice cube from her drink. She looked over at Justin. Uh oh. She had never seen that look on his face before. His eyes were so focused on Jill that she could've hit him with a bowling ball and he wouldn't have noticed. His mouth was slightly open and his thumbs were drumming to the song's beat on his knees. He was so far out on the edge of his seat, Bree thought he might slip off the front. The song continued and the audience was entranced. After a small bridge following the third chorus, the rhythm changed and sped up. She sang louder and louder, squeezing emotion out of every note. She continued to play and hopped off the stool while pressing her mouth up against the microphone. Her right heel kicked over the stool, timing it perfectly with an emphasized note in a way that had every member of the audience on the verge of tears and fist pumping at the same time. Finally the tune ended, "And sometimes I hope you feel that way toooooo!"

Her arm was still extended from stroking the final chord when the audience leapt to its feet with shouts and whistles that Bree had never heard at the club. Jill took a small bow and calmly walked back into the darkness of the patio. Justin was late getting back to the microphone. "Wow, people! That was, that was unbelievably great!" Had he been crying? His eyes looked glazed and there was something in his voice. "Jill Herman, everyone!" He stepped back from the mic as the cheering finally died down. "That will do it for this week's show. Thank you all so much for coming out and supporting our local talent. We'll be here every Thursday night at eight all summer long. Let's hear it one more time for everyone who performed tonight." The audience clapped again while some got up to pay tabs, use the restroom or make their way over to the performers. A group of people crowded around Justin, who of course was right next to Jill. Bree wasn't about to lose her prime seat at the bar, especially now that she would need a few more drinks to try to wash away what just happened.

A drink and a half later, almost nothing had changed. Justin was still over by Jill, and the crowd was barely thinning. She even caught an older woman getting Jill's autograph. At least she would have no trouble motivating Justin to try to sleep with Jill. He was completely smitten. She glanced over between heads every few minutes and could see it in his eyes every time. She spun around on her barstool and looked towards the patio's exit.

There he was.

Quinn was leaned over, packing up his camera into a small bag. Had he been there taking pictures? She did recall a few camera flashes during Jill's performance, but never thought to look at where they came from. Her pupils opened as far as they could to see the perfect body crouched down. He wore jeans, a black t-shirt, and black dress shoes, and didn't seem to notice her or anyone around him. He frowned and made faces at the back of his camera as he scrolled through the pictures he had taken. Finally he paused and smiled, probably finding one he liked. How many thousands of pictures had he taken of Jill? What would it feel like to have him photograph her instead? To have him note every detail in the angles, the shadows, the gaze of the viewer would be surreal. He would tell her to hold still, then lean in a little more, then snap a few more shots, all while yelling, "Beautiful! These are absolutely stunning! Make love to the camera—no, no—fuck the camera, make love to me!"

Just then he looked up and saw Bree's stare. *Panic. Do I keep looking? Do I pretend I wasn't staring and fantasizing?* It all rushed through her head and, before she could even decide, he gave her a little wave. Heart, blood, face, warm, hot, armpits. Dammit. She turned quickly to order another drink and then glanced back to wave her own hello. He was gone. *What kind of Batman bullshit did he just pull?* She had turned away for just a second and now her love was gone. Immediately she blamed herself. She was too creepy, she was too ugly, she was too fat, her teeth made him confuse her with a vampire. He probably already had a nickname like Stalker Ted lined up for her. Biter Bree. His would be more creative. Jill would probably come up with it and then write ten more beautiful songs to steal away her man, and apparently her best friend as well. She would never be able to compete with this girl.

As the fourth drink found its way to her mouth, she began to feel worthless. Others were so talented, and all she did was show people apartments. Her skills included unlocking doors, flipping on a light switch, and mentioning how all of the toilets had been updated to water-savers. God had shortchanged her. All she was given were an uneven set of boobs and some fangs to go with them. Thanks a lot, God.

She was staring down at her drink when Justin leaned up next to her. "Where to begin?" he said. She didn't even acknowledge him, yet he still babbled on. "I don't know how I'm going to pull this off, but I must have her. Perhaps

Quinn and I can talk over a cigar and trade you like fathers in those old cultures arrange marriages for their daughters." She wasn't amused. "Quinn, I'll take that little ball of talent off your hands and in exchange you get my lovely friend Bree, who—" he stopped there because he couldn't think of anything to say about her. Bree knew it, too. A tear splashed on the bar just below her sinking head. She covered her face with her hands and hoped Justin would just go away. He knew what he had done. He knew why she was upset. He knew she couldn't drive. He knew it was best to *finally* stop saying anything else.

"Let's go," he mumbled, and walked her back to his car and began the silent drive home.

13

Friday morning started with an unpleasant call from George. "Okay, Andrews, you're now well into June. You think you can actually throw a pool party for your residents this time?"

"Yes," she said, holding the phone away from her headache. George, or whoever his bitch was at Corporate, took it upon themselves to mail out newsletters to everyone in the four buildings earlier that week telling them about next weekend's pool party.

"Put out a few more signs from the PDF I'll be mailing you, and try to act happy about it to anyone who asks about it. Meanwhile, you've got a week to get on your boys about having the place spotless. And remember, no beer bottles!" he yelled. Did he mean no beer or just no bottles? She didn't care. It was going to be on the one Saturday of the month she had to work, so she would be planted in the office anyway, waiting for potential renters. All was not lost, though. Justin would be there drinking. For as mad as she was at him, she still needed to talk about last night.

The day kept her busy as she was able to show several apartments and lease three of them to young couples. One pair of newlyweds were only twenty-two years old and had the groom's father with them. He asked all of the important questions, while the two of them just held hands and giggled. She knew what they were thinking as they walked around the empty apartment, especially the counter.

She walked by Quinn's door three times that day but never heard a thing. The guy was a ghost. Sometimes his car was there, sometimes it wasn't. Any time a silver car went by, adrenaline would shoot through her entire body. Even the cars that looked nothing like an Accord still alerted her. She wouldn't even know what to say to him anyway. How was it that she had so few opportunities? It was like the universe was trying to trick her into thinking that it wasn't meant to be.

An email from George popped up. It was a copy of the newsletters from Stevens Chicago Properties being sent to everyone. Bree used to have to write up a newsletter for her building, but that had fizzled out months ago. George's letter rambled on about the pool party and the live DJ they were bringing in (nice to know). Then he lectured about safety and making sure no one brought glass bottles. Towards the end, the subject changed, and he explained that there would be random apartment showings with twenty-four-hour notices. His explanation was that the few empty apartments were being refurbished, so just for a limited time, "the friendly staff" would appreciate the residents' understanding. As a bonus, anyone whose apartment was shown would receive a twenty-five dollar discount on rent that month.

"Couldn't he have made it fifty?" she asked, knowing this was going to trigger some phone calls. And who was this DJ coming in? Did George want her opinion on any of this? Maybe a heads up about what was going on at least a few days before the residents would hear about it? Now even her insignificant job was making her feel even more worthless. She texted Justin: *Come over after your shows tonight.*

The rest of the day was quiet and she didn't even hear back from Justin. She hoped he wasn't already ignoring her as a result of falling madly in love with Jill. She figured she might as well get used to spending her Friday nights alone. She fell asleep on her couch to bad TV and didn't wake up until an infomercial around one.

"Are you sick of hiding your smile?" it blared.

"Yes," she said, opening her eyes.

"Too old for braces?"

"Uh huh, talk to me," she lifted her head.

"Call today to set up a free consultation for Smile Clear Orthodontics," the commercial continued. For the next twenty-nine minutes Bree carefully watched before and after pictures, testimonials, and beautiful smiles talk about what a life-changing experience Smile Clear caused. She wanted it. She needed it. It was time to change herself, and no one would even notice. She wrote the phone number down, but by the end of the infomercial, had it memorized right next to Quinn's.

By two in the morning she was going through bank statements and calculating her budget to see if she could afford some monthly payments for the life-changing product. Math wasn't making sense at this hour, but at least it was something to do. She felt like a grown-up looking at the various deposits and withdrawals (mostly withdrawals). Twenty-six and independent was a sugar-coating thought. She would barely be able to afford the pseudo-braces unless she made some cutbacks. She could drop her car to minimum coverage, since she barely had to drive it during the week. She could cancel the gym membership she had used four times. The Springview building had an ample fitness center, though she hated the idea of working out with the possibility of Stalker Ted wandering in. But was that where Quinn worked out? Why hadn't she thought of that before? Those shoulders didn't just grow like that naturally. She was wasting close to fifty bucks a month when all the motivation and eye candy she could ever want was free over at Springview.

Be over in five. Justin finally acknowledged her. How dare he assume she was still awake at this hour? But oh, well, he knew better than anyone.

She was waiting at the door with a blanket when he arrived. "Follow me," she whispered.

"Where are we going?" his voice echoed through the hallway.

"Shh!" she led him up the steps to her spot on the roof. "Okay, now you can talk at a normal volume, you drunk." It was weird seeing Justin this drunk. It wasn't because he never got this way, it was just that this time, she was sober for once. She lay the blanket down, smoothed it out, and plopped down, gazing up at the stars and the small crescent of moon.

"This is pretty fucking cool up here," he said, sitting down next to her. "Are you in your pajamas?" he mumbled. "Is this a slumber party?" It was going to be his last party if he didn't sit his ass down and start talking.

"Yes, I'm wearing shorts and a t-shirt. Is that okay or are you going to make fun of me some more?"

He swayed for a moment and then said, "Oh yeah, those Lilith Fair shorts you had on that one time were fucking great!"

"You're hammered, Justin. Dammit, I need to know stuff. I want you to be honest," she pleaded.

"Look," he burped, "I may have had some feelings when I saw you lying there naked that one night, but that was just, you know, you were naked," he said, and then hiccupped.

"What? No! Not that. Fuck, I *knew* you saw my boobs or something, you pervert."

"I wanted to do something, but I didn't. There, I'm being honest." He held out his arms and shrugged. "There, happy? I was honest."

"That's all fine and great, but I need to know everything about Jill."

"Oooh," he moaned. "That stuff. Yeah, I love Jill. Love her!" He was beyond drunk. "Jill is amazing. You should've heard her sing the other night at my show. Oh my god, it was amazing."

"I was there, you asshole! You drove me home," she yelled. "I'm wasting my time. Shit, is my car still there?"

"Yeah, um actually, no. I brought it home tonight."

"You drove like this?"

"No, of course not," he slurred. "I'm not stu—" He hiccupped again. "I'm not an idiot."

"Then how is my car here?"

"Okay, get this," he let out a little laugh. "Jill drove your car home with me in it."

Anger wasn't right word for the fumes that filled up Bree's body. She clenched her fists but her body couldn't move. There was something so invasive about that girl driving her car. Among the obvious, now she had the nerve to drive a stranger's car? He would pay for this dearly. Bree's natural reaction was almost never to physically harm someone. Sure, there was one mild scuffle when she was just out of high school, but that was after her first tequila experience, and that bitch deserved to be slapped. Justin deserved a different kind of punishment. She sat thinking and biting her tongue while he went on about all of the drinks he had. Infuriated, she kept picturing Jill behind her steering wheel. This wasn't part of the plan. Yes, her car was home and they had actually done her a favor, but why was it so infuriating? She wouldn't admit to any jealousy, despite what the little voice was saying.

"So earlier you were saying you wanted to touch me, yes?" she asked, masking the anger.

"I mean, we were drunk and it just felt like the right thing to do, but the wrong thing to do at the same time," he said, and then hiccupped again. She sat there with the cruelest of scenarios running through her head.

"Well," she said in a mischievous voice, "why don't you think about what feels right and what feels wrong and I'll be right back." She got up and started to walk towards the door. After a few steps she dramatically pulled her t-shirt off over her head and dropped it behind her while covering her chest with her left arm. She didn't look back, but she knew it would work. Once inside, she tiptoed down the steps and prayed to God no one in her hallway was up. Barefoot and topless all while sober, she dashed into her apartment. She dropped her arm and let the girls breathe before putting another shirt on. She brushed her teeth and even took time to floss for the first time in way too long. She inspected her face for blackheads, pulled her hair back for the night and took her sweet time returning to the rooftop. Justin was passed out on his back, shirt off, pants down to his knees and apparently really cold. Who would wake up naked and confused this week? To make sure of it she untied his shoes, pulled his pants down the rest of the way, grabbed his shirt and tossed everything off the side of the building. She left his boxers in the far corner near the edge and weighed them down with his cellphone and wallet.

14

At approximately five-thirty the following morning she got a text: *What the fuck did you do to me?* She decided to ignore it, like he had done to hers, until hours later.

Finally, after a Saturday morning of reading magazines in bed with a little coffee, she fired back, *Nothing. What happened?*

Whatever was his response. She felt better after knowing her little prank was quite vengeful. Had he even deserved that? He was trying to help her in a way, after all. Oh well, she could always lie and tell him whatever she wanted. For all he knew, he got laid. Keeping him wondering would give her a sense of power over him. He would be afraid to ask about it until next time they were drunk, which could be as soon as tonight. She still needed to talk to him about Jill, so she didn't want to mess things up too badly. Justin definitely had some leverage.

Lunch at Pete's Diner? she texted back.

Fifteen minutes later, an exhausted Justin knocked on her door. He was wearing the clothes she had thrown off the roof. "You're driving," is all he said.

"Hey there, champ. Are those clothes dryer fresh, or did you hang them out to dry?"

"Seriously," he said, "I don't know what happened. I don't want to know what happened. Just get me to some greasy food and a cup of coffee or I'll puke on you."

Bree was already in a better mood, but it was temporary. As she got into her car, she banged her knees on the steering wheel. "That bitch moved my seat up!" she said, pounding the dashboard.

"Easy. Please, I'm a little rough today. Would you rather your car still be at the club? Would you rather find me dead in a ditch from drunk driving?" he whined.

"Right now? Yes."

The first few minutes, the only spoken words were to the waitress. Bree was waiting for him to break the silence. She had no idea how to feel right now. Part of her felt sorry that she had done that to Justin. Leaving someone naked on a rooftop all night is a little much for a prank. He probably didn't even know what he had done wrong. She wanted him to sleep with Jill and she needed her car back, but why was she so mad about the way the plan was going? She knew Justin was attracted to Jill, but what was it he had said about her last night? That must have been drunk talk. She really couldn't tell, because Justin would say anything for sex sometimes. Even with her he would push it in a safe way. He either was acting like he was kidding or bluffing, and she never knew how to take it. She gave him one job to do, or rather he volunteered to do it himself, and it was taking too long.

"So," he said. "If you're done being mean and humiliating me, maybe I'll tell you what I can remember about last night's conversation with Jill."

"You mean be useful for once?"

"Then again, maybe I'll just add an extra order of bacon on—ouch!" she kicked his shin under the table. "Fine. Geez. What all do you want to know?"

"Are you going to be able to close the deal with this girl or not? Sorry for having my own purposes in mind, but as you can see I'm running out of patience."

"Jill's great. I no longer want to bang her to help you out with Quinn," he said.

"What?" Bree said, ready to leave him at the diner.

"No, no. It's not like that. I still want to bang her. I just want to do it for a different reason now. And I think I can."

"What was she doing at the comedy club anyway? Why wasn't Quinn with her?"

"All she told me is that he was really sick this weekend, so he told her to go out and have fun or something instead of staying home and catching whatever bug he had."

Bree thought about the ways she'd like to "catch that bug" and thought about how it wouldn't even matter if she was sick afterwards. She would cherish every ache and pain it brought, knowing that it had come from intimate contact with him.

"So anyway, as you can tell she's a really good singer. I guess the deal is she sings at weddings, usually just during the beginning of the receptions when everyone is still getting there, and he takes pictures of the entire day. Together they make really good cash."

"Can you tell me anything I can't Google?" Her mood wasn't improving as she listened to what a great team Quinn and Jill made.

"Well, like I said. After that, she didn't mention him all night. She sat in the back of the showroom for free because Jeff, the manager, was so impressed with her singing the other night. Then we hung out at the patio bar after the second show. We talked until whenever I texted you back."

"About what? You were pretty late on getting back to me."

"That's the thing. I don't remember it all that well. These people in the second show sent me two shots while I was on stage, and then found me afterwards and gave me two more. Plus I was drinking in between."

"God Justin, you don't even know how well it went?"

"I mean, I think it went well. I remember her laughing at me on the drive home."

"Was she drunk? 'Cause if she had wrecked my car—"

"No, I don't even think she was boozing at all. I think it was just Coke in her glass all night."

"So then why do you like her so much?"

"Well, she's cute," he said. It hurt. It shouldn't have hurt. It made no sense that it hurt. But it did. He was right. She looked cute belting out her amazing song that had everyone melting and applauding all at once. Bree had done nothing but obsess about Quinn's appearance, and if she wanted to have Justin she could've . . . at least last night on the rooftop. So why did it hurt so much to hear about this girl? "Obviously her singing and guitar playing is attractive."

"Obviously," Bree said in a mocking voice.

"Look, I thought this was the plan. You can't hate her for no reason other than your jealousy. I actually like her, and if all goes as planned, that means destroying her relationship with Quinn. Have you even thought about the repercussions of all of this, seeing as how the four of us live in the same damn apartment complex?" Bree put her coffee mug down and crinkled a packet of sugar in her left hand. She glanced out the window that was adjacent to their booth and sighed as an old woman crossed the street with her dog. "I know a lot of this is my fault for not taking it seriously until now, but we have got to think this through."

"Well, did she seem happy with him?" Bree asked instead of telling Justin he was right. The fact that her tone was defeated was her signal to him that she understood.

"Like I said, she only mentioned that he was sick. After that, it wasn't much other than his photography stuff." Bree's mind flashed back to Quinn squatting down and putting his camera away before she was spotted, his tan arms and hands working meticulously at inspecting his work while she noticed everything else about him. The way his black sleeves hugged—no, squeezed—his bicep. The way his shirt didn't reach all the way down to his jeans in the back, leaving just a sliver of flesh and gray designer underwear showing. All of it amazing and permanently engraved into her memory.

"Do you feel like you have a chance with her?" If Justin had a chance with Quinn's girlfriend, then she felt she had a shot with Quinn. She'd settle for being his revenge fuck, his rebound, even a shoulder to cry on at first. She just needed one chance with him and he'd be hers forever.

"Honestly Bree. I do," he said with a mild laugh. "From what I remember she was into me somewhat . . . and she was sober. Maybe my judgment was a little off, but she made sure we got home okay. I don't exactly recall the ride home or much of why I ended up naked on our roof, but—"

"I'm sorry," Bree finally said. "I was mad, a little drunk too," she lied, "and you said some mean, weird stuff." He couldn't argue. The beauty of not blacking out.

"Like what?" Uh oh.

"I don't know, just stuff."

"Well, it must've been something, 'cause you left me naked on a roof. What the hell did I do that was so awful?"

112

"Look, you're the one who took your clothes off, not me," she said. *There. Explain that.*

"Well, what prompted me to take my clothes off?"

"Probably all those shots people were feeding you." Wow. She had taken her shirt off in front of him and he didn't even remember it. That would be her little secret until they were old and gray.

"So what's the next step, Bree? I think we're even. We both want someone we can't have right now. Patience? Is that what we need? I mean, they're young too. Relationships have problems."

"Their relationship has a lease for another nine months. I ain't waiting that long." She never said *ain't*, but thought it would show Justin how serious she was. "When's the next time you'll see her? Thursday's open mic night."

"Probably. Are you going to go?"

"I don't know, Justin. He didn't even come talk to me last night. He just waved and disappeared. I don't even know if he was waving at me or one of the other twenty girls proba-bly gawking at him. I can't stay calm whenever he's around, and especially if *she's* around. I'll say something stupid, or just turn green with envy. Plus I'll have drinks in me and we know that never leads to good decisions. If I go, I'll just hate her even more."

"You've got a point. Can you just wait a week or two while I see what the Jill situation is?"

"Wait. Yes. That's all I've done." Was it? So far she had done shots of rum during the workday, dressed like a prostitute in the laundry room that she had sabotaged, attempted a slutty carwash scene, gotten naked in front of Justin, let him get naked in front of her, and then chucked his clothes off the roof of their building.

"Do you remember what we talked about that one night? Having a passion other than another person? Remember that heart to heart?"

She paused. Shit, he was bringing that up before she had found one. "I know I need to become a better person," she said.

"I didn't say that. I just said find a passion."

"Have you ever heard of that Smile Clear Orthodontics thingy?" She liked to change the subject when he was right.

"That what?"

"I saw a commercial for it and I think I want to get my teeth straightened. I know that's why I'm ugly."

"Aw, is the baby feeling sorry for herself?" he asked in a whiny voice.

"Shut up, I'm serious. I've got some money saved up so I'm going to go in this week for a free consultation."

"Fine, whatever you feel you need to do. I'm going to wait until Thursday night and make my move then. Friday and Saturday I have shows again, so I'll see if she'll come out to one of those alone and put their little relationship to the test. If worse comes to worst, she can always live with me for the next nine months," he laughed.

"No, no, she's staying there. Quinn will move in with me!"

15

The following Thursday, Bree rushed over for her appointment during her lunch hour. The office was in a small strip mall next to a sports bar and a drug store. She signed in and took a seat next to a father with two young boys. The father was buried in his *New York Times* while his two sons, whom she guessed were around the ages of twelve and ten, stared at her.

The first boy whispered to the second, "She looks really old to be getting braces." Bree pretended not to notice the metallic smiles. "But it also looks like she needs them."

"What the hell, dude?" she snapped at the older child.

"Dad, she cussed at Mike!" yelled the younger one.

"Teach your boys some manners and I'll clean up my language," she said defensively.

"I apologize. Boys, do you need to wait out in the car?" the father said sternly. Good lord, was this going to be how every visit was? Weren't there other grownups there getting their teeth straightened?

"Breezy Andrews," an assistant popped out and called her back.

"That's a weird name," the younger boy whispered too loudly.

"Be quiet!" he said. "She works at our apartments." Oops. This community was getting too small or the apartments were getting too big.

Finally she was able to talk to the doctor. He poked around in her mouth, looking at her teeth from all angles like a dentist normally would. His gray hair didn't fit his young face. With his green eyes he almost looked like an actor in costume. At the conclusion of the exam, he raised her chair back up and broke things down for her.

"Well, Breezy, you definitely need to fix that class two, division two," which she assumed was the technical term for snaggle-tooth. "The Smile Clear system won't work for your extreme case, however, so we'll need to put on braces for a year or two." Extreme case? A year or two?

"My teeth are that bad?"

"Oh sweetie, it's not your that your teeth are bad, they're just a little crooked. We'll get 'em straightened out in a few months, and then the braces keep them there until they're permanently straight. Well, you gotta wear a retainer at night after the braces come off, but that's not so bad."

"But the infomercial had people with teeth ten times worse than mine," she said.

"Well, that's the magic of television. It would not be wise to even consider Smile Clear in your situation. Would you like to talk pricing, or do you want to think it over?"

"What's a ballpark figure for braces?" she said, just to see.

"Thirty-five hundred, but that covers your retainer and all your visits as well. We'll tighten them up every few months and make sure everything is moving how it should. We also have a monthly payment plan, but there's a small finance fee with that, so it goes up to about four grand."

"Damn," she said, thinking back to her bank statements. "Let me sleep on it a few nights and get back to you." She could afford it, but he wasn't quite selling her on it. "I'll have to think about it. I hope I'm not wasting your time."

"No no, Miss Andrews, I understand. No one at your age has ever regretted it, though. Kids are a lot nicer in their twenties, right?"

She thought about the cracks Justin would be making from day one. "I'll get back to you," she said. As she walked back through the waiting room she envied the two brats for having a father who took care of this when they were children.

After hurrying home through lunch hour traffic, Bree had just enough time to heat up a Hot Pocket that had been in her freezer for close to a year. It sat next to the box of fish sticks that she always bought but never ate during Lent. One to two years and close to four grand would be the cost of fixing her smile. She had close to five thousand in savings, but would need that for a different car someday. She remembered all of the testimonials from people who had straightened their teeth. No one regretted it. But would Quinn be able to overlook all that metal in her mouth? He wouldn't have to settle for a girl like her when he had his choice. He chose Jill, though. Bree had a chance.

As she returned to the office she texted Justin, *Good luck tonight!* The luck wished had nothing to do with his performance on stage, just his interaction with Jill. The afternoon was filled with phone calls from residents.

"What's this about showing our apartments?" was the typical question.

"Sorry, Mr. Wise," she said. "It's just that Stevens Chicago Properties isn't always able to show the empty units because of remodeling. You get a nice discount on rent if we use yours, though."

"Sounds like bullshit to me, ma'am."

"Well, I'm sorry you feel that way. If I can help it, I'll try to make sure yours doesn't get selected," she said to a click on the other end. A few other calls went the same way.

She was just about to leave for the day when the phone rang one more time. Two minutes later and she would be out the door.

"Stevens Chicago Properties, this is Bree. How can I help you?"

"Yeah, I just read about the twenty-five dollar discount for letting you show our apartment," the female voice said.

"Yes, I apologize. We're getting a lot of complaints about it. I'll talk to corporate and see if we can up that to fifty or figure something out."

"No no, you can use ours. Twenty-five bucks off would be great."

"Really?" Bree said. This was a pleasant change.

"Yeah, I'm a bit of a starving artist," she said.

"All right, let me get your information." She got a pen ready to write the name down but wouldn't need to.

"Jill Herman, I'm over in Dogwood." Bree said nothing. "Hello? Are you still there?"

"Sorry, yes. I will note that and if we need, we'll shoot you a notice. Are you gone during the daytime?"

"Almost always. We're both usually not here in the afternoons. Mornings, I sleep late, but by lunchtime we're both at work somewhere on Monday through Thursday."

"Got it. Thanks, Jill." The conversation ended but her heart was racing. Seeing their apartment would hurt, but could also answer so many questions. What kind of bedroom did they have? What kind of cereal does Quinn eat? What does he drink? Would there be posters on the wall, and would they have frames? She would be able to tell so much by what was in there. Antiques, books, or any other interests she could fake were all potential conversation starters.

That night Bree stayed home and stared at her phone. Justin was texting updates about the night. She had given him specific instructions on staying sober enough to remember what they talked about. Jill was there with an attractive blonde, but Quinn wasn't around. She sang a different song, but no standing ovation this week. There was a much smaller crowd somehow. Just before midnight Justin woke Bree up with a text that read, "Nothing major tonight, but she's going to swing by my shows tomorrow."

That seemed major. Justin was downplaying it so that Bree didn't force him to explain everything tonight. She was thrilled that Jill seemed to be bonding with Justin, but who knew what Justin would actually go through doing. She lay awake in bed until well past midnight. A few times she went to Quinn's business webpage and looked at his picture on her phone. She considered going up on the roof, but it was still too hot to be comfortable. The weekend was forecasting near-record highs; at least the pool party would be a success.

She finally dozed off and dreamt of her reflection in the mirror. Instead of her normal smile, she had two large tusks jutting out of her mouth. Everywhere she went, people were staring at her. Justin was the only one who wouldn't say anything, but he was just being nice. She knew he felt embarrassed to be seen with her, but he stuck with her anyway.

Bree needed three cups of coffee to wake up on Friday. After her nightmare, she called the orthodontist and told him she'd like to talk about the whole braces procedure again. By ten-thirty she was buzzing around the office on a caffeine high when a younger guy came in. There was something familiar about him, but she couldn't place it. He had brown eyes with a slightly shaggy head of brown hair. What little facial hair he could grow was spotted around his cheeks here and there. He had on a dirty white t-shirt and khaki shorts that looked almost as old as he was.

"Hello, are you interested in renting?" she asked, putting on her facade of Friendly Leasing Agent.

"No, I'm the DJ at the pool party tomorrow. Mark Owen, nice to meet you," and he reached his hand out. She was sure she had seen him before, but didn't want to ask because he seemed so young.

"Oh, thanks for stopping in. I guess you're here from what, ten until one tomorrow?"

"Noon to six actually. I threw in a couple free hours for some plugs in your newsletter next month." Six hours? She had no idea it was an all-day thing. Usually these little events were a couple of hours in the late morning. She had visions of Justin running around naked after six full hours of pool drinking.

"Wow, I guess I will be there," she said. Quinn or no Quinn, what did she have to lose?

"Cool. Mind if I take a look around?" he asked, keeping a business tone in his speech. He was young but handled himself like he was thirty. Bree escorted him to the pool area where not much was going on, just a small child playing with his mother in the shallow end. She opened the gate and let Mark walk around. He stared at some of the tables and asked if it would be okay to move some things around so that his equipment wasn't too close to the water. Bree showed him the nearest electrical outlets and let him measure how many feet of cord he would need for power. There was something relaxing about his deep voice. It didn't feel like it belonged to his body or boyish face. *He's just so petite for a guy*, she thought. Cute enough to put in her big fake Chanel purse and carry around whenever she needed someone to . . . hold?

"All right, Miss Andrews, this place looks fine. I think we're good to go for tomorrow. How many people are you expecting?"

"I'm not sure. It could be a dozen, it could be capacity." She looked over at the sign that labeled that at forty-eight. They only had thirty-some chairs, so that could get interesting. "Most of the complex is small families with a kid or two, and the rest are older divorcées. What kind of music are you playing?"

"Oh, I guess I'll have to stick with the popular crap, but I can always slip in something good from the last one or two decades. I'm pretty good at reading crowds." Mark had her sign some paperwork that had to do with her company paying him five hundred dollars for his time. He left, and she pounded her brain as to where she knew him from.

A few minutes later she returned to her office slightly sweaty. The air-conditioner felt great, and she just wanted to relax the rest of the afternoon. A half-hour later, the phone rang. It was the local pizza shop, Jimmy's, confirming that they would be ordering somewhere between five and twenty pizzas tomorrow at one for the party. Sure would have been nice if George had mentioned *any* of this to her. Was she supposed to place that order? How much was she supposed to get? She played along like she knew what she was talking about. Right before she left for the weekend, she remembered to check her email and, sure enough, George's note was waiting. Tomorrow she was to oversee the DJ, provide him bottled water, take a pizzas order depending on the number of people there—divide by three, he said—and then help shut things down at six. And most importantly, she had to make sure there was no glass on the premises. None of that mattered.

She followed her recent Friday night routine and fell asleep on her couch before six. She woke up starving and thirsty after midnight. "All caught up on sleep with nowhere to go." She heated up a frozen pizza and poured herself a glass of wine from a box she had picked up earlier in the week. Hopefully Justin would be giving her some news on things shortly. She opened a window and peeked out at the moon, which was now much fuller. The air felt a little more pleasant, so, while the pizza was still cooking, she walked her glass of wine up to the roof.

The door was already propped open. Who else had discovered her spot? Before she made her way out, she thought about Quinn. Once they started dating he would set up little surprise picnics up there. There would be flowers and candlelight on a table he would miraculously fit through the door. There would be a small set of speakers for background music, and they would slow dance while fireworks went off in the distance. She would happily throw Quinn's clothes off the edge of the building and spend the rest of the night on top of him until the sun came up. Then she'd do him some more. She smiled and peeked out into the roof. Across the building, she saw what appeared to be a figure on the ground. A cloud covered the moon for a brief moment, so that only the light from the parking lot in the distance made anything visible. The moonlight returned and it turned out to be two figures. She ducked her head back inside and then peered out again. Familiar noises from the past solved the mystery. It was Justin having sex, but with Jill! He had done it. She saw his bare ass in the moonlight and then ducked back inside. She hurried back to her apartment, where a pizza was starting to burn in the oven.

She burnt her hand while trying to cut the pizza but didn't feel a thing. Holy shit, he actually went through with it. He stole Quinn's girl! This was huge. How long until the dominos started to fall? Surely this Jill would be honest. Or would she need Justin to make it obvious? This could get really ugly, but she figured the uglier, the better.

She would definitely make her way to the laundry room next Friday and lock the door behind her. "Allow me to help you get even with her," she would tell an upset Quinn. "Can you add these to your load?" She'd take everything off and be stuck naked with him for an entire wash and dry cycle. That would take the frown off his beautiful face.

She wondered if Justin would contact her tonight after he "finished," or if she'd have to wait until tomorrow. Apparently her Saturday hours were an all-day thing, though she could relax at the pool after the pizzas were taken care of. Going to the pool party was not in doubt now. It was the beginning of the end of Quinn and Jill, and she needed to start the ball rolling as soon as possible. For the first time in weeks, she went to bed feeling hopeful.

16

Bree pounded on Justin's door on her way down to the office. After a minute, he cracked it open, looking like a baby farm animal opening its eyes for the first time. He opened his mouth to say something, but all that came out was a yawn with a heavy stench of morning breath. "Be down in my office in ten minutes, Romeo," Bree ordered. She was dead serious and he could see it in her face.

When he finally entered her office, she had a woman and her child at her desk reviewing the different floor plans of each building. A young couple waited in the seats near the door. Bree would be tied up with potential renters for another half hour at least. He flashed a small smile her way that she happened to catch as she looked up. She gave him a look that screamed, *"Don't you dare go back to bed, you asshole!"*

He held up his phone, which was her signal to text him when she was free. Needless to say, neither of the potential renters got her undivided attention. She hurried through the charts and didn't even offer to show them the last remaining two bedroom apartments. As of Monday, she could officially start showing the units in use; she just needed potential residents. Then it would be hello, Quinn's apartment!

The office finally cleared out, and, after four texts—the last one explaining that he needed to *hurry the fuck up*—Justin was finally seated in front of Bree's desk.

"So it wasn't Santa's reindeer on my roof last night, was it?"

Justin blushed. "Wow, nothing gets past you." He was smiling, but a bit embarrassed. "Yeah, I held up my end of the plan and enjoyed every minute of it."

"Oh, you lasted a full minute?" Justin jokingly got up and pretended he was walking away. "Sit your ass back down here!" she laughed.

"Well, yeah, so she came out to the club and watched me have probably the best two shows of my life."

"Was she drunk?"

"I don't think so. This time she drove her own car home with me in it. By the way, I'll need a ride to the club tonight. She didn't feel like saying goodbye yet, so I showed her that spot up on the roof. She didn't mention Quinn once, other than the fact that he was shooting a wedding. I tried to bring him up, just to test things, and she said she'd rather talk about me."

"Wow, that relationship was in bigger trouble than we could have ever foreseen. That's what happens when couples live together, I heard. So when are you going to see her again?"

"She's going to the pool party, which starts when?"

"Soon. I have to help some DJ set up and then order pizzas for everyone and then I can come down. What are you going to do if Quinn is there?"

"Just play it cool. He probably knows we're friends. I'll let her get out of the relationship however and whenever she wants. Preferably sooner than later." He kept going. "Although the whole rooftop under the moonlight thing was awesome. Thanks for the idea. May I go now and get a little sleep before my big day at the pool? Also, what time do the pizzas get there? And should I save you a seat?"

Bree ignored his questions and erupted with nerves. Quinn would probably be down there. Shirtless. If Justin was going to become part of their little clique, he would probably be sitting with them. She was going from almost no interaction at all to an all-out *hey-look-we're-half-naked-and-drinking* encounter. This was too much. She pondered how much to drink ahead of time. Too much, and she could permanently ruin things with one dumb comment. Not to mention she probably shouldn't be trashed in front of all of her residents.

"So what time, and do you need a seat?"

"Pizza's around one, save me a seat."

Justin turned to leave, mumbling under his breath. Bree was done thinking like a sane person. She stared into space, plotting and scheming, running through various scenarios in her head. The phone rang and she almost ignored it.

"Hey it's Mark. I'm here to set up."

"Already?" She hadn't looked at the clock for once.

"Yeah, it's ten till. Are there people showing up yet?"

"Shit, my fault. I'll be out there in a minute." She hung up and did her best speed-walk out to the pool. Groups were already showing up and the chairs were filling quickly. The "good seats" that the parents all battled for by the shallow end were nearly full. Off to the other side by the deep end, Mark was sliding tables and chairs out of his way so that he could fit back in the corner. She scanned around the middle and counted two dozen people already there. They were at half capacity in the first few minutes, and the free food hadn't even arrived. She hoped Justin would get there soon. If he was back in bed catching up on sleep, she would kill him.

Mark quickly got the music started with some generic dance song she had heard on commercials, and she hurried back to the office to lock things up. On her way back to the front of her building, she ran into Justin.

"It's filling up fast, hurry!" she said with urgency.

"What's that? The Titanic is sinking? There's not much time? I better sprint!" He walked even slower.

"Seriously, smartass. It's already halfway full. Where are you going to sit?"

"Right next to her," he pointed at Jill who was carrying a towel and a small tan bag of poolside supplies with her. She was having a hard time getting the gate open with her hands full. "I'm needed," Justin said and ran to assist her grand entrance.

"You never moved that fast for me, jerk," she said. Justin was already going above and beyond for this girl. The weird thing was that he had already slept with her. Usually that was Justin's cue to stop caring about someone. *Uh oh.*

Bree ran up the stairs in her building, figuring the extra few calories she could burn wouldn't hurt for the first day at the pool. She found her shades, flip-flops, and a magazine to pretend to read while eavesdropping on Justin and Jill. Maybe she would just be a third wheel and Quinn wouldn't show. Perhaps Jill had let him down gently and been honest from the start. She wouldn't mind being a third wheel if Quinn was an emotionally damaged fourth. Jill could've lied and just pretended something was wrong with the relationship. This would lead to the two of them not talking at all and Quinn turning to Bree for good conversation. Sure, make Jill jealous, that was the plan. The four of them could chicken fight in the pool! She could mount Quinn's shoulders while Jill got on Justin's and then simply beat the hell out of her. She dropped everything in her living room and actually closed her eyes for this fantasy. It would be orgasmic just having her legs wrapped around him. He would hold her steadily and never let her fall. She would create friction on the back of his neck and—

"Fuck, the pizzas!" she said, snapping out of it. She still had a few obligations before dry-humping Quinn's vertebrae. And by the way, *what the hell was she going to wear down there?*

Her bottom dresser drawer had three buried options. The first was a dark-blue one-piece that was so-so but looked like something an old lady would wear to swim across the English Channel. Her mother had bought it for her when they were supposed to take a trip down to Hilton Head the summer after her college graduation. It never progressed beyond an idea and a few compulsive purchases.

The second option was a red bikini that fit fine up top, but showed her butt crack whenever she turned around and caught her reflection in the mirror. Justin would remember it from all of the group vacations they took when they were younger . . . and smaller. He would laugh his ass off if hers was sticking out like it was. Zero for two.

The third suit was a bikini that she had only worn once or twice towards the end of her relationship with Brad. It was white, simple, and would probably fit just well enough to not make a scene. It still smelled of the chlorine from a hot tub they enjoyed in a hotel on their final Valentine's Day together. She had drunk too much and passed out as soon as they got back to their expensive hotel room at five in the afternoon. Brad sat on the bed in a bathrobe all evening while she slept motionless until the following morning. Ah, the romantic memories.

Bree slipped on the white suit and reviewed herself in the mirror. She inspected every one of her flaws and almost talked herself out of going at all. She pinched a layer of skin where abs would've been six years ago. The backs of her thighs weren't doing much for her either. But compared to Jill, she wasn't *that* bad, right? She continued to review every curve, and spun so many times in front of her reflection she became dizzy. Her dark apartment was a safe cocoon, but she would have to leave it and face the inevitable judgment of her lover's eyes. Seeing him shirtless would be worth it. Fuck, would it be worth it!

She threw on a long t-shirt that hung down almost to her knees as a cover-up and marched her way down. She kept a beat in her head and forced each step to keep up with it. Maybe she could fake the confidence like those ugly girls at dance clubs always managed to. She had to play it cool. If she thought the bikini looked good on her, no one else could disagree. She had read that somewhere. Sure it was probably some Cosmo article written by a swimsuit model who never had to worry about her appearance, but it applied to twenty-six-year-olds on the verge of finally having a meaningful conversation with the guy they were going to marry someday.

Still a half-parking lot away, Bree could see that the pool was almost at capacity. She called and ordered the maximum number of pizzas and made sure the clubhouse was equipped with paper plates, napkins, and cups. Now all she had to do was face the world with every inch of pale skin.

"Is this seat taken?" she asked Justin.

"Hey Bree!" Justin said with enthusiasm. "I was wondering if you were going to make it down. This is Jill." Jill sat up from her tanning posture and said hello.

"Nice to meet you, Jill," Bree said. So far, so good. Jill's body was better than hers, but not by much. She had smaller thighs, but smaller boobs too. She could hang. Jill's suit was pretty amazing, though. It had splashes of aqua and other shades of blue in a pattern that looked like organized chaos. Even her sunglasses were some weird brand she had never heard of. She envied those too. She glanced under the chair that Jill was reclined on. Wedges too? She wore wedges down to the pool? Was this for Quinn or Justin? Then she saw the most important thing of all. Jill had placed a large gray towel on the chair next to hers. He would be there, but three spots away from her seat by Justin. That might be for the best, she thought. She had to let things happen, not force them. Seats would rearrange through the day as they drank and chicken-fought in the pool. Bree realized she was already shaking. *Calm down!*

Justin noticed it too. The two of them exchanged an entire conversation with just looks in a matter of seconds.

When's he coming down? Does he suspect Jill cheated on him? Is he going to talk to me? Can we switch seats eventually? Can I have some of your beer? Does my bikini look okay? What should I talk to her about? Should I talk to her at all? Should I try and make her jealous? When is he coming down?

Justin shrugged back as if to say *I don't know, chill out,* to all of her questions at once. Worthless!

The sun was almost straight overhead and beaming heat on them. Bree took off her flip-flops only to burn her feet on the pavement. She looked around at everyone enjoying themselves. Stalker Ted was already bothering the DJ, mothers were yelling at their children to stop running, and many other new faces from the other buildings crowded into the water. She was the only one there not relaxing. In fact, she was almost in a panic.

"Justin, can you beer me?" She needed to establish some kind of jurisdiction back over him. He didn't belong to Jill just yet.

Jill watched as Justin pulled out a can for Bree. "You need one too?" he asked her. Dammit.

"No, I don't drink beer," she said. *She doesn't drink beer? Whoever heard of a musician who didn't drink beer? Was she above that? Did she only sip summer cocktails with fruit and umbrellas in them? Ah, umbrellas.* She thought back to that first rainy day on Quinn's arm.

"I've got the hard stuff!" Jill lifted up a quart-sized jumbo mug with a red straw coming out of the top.

"That's my girl!" Justin said. *That's his girl?* Oh this was going to get super-interesting as soon as Quinn showed up. Bree thought of all of the little jabs she could throw in. "Justin, why don't you see if *your girl* needs a refill?" she would say, just loud enough for Quinn to hear it. It can't take long for a relationship to crumble when the other person is cheating.

Bree let the beer run to her liver. She stopped shaking and felt the warming presence of the sun on her arms. It was time to take off the t-shirt and let everyone at the pool see her in a bikini.

"Pizza's here!" somebody yelled. Perfect timing. She quickly removed the shirt and tossed it aside. No one was laughing, no one was staring—check that. Stalker Ted's prescription sunglasses were aimed right at her from across the pool. Though he was probably having a *fascinating* conversation with the DJ, Bree's cleavage and pizza were a higher priority. He spotted her and almost ran to their spot.

"Are you getting in the water, Bree?"

"Hello to you too, Ted."

"I like the water, but I'm not a great swimmer. Do you teach lessons?" His oddball questions didn't even faze her anymore.

"Nope, not a great swimmer myself. Are they going to run out of pizza?"

"They better not!" he said and continued over to the clubhouse.

"Well done," Jill said. A compliment. She was nice enough to acknowledge the favor Bree had just provided to the group.

"Yeah, he's a character," Bree said, unsure as to how politically correct she needed to be.

"That's Stalker Ted," said Justin. He started to explain to Jill all of the crazy things Ted had said and done over the years. Jill laughed with each anecdote and couldn't take her eyes off of Justin. He had her eating out of the palm of his hand, and they hadn't even been on a date yet. Justin was funny and all, but Jill was doubling over. This was a completely different persona than the singer who expressed so much sincerity and had everyone under her spell. Now she was the one being entertained. It was nice to see her vulnerable. Plus, her boobs weren't even big enough to jiggle when she laughed. Bree would have no problem replacing her in Quinn's arms . . . okay, bed.

She had an impulse to ask "Where's your boyfriend?" and put their Hallmark moment to rest, but thought better of it. How great would it have been to be able to pause time and have a quick chat with Justin. They could orchestrate something to get the couple apart at each other's apartments. Bree pictured the overhead map of the four buildings and a series of Xs and Os planning sexual romps and escapes around Stevens Chicago Properties.

"Anyone want some pizza?" Justin offered.

"Nah, I'm good," Jill said. Too good for pizza too?

"I'll go with you," Bree said. Finally, a moment.

"Bree, I have no idea what's going on. He's going to be here like, anytime now, and she barely mentions him. I don't want to ask and screw things up. As it goes, I'm just acting like a buddy right now. Don't say anything suspicious or take any jabs, got it?"

Wow, when Justin was getting some, he was suddenly mature and focused. How convenient. Bree looked down at the table of pizzas and chose a slice with extra cheese. Maybe it would all go to her chest. When they returned to their chairs, Jill was checking her phone.

"He'll be here in a few," she said.

"Cool," Justin said, trying to think of something else to talk about.

Bree's heart started racing. How could she shove this massive slice in her mouth when a man with perfect physique was going to be here any minute? Focus on the positive. Enjoy the free show. Keep drinking.

"Another beer, pumpkin?" she asked Justin. He raised an eyebrow. Where the hell did *pumpkin* come from? Instead of making a joke about it, he gave her a weird look and handed her the can.

Bree took a small bite of pizza. It burnt the roof of her mouth and she almost had to spit it back out. She slipped her finger under the tab to open her second beer.

"Hey, Quinn," Jill said.

Crack! The can opened and foam spilled out all over her. *Son of a bitch!* "Whoa there," Justin said. "Get a little excited?" Half the can ran down her lap and spilled onto her pizza. Her heart, her adrenaline, and her beer all erupted as Quinn sat down next to Jill.

"What's up?" he asked, somewhat quietly. Two words. *Two words and they came out so sexy!* Bree couldn't conceive how she would ever be able to get past hello. He took off his Cubs hat and let his messy hair shine in the sun. She tried to look away, but couldn't. His forest green suit went down just far enough to show the bulge of his quadriceps. They had a perfect curve, and, for a moment, Bree understood men's fascination with breasts.

"Beer?" Justin offered.

"No, thanks." He held up a mug just like Jill's but without a straw. Bree would have paid a hundred dollars to know what he was drinking. Whatever it was, she would spend countless hours researching for the top recipe of it on the internet. She would turn her kitchen into a chemistry lab to experiment with the best way to make it taste better while doubling how potent it was. Somewhere in this fantasy, she acquired a lab coat that she would wear nothing under while anticipating his arrival.

Instead of saying hello well after he sat down, Bree took another bite of pizza. It had cooled off a little, and she took another swig of beer. It wasn't the most lady-like bite either. *Oh no, too big,* she thought. *Chew. Chew!* The cheese seemed to be expanding in her mouth. The more she tried to chew, the further back into her throat it slipped until she felt herself failing to swallow. Her eyes widened in a panic, but she couldn't make a sound. The DJ's music blared as she tried to make even a gasp. Justin was lost in Jill's eyes, and she was laughing about something else. Finally, Quinn glanced over to see Bree with both hands around her neck. He jumped up and ran over behind her and picked her up. Despite the oxygen slowly leaving her brain, she could only think of his hands on her bare flesh. He clasped his hands together and gave a solid thrust on a stomach she wished wasn't so soft. The cheese shot out several feet and almost hit Justin. Her vision cleared as she coughed and took a few deep breaths. His arms were still around her. She wanted to fall back into him and let her butt feel whatever it could. He finally released her and turned her towards him. She looked into his eyes and almost cried. It had nothing to do with the near-death experience. His eyes were just so beautiful. The brown was perfect in the sun. The way he looked at her with such care, concern, maybe even passion, overcame her. His left hand swept the hair from her forehead and pushed it back away from her face. His thumb caressed her temple ever so softly. No one else was around and there was definitely not a large piece of regurgitated pizza on the pavement just a few feet from their magical moment. He had touched her hips, her stomach. If she could do it over, she would somehow get her boobs involved.

"You okay?" he asked. She said nothing.

"Bree, what the fuck happened?" Justin chimed in, unsure whether it was okay to laugh about it yet.

"Thank you," Bree whispered back, still in a hypnotic trance. She gathered herself and took a seat. She grabbed a napkin and disposed of the mess she had left and the rest of her pizza.

"Are you okay? Drink some beer," Justin said. "It'll make you feel better." She didn't hear him. She was replaying the events over and over while she mentally pleaded with each of her nerve cells to never forget what his arms felt like around her.

What could she say? "Well, I guess I don't need to wait a half hour before swimming." The other three paused, and then laughed once they got the joke. She needed a moment to collect herself. The pool would wash away the daze she was still in. Plus, she knew her hair looked better wet and slicked back. She eased herself into the warm water and dodged a small girl doggy-paddling by. Slowly she regained her full awareness. She could still feel his grip around her. She stood still, cherishing it in a moment of peace.

"Cannonball!" Justin yelled, and her peaceful moment was over. He landed right next to her and dunked her like a baptism in the Deep South.

"Thanks," she said, trying not to be too pissed off. "I just got my breath back and you're already trying to drown me." She squinted back at Justin and then up at the chairs. Quinn wasn't there. That shirt was off. He was in the water. Where was he?

17

Bree finally caught a glimpse of the brown wet hair in the deep end. She had the urge to swim straight to him. He was up to his collarbone in the water. As the water dipped, it revealed brief portions of muscles that ran from his neck to his shoulder. From a distance she could tell it was rock hard and gently tanned.

"Easy there," Justin said. "Keep your bottoms on." Even with her sunglasses on, Justin knew what she was doing. "You may want to tone the gawking down just a bit. Sure, he saved your life and all, but his woman is right there next to him." Bree finally noticed Jill swim into her view. She wasn't tall enough to stand in the deep end, so she was treading water next to him. Finally, the two sat on the edge, with Bree still gazing.

"What's the plan now?" Justin asked.

"Go chat her up so I can finally have a real conversation with him."

"What do you want me to do, just push him aside?"

"I don't know. They're not even near their drinks."

"So go slip a roofie in his, why don't you?" Justin laughed. He couldn't be serious even at such a key moment. "Wait, he's getting up and she's following him back to the chairs."

"Is he leaving, Jill?" Justin asked. Bree noted that he could've just asked Quinn himself, but he went through Jill. Was Justin intimidated too? He was a muscular guy, but, if you compared his shoulder width to Quinn's, he looked boyish. Bree followed Quinn's steady walk back to his seat. The line above his hip moved perfectly. He was just so much . . . mass. All perfectly placed with amazing eyes that guided a flawless face. He reached for his phone and frowned at a missed call.

"I'll be right back. I gotta return this," Quinn said to whoever was listening. He exited the pool area, still shirtless and dripping. Bree would've bottled the droplets that fell from his slicked hair. As he left, she felt like a toddler whose mother disappears for just a moment. Was this it? What if he doesn't come back? Then she saw that his things were still by his chair. His shirt and mug were unguarded.

Justin swam his way over to Jill and leaned up against the edge of the pool facing Bree. Jill turned away so she could face Justin. Bree wondered if he meant to do that or if it was just dumb luck. She eyed the plain grey t-shirt. It looked soft, but worn out. Hell, she'd settle for a night with his shirt. Holding it. Smelling it. Absorbing him through the years he had worn it. Then her eyes moved to the mug. Jill wasn't looking. Justin could keep her interested for a few more moments. It just sat there, waiting for her to taste and figure out what was in it. She could discover his favorite drink. She could tell how strong it was. She could offer to make a refill. She could win his heart one tiny favor at a time.

She climbed over the edge of the pool like a child. There was no time to swim to the ladder. She looked back at Justin, who simultaneously suspected something. He cracked a smile and then moved so that Jill's view wouldn't catch Bree. He even started using his hands to animate whatever bullshit story he was working on.

Bree hesitated, but only for a moment. She picked up the large mug with two hands and sipped from it. She thought about his lips being there only minutes ago and how hers touched the same spot. Maybe she could spend a night with his mug, too. The mystery liquid was cold and ran down her throat, but in a familiar way. Water? He only brought water to the pool party? The same tap water that she filled her cups with in the middle of the night to battle hangovers was worthy of filling his mug all day? Oh well, mission accomplished. She scooted back to her seat and gave Justin a quick wave.

He got out of the water with Jill behind him. She envied every other person there. Their future wasn't at stake; they were just there to have a good time, enjoy free pizza, and music that was being played too loud. She wasn't the only one to notice. As she waited on Justin and Jill, Stalker Ted found his way over to their spot.

"Bree, he's too loud. I told him to turn it down, but he won't."

"Ah, c'mon Ted, you sound like an old man. It's not that loud, is it?" Could she get rid of him before Quinn got back? Too late. He was already at the gate, still shirtless but making his way back over.

"What's up, Stalker Ted?" asked Justin. Jill smacked him for being rude like they were already a married couple. They even sat next to one another. Jill took the seat that Bree was in and Justin almost fell into his. This was going perfectly. She owed Justin; or maybe they were even for all the smartass comments he'd made over the years. Bree sat down between Justin and Quinn's open seat, which would be filled in a matter of moments. His grand chest led his beautiful body back to their spot. His figure eclipsed anything else in her stare. Good Lord, she would be sitting by him with a chance to talk. How was he okay with Jill sitting down by Justin?

"Bree, please!" Ted pleaded as Quinn sat down. She was close enough to reach out and touch him. If only he needed the Heimlich maneuver this time. She would just barely be able to get her arms around him, if at all. He could cough out whatever it was that choked him while she pushed her fists into his lean, cut torso. "I can't hear anything!" Ted yelled.

"Ok, Teddy. I'll have him turn it down." Ted had a point. The music was blaring and, if she was going to have a real conversation with Quinn, she'd need to hear his sexy low tones. She smiled at Quinn and walked around the pool to Mark. *Don't trip, you've made a fool out of yourself enough today.* She got within a few feet of the pounding speakers and waved for Mark's attention. She gave him the universal signal *for turn it down a bit*, which he obeyed. She scampered back on the hot pavement. The sun was relentless and she became aware of the discomfort the warmth had brought. Another beer would fix it.

She was almost back to their side of the pool when she noticed a tall slender figure enter by the gate. Her hair alone turned the heads of everyone she walked past. It looked like part of the sunlight and moved in slow motion like hair in a shampoo commercial. *No.* The word *blond* didn't do it justice; this hair was golden. A silver tunic hung on the size-two frame, which turned the poolside into a catwalk as it strutted by in wedges. *No.* She paused and looked around at all of the people, most of whom were staring back at her. She took off her large black sunglasses to reveal a face that belonged in a makeup ad in a magazine. *No!* She turned again and finally found who she was looking for. Quinn smiled and patted the chair that was still damp from Bree sitting there just moments ago.

18

It was the second time Bree had seen Justin with a dazed look on his face in the past two weeks. The first instance was when Jill opened her mouth to belt out a Grammy-sounding tune in front of a mesmerized audience earlier that month. This time his attraction was pure superficial. That hair. Was she royalty from some ridiculous line of Scandinavian princesses? Had she had a nose job, or was that from her perfect lineage too? Bree usually didn't feel short, but she would only come up to the perfect tan breasts that peeked out from the tunic. Teeth, cheekbones, chin, ears, legs, all perfect. But she wasn't a Barbie. This girl had something about her that was unique with her beauty. It was all put together so well that to dismiss her as a Barbie doll wouldn't have done her justice.

Justin finally snapped out of it long enough to glance over at Bree, who was finally turning away.

"Sorry I'm late," the girl said to Quinn.

"That's okay, you didn't miss anything," he said back in a happy-go-lucky tone that Bree had never heard him use. In moments it was like he had burst from a shell of mystery and this girl, this fucking goddess, had flipped a switch to give her, and only her, the access to Quinn's true personality.

"Everyone, this is Prentiss," Jill said, finally introducing her. Seriously? Prentiss? Did she hear that right? Bree turned away and walked towards the edge of the pool. Justin stood to follow her, but then paused as Prentiss stood back up. With one graceful motion her tunic slid over her head and onto the chair, revealing a body that bested her hair and face. Justin's eyes bulged before he caught himself and looked back at Bree. Then he realized the full irony of the entire situation. They were wearing the same white suit. Bree stepped off the side and into the water like a hopeless madman taking a final plunge off a bridge.

It was only four feet deep, but she stayed under as long as she could. Her eyes were wet with tears and it would be the only way to disguise the pain. She felt someone land near her and opened her eyes, expecting to see Justin's blue trunks. Instead it was Jill. She came up for air and tried to move away. Nothing to see here. It's not like her heart was bleeding throughout the pool. She couldn't get herself to look back at Quinn's perfect body. This girl, this Prentiss, had taken even that from her.

"Follow me," Jill said as if the two were best friends. Oddly enough, she listened. Jill seemed like a different person now. Of course she wasn't Quinn's girlfriend. She had as little a chance as Bree compared to this girl. All of the plans and schemes that she and Justin had coordinated and followed through on had been a waste of time. She had no idea she was up against the impossible. Get braces? Shit! She'd need braces, veneers, liposuction, and more plastic surgery than a reality star to even come close to getting Quinn's attention next to this girl.

"Where are we going?" Bree asked in a meek voice. She was trying not to cry but even those few words gave her away to Jill.

"Bree and I are going to head up to her place for a drink real quick," she called back to Quinn.

"There are drinks here," said Justin. Was he that oblivious? Some friend.

"Yeah, we're getting some other ones."

Justin still wasn't getting it. "I can get you whatever. Let me know what you need."

"I need a fucking tampon, okay?" A few heads turned and a mother covered her son's ears with his floaties. Jill climbed out of the pool, grabbing her stuff along with Bree's, and marched to the gate with Bree following. Holy shit, she had a new friend.

"You didn't have to do that," Bree said as they neared her building.

"Yes I did. I've seen you before and well, your nipples are showing right through that suit. Wrap your towel around you."

"Yeah, I remember you from the laundry room that day. I guess that's where you saw me," Bree said, feeling pushed into her new friendship.

"No, I mean, I've seen girls like you before. When it comes to Quinn. You're not the first one to be infatuated with him."

"I'm not infatuated with—"

"Bullshit. Look. I like you, but if you're not going to be honest with me you'll just turn into every other psycho that's been in your shoes." Bree let Jill into her apartment. They were both still wrapped in towels and sat on opposite ends of the couch. The apartment seemed dark compared to the bright sun that had been shining on them all day. The bass from the music still boomed in the background along with a white noise of chatter from people having a wonderful day.

"I thought you were his girlfriend at first," Bree began.

"Yeah, everyone thinks that. I get the same expressions from women everywhere. Random scoffs, glares, and confused looks wherever we go."

"Well, you do *live* together, right?"

"Yes, but that's it. We're roommates. We sometimes work weddings together. It's more of a professional relationship than anything else. We moved here not that long ago so that he could expand his business and I could find some better stages. Wisconsin wasn't doing it for either of us."

"But, how do you—" Bree tried to choose her words carefully. Jill could become the ally she needed.

"What? Not want to jump his bones?"

"Well . . ." Bree forced the honesty out.

"I don't know. I guess once you've known someone for that long, you learn not to think of them that way. We met in fifth grade, so I kind of knew him before he turned into this lady-killing heartthrob. Wait, that's not the right phrase. You know what I mean though: attractive."

"That's an understatement," Bree laughed. "So you just magically have no attraction to him? Is there something wrong with him?"

"No, nothing wrong with him. I just know better. For one, he's not ready for anything serious, thus he's with a twenty-year-old. It's a long story but, for now, you can't get upset about it or he'll break your heart before you even have a normal conversation."

"I've tried. The day we met we had a somewhat normal conversation." Bree felt like she needed to argue her case, but wasn't sure what she was disagreeing with.

"Well, he has a lot of conversations with women, and almost all of them go the same way."

"I don't know what you mean."

"Yes you do. Women don't have any game, especially with guys like Quinn. Let's get back to the pool before Justin says anything stupid."

"Hey—by the way!" Bree had so much to say about the budding relationship Jill seemed to be forming with her best friend.

"Ha—no time! Must get back to pool, my friend." She was already out the door before Bree could even ask her about the rooftop.

My friend, she said. I have a new friend. The swirl of emotions left her feeling confused but currently happier than five minutes ago. "So what should I do today?" Bree said as they skipped down the steps. "And if you say 'just be yourself' I'm going to push you into the pool."

"Get drunk then," Jill shrugged when they reached the ground floor.

After ordering Justin to fetch more drinks, the afternoon became a little more tolerable. Bree made her rounds, socializing with residents around the pool. She chatted more with Mark about this and that and fended off Stalker Ted a few more times. She was doing just fine until the final few songs of the party came on. Mark was trying to wind things down, so he lowered the volume and started playing sad songs. Maybe they weren't sad to everyone else, but to Bree they were the most depressing melodies she had ever heard. She didn't even recognize them, they just kept streaming out of the speakers like the tears she had tried to hide earlier. The euphoria from the drinks had peaked and tipped long before, and the downside of her buzz came rushing in. The sun was on its way into that early-evening yellow phase, and a shadow from the Dogwood building covered half of the pool.

She didn't want the afternoon to be over. *Come back, buzz, come back, sun, come back, socializing with residents.* Come back, any distractions from her hopeless future. She looked around and saw that most of her neighbors were packing up and heading out. A few children protested the pleas of their mothers, but gave in to promises of ice cream and an evening movie.

She glanced over to the inevitable and saw Quinn with his arms around Prentiss. She sat lightly on his right thigh and they could've posed for a Nautica cologne ad. What hurt worse was that Justin and Jill were facing each other, holding both hands. Everyone else was in love? "Last song!" Mark yelled out. It was something about "tearing in my heart" accompanied by a slow waltzing beat. The shadow was now covering almost the entire pool, making it look later than it actually was. Bree debated getting back into the water one last time to hide the oncoming tears, but then remembered that under her shirt her bikini top did little to cover her nipples. Prentiss hadn't put her cover-up on yet, and she wasn't about to become part of a "who wore it better?" competition with her.

With her head down and flip-flops scraping against the pavement, Bree slowly exited the pool area, defeated beyond belief. The pool could close itself. As she got near her building, she heard a beer bottle crashing onto the pavement.

The late afternoon naps that lasted way too late were becoming more common. Bree woke up on her couch and glanced out to see nothing but fireflies in the apartment yard. She walked to the bathroom in some sort of new physical pain that seemed to be expanding with every step. She did a double-take as she neared the mirror. Her face was beyond red. She took off her shirt and saw that she still had her swimsuit on underneath. Everything else was red. A painful red. A red that would prove to be relentless pain for hours, days. She hadn't even thought about putting lotion on today. She had been concerned with other matters that seemed so much more important than sunblock. Shit. Everything hurt. The tops of her feet, her arms, her ears, her face. Despite having her shirt on for the good part of the afternoon, her shoulders still burned. "Dammit, you idiot!" she yelled at herself in the mirror. "You fucked up everything today." She made an ugly face at herself. She hated everything she saw: her scarlet forehead, the bags under her eyes, and her teeth—oh her teeth. They were going to pay for this. "What a loser," she said, and continued to stare herself down. "A fat fucking loser. A snaggle-toothed has-been. A single unattractive, drunk-ass, ugly loser." The song about tearing in her heart was still stuck in her head as she finally fell asleep on her floor. She had decided she wasn't good enough to sleep in a bed that night.

19

On Monday morning her first phone call was to her orthodontist. During her lunch break, she called her bank and moved all of her savings to her checking account so that she could pay for her braces up front. There was no going back this way; she had to get them. She pondered what it would be like to be twenty-six years old and have a mouth full of metal, but what was the worst that could happen? More guys could not date her, big deal.

Later that week she went in for one last consultation for measurements and payment.

"What is it do you do again, Bree?" her doctor asked.

"I work for an apartment complex not too far from here," she said.

"Yeah, I remember that, but what else do you do? You know, for fun?" She had no answer. "I guess what I'd like to know is what made you finally get the braces? I think it's an excellent choice, obviously, but I always like to hear why my adult patients choose to fix that smile at whatever point they're at in life." Fix that smile? Hers was broken for sure, so broken that she didn't smile all that often these days. Maybe when she was drunk or having one of her never-going-to-happen fantasies about Quinn, but she sure wasn't smiling during the week.

"Well, Doc." Her tone was blunt. "I'm not getting any younger. This body isn't getting any thinner. And my life has become a pathetic routine of letdowns. Oh, and as my best friend pointed out to me last week, I have no passion." *There, satisfied?*

"No passion?" He didn't even flinch at her pity party. "Well, that's too bad. How's Friday afternoon work, say three-thirty?"

"I think I can get that off. I'll be here." She would just email George and tell him she was feeling sick. She hadn't used a sick day in forever, so he would have to let her.

That night Justin came over on his way to Jill's. "What? You're going through with it?"

"Yep. Friday I start moving these teeth back to where they belong," she said, trying to sound confident in her decision.

"But your smile is part of who you are," he said.

"Crooked? Yes, that's me. Snaggled and ugly. If only I could stay this way, right?"

"You know what I mean, Bree."

"No, honestly I don't. How are my fucked-up teeth part of who I am?"

"Don't get all pissy with me. I wasn't trying to be mean."

"I get it, it's part of my identity. I don't have a passion, just a messed-up smile. It's part of who I am. Single. Alone. Not attractive enough to win anyone's heart. I'm just that girl in the background. But hey, people can say that I'm cool."

"Well, you are cool," Justin said, trying to help. He was starting to understand that he wasn't going to win this conversation. She was hurting. She was jealous. She was lonely and destroyed by what happened the other day at the pool. She was let down from the weeks of emotion she had put into Quinn for nothing.

"Yes, cool. You know what the opposite of cool is? Hot! So yes, I am cool, and I will stay that way unless I change myself."

" I don't think you need to change," he said. "I love you just the way you are."

"Well, thanks, Billy fucking Joel, but that won't get me anywhere. Don't you see those people who stay alone their whole lives? The virgin guy who's thirty-five years old? The cat lady who's pushing forty but never bothers to do anything about it? That's what's wrong with this world. People drift through life thinking that love will just happen one day while doing the same thing over and over. I'm not going to be like that. I need to become more attractive. I need to find meaning in my life. Living and working at this shit apartment complex isn't going to get me anywhere. From this day forward I'm going to become a better person. I'm going to become more attractive! I'm going to become more interesting! And you better fucking believe that I'll find my passion in something!"

Her yelling echoed on her kitchen walls. She considered whether her entire hallway had heard that monologue. Oh well, that would just make her stick to it more.

"Well, I hope that works out for you," Justin said accidentally sounding like he was patronizing her.

" I hope Jill works out for you," she said mocking him back.

"Hey, Jill *likes* you, okay? There's no need to be mean to her," Justin said.

"I'm not," she said, finally lowering her voice.

"You should come hang out Thursday night. She's going to sing again and would like someone to chat with while I'm busy running the show."

Bree opened her mouth to decline, but when was the last time someone other than Justin invited her anywhere? And without the jealousy, she could actually enjoy Jill's vocals.

"Yes, I will go. From here on out I am going to be more active socially. I'm going to leave this apartment complex whenever I get the chance. Tell her I'll be there."

"You could just ride with us, you know."

"Tell her I'll be there."

"Okay then. Everything's cool?"

"Wait, is Quinn going to be there with that, that—" Bree didn't know how to end the sentence.

"With that what?" Justin asked. He wanted to hear what she could possibly say about Prentiss.

"He won't be there, will he?"

"Doubt it," Justin said, and then left before he said anything else wrong.

A half-hour later Bree received a text from a new number that read, "Thursday night you're riding with us—Jill." That was that. She agreed in her reply and then felt a little better. She wouldn't have to worry about driving home, at least. Quinn wouldn't be there. She could sit by Jill instead of her usual lonely spot at the end of the bar. She could appreciate Jill's music. It would be the last night of going out with her teeth looking like can-openers. Were things looking up?

That night she found an old green notebook still empty from a journal she never started, along with a pencil with still half an eraser left. She threw a blanket over her shoulder and carried the writing materials up to the rooftop. It was getting cooler as the last of the sunlight disappeared. With the faint amount of light she had, she started doodling in her notebook. Generic smiley-faces, flowers, and cats filled a page. That "talent" hadn't improved since grade school. She flipped the page and began to etch a giant mouth. She exaggerated the teeth and made fangs to dwarf even the over-sized incisors. She then drew little boxes that looked like jail cells on each tooth. By the time she finished it looked like a series of angry scribbles with hardly any room left on the page for the rest of the face. In the bottom corner she carefully wrote "12–18 month sentence for being ugly."

She turned the page once again and began free-writing. *"The worst thing about getting braces at twenty-six is all of the little kids staring at you in the waiting room. 'Look how old that lady is to be getting braces, daddy!' 'Shut up or I'll take your daddy home. You'll only see daddy every other weekend!' Tom Cruise got braces and he still got any man he wanted. Mine are going to be glow in the dark in case I ever want to fit in at a rave. I hope my face doesn't feel like a teenager again and break out in zits. Or even worse, my boobs will shrink back to their 8th grade size. Of course, if my ass follows suit' that's a tradeoff I'm willing to consider."*

She realized she was writing jokes. Had Justin rubbed off on her over the years? Hell, she had sat through enough comedy shows to see how it worked. Make fun of yourself, your appearance, and anything else, and throw in some punchlines. The audience can relate, so they laugh. How hard could it be? Justin was always complaining about tough crowds, but sometimes she agreed with them instead of her friend. He wasn't always that funny. He was even less funny off stage.

She started filling the pages with ideas to joke about. Her name, Breezy. *"It's like my parents expected me to be an airhead. Or a porn star. I was more than happy to follow mom's footsteps."* She thought about where the audience would be laughing and paused for her imagination.

She filled the next few pages with a list of things that bothered her. *"So the lady in front of me at the store is buying brand name cereal with food stamps, while my broke ass has to buy the generic stuff that's so bad I actually still use my appendix. I'm sick of settling for Raisin-y Brand and Freezer Burnt Flakes. I'm never going to be able to retire, but the good news is, my food will kill me long before I turn sixty-five. That's okay, I won't have any money saved up anyway. Up until last week I thought 401K was another cereal I couldn't afford."*

Were these funny? Did they make sense? She kept going, page after page. Her handwriting was a cryptic cursive that only she could read. It had been so long since she had to handwrite anything. The creativity seemed to come out more without a keyboard, though.

She brought her notebook to her office on Thursday and found herself writing with each break that she had. The jokes were coming easier and the venting felt wonderful. No wonder Justin refused to settle down and get what everyone else considered a "real job;" this was fun.

That afternoon he texted her to confirm plans. *Still going with us, right?*

She told him to stop by the office when he had a chance. He came down five minutes later with a t-shirt on backwards.

"What's up, Bree?"

"First of all, are you bringing back the Kris Kross look or were you just in a hurry?" He glanced down at his shirt.

"Shit." He laughed and quickly pulled his arms in to flip the shirt around.

"I want to try something tonight," she said.

Relieved she was in a happier mood for once, he nodded. "Okay, what?"

"I want to try stand-up at your open mic show," she said with her eyes closed.

"Oh. Jeez, Bree, I don't know. It's a lot harder than it looks. Can I hear your jokes first?"

"No, I don't give a shit if I'm funny. I'm trying something new. I wrote a bunch of stuff down last night and I've been memorizing it all day." She stood up firmly from her desk.

"What's causing this? I mean, why now?"

"Oh, there's a lot of reasons. My life has gone to shit. I get my braces put on tomorrow. I'm going to get laughed at anyway, so I might as well invite it."

"Are you trying to impress certain people?"

Busted. That thought had gone through her mind several hundred times. Quinn's little angel couldn't have had any real talents other than looking hot. This gave her at least something to be proud of. "I'm doing this because a certain friend told me I needed to find my passion in life."

"Your passion or mine?" Justin snapped back.

"Oh, so you're the only one who's allowed to do stand-up? I thought you'd be happy about this. I thought I could get some tips from you. I thought you'd be proud of me for trying something."

"Bree, it's just…it's just hard to explain. It takes a long time to get good for most people and I don't want you to get upset about something else if it doesn't go well."

"I know it's not going to go well. It's my first time, duh! I've seen all the first-timers you bring on. They suck. I'll suck. You probably sucked your first time. I'm okay with that. What I'm not okay with is being the same person day after day, month after month, year after year. I'm getting older, fatter, and lonelier every day, and if I don't do something about it I'm going to wake up and be forty with no one around me."

"So you think trying stand-up will prevent that? It's not something that attracts people. In fact, you have to hurt a lot of relationships to do it professionally. It's a lot of nights out or on the road. Don't you see how crazy and unhappy even the famous comics are?"

"Well, thank you for worrying about me once I'm famous. May I try three minutes tonight?"

"Fine. But I don't want to hear any whining or pouting afterwards."

Jill entered the office as Justin finished agreeing. Her hair was messy and she was wearing one of Justin's t-shirts. It was three sizes too big and hung down almost to her knees.

"What's up?" she asked in a raspy tone.

"Oh, I get it."

"What?" Justin said.

"She's wearing one of your shirts and you came in with yours on backwards," Bree said, turning away.

Jill blushed and playfully punched Justin in the stomach. He laughed and said, "So it sounds like all three of us will be performing tonight."

"It looks like you two already have today," Bree said, keeping Justin unsure if she was really upset or not.

"You're going up tonight?" Jill asked as the red finally faded from her face.

"I've written some jokes. Butthead here doesn't think I should try it."

"I said you could do it," Justin said, holding his hands out.

"Well, then thank you for your permission, kind sir," Bree said.

20

Bree wasn't nervous until she got into the car with Jill and Justin. Jill drove a stick shift, which jerked and jolted way too frequently. Seeing them both with their game faces on made her feel very unprepared. At one left turn, Jill's guitar case leaned over against Bree like a passed out drunk. She quickly pushed it back to its own side. She glanced up into the rear-view mirror and caught Jill's made-up face. The radio was off and she was warming up her vocals with scales. Beautiful scales. She had so much talent even in her warm-up. Justin was scribbling in his joke notebook and mouthing bits to himself. Bree had left her notes on the back of the toilet. That was the extent of her final rehearsal. Relieving herself while practicing punchlines. Probably how the greats prepped, too.

Her prayers for a small crowd were answered, as it was a fairly humid night. Had she put on deodorant? Yes, but was it enough? Her light blue shirt would surely show any traces of perspiration. She should've gone with her black shirt, or navy, or any other color. She had dozens of options and chose the one shirt that would betray her.

She was about to settle in to her usual seat at the end of the bar when Justin signaled her to the empty inside showroom. "It's our pre-show meeting," he explained. Close to a dozen other performers were already there, chatting with each other and comfortably joking about old stories. Jill seemed to already know most of them from her short time on the scene. Bree stood in the back of the room as Justin addressed the group, who immediately got quiet for him. His tone was different and he looked so much more important than any context she had ever seen him in.

"Okay, everyone gets five to seven minutes tonight unless I tell you otherwise. We had a few comics go over their time last week, so please don't repeat that. It's a smaller crowd, but I expect you all to treat this like a professional show. We have an addition to the list: Bree Andrews is trying comedy for the first time. Other than that, nothing too different this week." That was it? A subtle mention of her like she was just some random wannabe whom he didn't really know. She didn't want the spotlight already, but maybe a brief hello or a mention that he was good friends with her. Something to set her apart from the rest of the twenty-somethings who probably still lived in their parents' basements. Yet the distance between her and this in-charge Justin made him seem kinda hot. The shadows from the one light in the front of the room highlighted his firm frame and his jaw line.

Oh no, was this happening with the void of Quinn? Snap out of it.

She ignored the rest of what Justin had to say and she daydreamed about Quinn and Justin getting into a fistfight over her.

"I knew her before she was famous!" Justin would yell.

"You had your chance and never wanted more than a friendship!" Quinn would yell back while ripping his shirt off in a fury.

She would pretend that she was against the fighting and would yell for them to stop, but in truth, it turned her on.

"Andrews, you'll be fourth," Justin called out. "Matt, you go fifth. Mark is sixth . . ."

Mark? She knew him. The DJ. That's why he looked familiar. He was here the last time she came. She glanced over at him, hoping to make eye contact with someone else she actually knew. He looked different as well. His casual wardrobe from the pool was replaced by a pink shirt only his face could get away with. He still looked young, maybe the youngest in the room. He was sipping from a soda instead of beer like every other comic. Shit, he looked cute too. So did that Matt guy. Uh oh, hormone surge. Just in time for her braces procedure tomorrow afternoon.

The meeting ended and the nerves in Bree's stomach hit a new gear. The patio had maybe a dozen or so spectators, but it felt like many more. She envied them for their lack of responsibility to the show. All they had to do was sit back, sip and have a good time. She was one of the clowns in charge of that. This was a mistake. She should have listened to Justin, but couldn't go back now for that exact reason. If she bailed before she even tried, he'd never let her try again or hear the end of it. A cloud was making its way across the horizon as the sun was setting into twilight. Maybe it would rain and they would just cancel the show. No, they would just move it inside to the regular showroom where the spotlight was even brighter. There was nothing that could stop this show from happening. *I'm getting braces tomorrow, I'm getting braces tomorrow*, she repeated to herself. If she could just remember those lines, she had the rest of her three minutes down.

"A drink please!" she signaled to the bartender, who knew her well enough to see she needed a rum and Coke. Justin began the show with some comedy up front. His new jokes were bombing, but he slipped in a few of his usual trusty ones so that he didn't lose the crowd completely. Finally, he started bringing up the amateurs. The first act was a solid comic who took things a little too far with an edgier joke about race. The next comic completely ate it. "I can do better than that," Bree whispered to herself. The third act, the one she had to follow, was an older guy, maybe forty, who strummed some chords but never ended up singing anything.

"Coming to the stage next," Justin eyed Bree from the microphone as she hustled her way over to the side of the small stage, "is a good friend of mine debuting her comedy chops for the first time in her career. Please put your hands together for Bree Andrews."

Polite claps from the crowd felt like thunderous applause which she could never meet the expectations of. She walked up to the stage in her flats—not even a chance of risking a trip in heels—and shook Justin's hand. She didn't want the handshake to end. He just left her up there on her own? Why couldn't he stay and just open his mouth so she could make fun of him? *Be funny.*

"Keep it going for Justin," she said as the clapping died down. "I was there for his first time too. I'll never forget those ten seconds." The audience erupted into laughs and howls. She wanted to start her first joke but the entire patio was in an uproar from her slam. Even the other performers were losing their minds. Justin laughed as well, seeming not to care. "So I'm getting braces tomorrow . . ." Her three minutes turned into five as she received laughs on almost everything she said. She laughed along with the crowd at some spots. Someone held up a flashlight from the back of the patio and she finished on that joke to a higher level of applause. "Thank you!" she said and then quickly walked off the stage before Justin could reach her to shake hands.

He finally reached the microphone. "Keep it going for Bree, everyone. She's obviously in a hurry to get to that next drink and tell everyone about her first time. This one didn't involve an eighth-grader!"

"Ohh!" the crowd moaned and then laughed as loud as it had for any of her jokes. Ouch. Why did he slam her like that? He must already be jealous. What a prick he could be.

Matt followed her just fine, although he was more of a story-teller with a big payoff of laughter just at the end. Then it was Mark's turn.

Justin introduced him in a calmer tone. "Ladies and gentle-men." The crowd seemed to have doubled since she had last taken count. The sun was down completely, and other than the stage spotlight, there were only candles on the tables with a few tiki-torches near the entrance. "This next performer is not only a very talented DJ, but he's also an amazing writer of poetry. Please welcome Mark Northern."

Mark walked out with a short humble stride, keeping his eyes glued to his notebook. His persona was different as well, but very much working for him. He cleared his throat off mic and then leaned in and began reciting some lines about the ocean. The crowd seemed to be enjoying it, though the juxtaposition of their response was odd. Complete silence from everyone somehow still filled the patio. An engine revved blocks away, but no one heard it. He had captured them all in his hand with the simplicity of his free verse. Then, just like that, it was over. Sincere applause and even a whistle followed him off stage. Bree was swept up with the rest of the crowd, but she wasn't sure which words had done it. Or was it his tone? His voice? The mild alliteration in the last line? What the hell worked on her that made her see Mark as a man she now wanted? This was getting out of hand. The summer air was driving her crazy and she couldn't have any of these guys.

She took a deep breath and found something she could have: another rum and Coke. And maybe a shot of Jack to make up for the liquor her nerves gobbled up earlier. The show continued and she couldn't decide if she wanted to punch or have sex with Justin. Two drinks and five acts later, Jill was up to close the show out with yet another song that earned her a standing ovation. It was like she had scared all of the other musicians away from even trying, and rightfully so. She was way beyond most amateurs. After her set, Justin closed the stage out with an extra round of applause for Jill which made Bree jealous—and more attracted to Justin. She looked down at the expensive bar tab that was left in front of her and pondered one more. It was her last night without braces and she had a ride home. Maybe Justin could help her get to her door and she could take things from there. She had to get laid. She was sure of it. If she was going to think of herself in terms of being "horny," she may as well phrase it like a guy—and drink what a guy would drink. "Wild Turkey?" she asked the bartender. He shrugged, gave a disapproving nod, took her credit card to close out her tab, but poured the shot anyway. She wasn't sure why she had ordered that particular drink other than she always noticed the bottle in the arsenal of liquors and no one ever seemed to order it.

She held the shot in front of her as if she was grading it for clarity. "Poor little turkey," she said with a slur. "Nobody loves you either. Well, we'll see how we can help each other tonight." Justin would have to drop off Jill and her fucking-magical guitar and then walk Bree up to her apartment, her room, her bed. It would just be a one-time thing to break this curse of urges. *Hmm, curse of urges. Sounds like cool phrase. Maybe Jill could write a song called that. Or better yet, Mark could write a poem with that title.*

Bree fell into the backseat of Jill's car. "I thought Justin drove us?"

"How drunk are you?" Justin said. "We rode in Jill's car on the way here. Do you remember squeezing in my truck?"

"Oh yeah! I'm gonna need some help," she said. Justin would take care of her when they got home.

After a two to one vote against stopping for food (Justin was craving tacos), they finally reached the Stevens Chicago Properties lot. "Here's our stop," a belligerent Bree said. "Let's go home, honey."

Justin walked her to the door and then let her in. "Take the elevator, Drunky," he said—and then got back into Jill's car. Bree watched as the lights headed down to the Dogwood building. They had ditched her so they could go do what she was incapable of. And at Jill's place, or would they find somewhere else on the property? *He'd better stay out of that laundry room.*

Logic and decision-making skills were long gone. The weeks of longing for someone she couldn't have, the excitement from performing, and of course the half dozen drinks in the last hour all came to a head as she stumbled over to her office. It was weird seeing the clock on the wall without the usual light from outside. She clicked on the seldom-used desk lamp and dug through her Rolodex until she found what she was looking for. "Mark, DJ service," she read aloud. It took her fingers three attempts to get the number right before someone finally answered.

"Hello?"

"Hi Mark. Do you know who this is?"

"Um, no. I recognize the number from a business call, but—"

"It's Bree!" she laughed. "You were so awesome tonight. I just wanted to call and tell you."

"Oh, uh, thanks," he said. She wasn't hiding her intoxication at all.

"You should come hang out with me."

"I should?"

"Yep." She popped the p as loud as she could. "I have to get braces tomorrow, so it's the last night I can do things without them."

"Um," he paused. "I can't really make it over tonight. You should probably get some sleep, okay?"

"Whatever!" she said, hanging up on him. Rejection? *What a loser,* she thought. Her next impulse led her across the parking lot towards Jill's car, which still had a warm hood. She knew exactly which apartment was hers from the hundreds of times she had brought up that apartment's address: 1D. It wouldn't be that easy for Justin and Jill to get rid of her. She would crash their party until Justin realized it was his job to tuck *her* into bed, not Jill. The walk seemed to take forever and had obstacles on the way. Someone parked their car right in her path, so she kicked its tire, which set off an alarm. At another point a fire hydrant jumped out and banged her knee. Then a cat ran out of nowhere to try to scare her back home. "It won't work, kitty," she said. "I'm going to find them." Once inside the building, the hall lights seemed blinding. "I should get these removed," she told herself, hoping she'd remember the request to maintenance in the morning.

Finally she reached the apartment. The 1D spun as she stared at it. The floor started to tilt and her ears were ringing. What was the smell? Where was she again? Oh yeah, Justin's . . . or Jill's. She knocked eight times. Each knock loud enough to wake the neighbors. Finally the door cracked open. "Bree?" said a deep voice. Quinn was standing in front of her in nothing but his gray boxer briefs. A moment of clarity pleasured her eyes as she counted each muscle in his abdomen.

She followed the chiseled crevices up his chest to his beautiful face. God. Damn. Look at him.

"I—I love you," was all that came out before she collapsed to the floor next to his bare feet.

21

Bree somehow woke up in her own bed, wearing the clothes from the night before. She remembered her set going well. She remembered pounding some drinks, a ride home, and maybe a trip outside? Her leg was bruised and very sore, but what had she run into? As she sat up to think, she realized it was much brighter than usual outside. "Oh shit!" It was quarter after nine and a jolt of adrenaline washed out most of her potential hangover right then. She scrambled to put on a different outfit, though she ended up staying in her jeans. The mirror had to be ignored as she brushed her teeth and grabbed a little makeup to put on at work. She scurried down the steps and over to her office, which was already unlocked. George was waiting inside.

"What the hell kind of operation are you running here, Miss Andrews?"

"Sorry, I had food poisoning and was a little sick this morning," she lied.

"Is that any reason to leave the office door unlocked?" he asked, raising his voice. "Do you know how much confidential information we leave in here? How much this computer costs? How many security codes are kept on file? Do you have any idea the shit you're in?"

"It was unlocked?"

"You're damn right it was, and unless you're illegally giving out copies of the key, you're the only one who could've done it! Is this how late you're coming in every day? Are we missing potential leases because you can't get your lazy ass up in time?"

"No, sir, I apologize."

"You're making me question whether I should even keep you around here," he scoffed. So now was not the time to ask him about leaving early for her orthodontist appointment. "I better see some numbers put up by the end of the day. I better see some even more amazing numbers put up by the middle of next week. I better see this place fill up soon or I'll find someone who can do it for me!" He stormed out of the office, slamming the door behind him.

Moments later Jill walked in. "Bree, what the fuck?"

"Just my boss threatening to fire me," she said with tears welling up in her eyes.

"No, I mean what the fuck was that last night?"

"I'm sorry?" Uh oh, what now?

"You came pounding on our door and then told Quinn that you loved him."

Bree's head fell to her desk and the tears couldn't be held back any longer. She remembered the encounter now. Even as she cried, she thought back to Quinn in his underwear. Despite the tears, she was starting to tingle at the image that her drunk brain managed to restore. Shit, it might have been worth it. That might be the last time she got to see him for a while. She certainly couldn't face anyone at the pool ever again.

"I'm sorry. I'm sorry. I'm sorry, okay? I already got yelled at by my boss. Yes, I'm a drunk idiot who is apparently stalking your roommate and madly in love with him, but then again you already knew that. I fucked up, okay? I can't do anything right. I'm getting my braces on later today and then I'll just climb in a hole for the next year and a half."

"I wouldn't go that far, Bree. What's this about your job being at risk, though?"

"No one is renting, so it's my fault, somehow."

"Well, I said you could show our apartment if you needed to. Quinn left this morning for some wedding he's shooting back in Wisconsin, and I'll be gone most of the day."

"Thanks, but that will require people to actually want to see a place."

"It's still early. Use ours, it's clean. Neat freak had to organize everything before he left and it even smells good. I promise, no one will be there all day. We still get the rent discount, right?"

"Yeah." Bree was still sobbing somewhat between answers.

"So things aren't that bad. You'll rent some apartments, get your braces. Oh—and I think Quinn was rather flattered at your final words before crashing to the floor at his feet."

Flattered? What's this? He liked it? He liked her? He felt the same? He wasn't madly in love with his girlfriend? She didn't interrupt their passionate lovemaking to make a fool of herself? It was very easy for Bree to read into this what she wanted. Suddenly the tears dried up and her tone changed.

"He was flattered?" she said trying not to give away the absolute joy Jill's word choice had injected into her.

"Yep, flattered. But I'm only telling you that so you'll stop beating yourself up. Don't get any crazy ideas. Remember what we talked about the other day. Pursuing him is only going to frustrate you and break your heart. It's not worth it."

"Like, what else did he say, though?" Bree only heard what she wanted when it came to Quinn.

"Bree, are you not understanding what I'm getting at?"

"I just want to know what he said about it. How do you know he was flattered?"

"Forget it, Bree. I've gotta run. Don't get any ideas!"

"Wait!" but Jill was already out the door. Before it could even close all the way, a young girl with an expensive outfit came in, popping her gum. Her jeans must've been several hundred dollars, her hair had highlights and extensions worthy of a runway, and her makeup was caked on.

"I need an apartment," she said. Bree took her through the usual spiel, got her name, Amanda, and then casually invited her to see a place in the Dogwood Building.

"Why do I have to go down and see a unit in that one? What's wrong with here?"

"Um, nothing, we just have a lot more open units in that building. In my opinion, it's a little quieter there too." *Not to mention that there's a six-four god named Quinn who frequents the laundry room, but if you even think about making a move on him, I'll cut a bitch.*

"Fine," the girl huffed. Halfway down, Bree realized Amanda's problem. She was wearing heels. Who wears heels to go apartment hunting?

"You're dressed awfully sharp this morning," Bree said, trying to be friendly and improve her chances of signing a lease.

"Thanks, I just like to look good. You never know, right?" she said lightening up with the compliment. Never know what? When a man like Quinn is going to walk into your life and take over your heart, your thoughts, and your sanity? She wanted to judge the girl for being so deliberate with her wardrobe, but then recalled only a few weeks ago that she was climbing around in thigh-highs in a laundry room. Her rules were different, though. She struggled to keep up as Amanda's heels echoed through the hallway.

"Okay, we'll look at D today." She knew full well from talking to Amanda that she wanted a one bedroom, but oops, she would be showing her Quinn and Jill's place first, and then they would find a suitable one-bedroom. Bree just had to play dumb, which she seemed pretty good at lately.

Her heart raced as she knocked on the door to make sure no one was still there. She put the key in the lock and turned. The door opened so easily, why couldn't Quinn be the same way?

"Wow, well, it smells good in here," Amanda said. She started talking about the amount of sunlight, the coat closet, the spacious kitchen, but Bree was in her own world. This was his home. This was where he walked around in his underwear cooking egg-white omelets after doing planks and sit-ups on the living room floor all morning. She glanced to the side of the black couch and saw an ab-wheel. So that's what did it? She must get one of these powerful exercise tools. She followed Amanda into the bathroom. It was still slightly steamed up from a morning shower. Bree inhaled it as deeply as she could. It smelled of a manly body wash. Those water droplets had cleaned his perfect skin. His towel hung on the back of the door. Amanda squeezed by to return to the living room while Bree secretly indulged her hands in the dampness of the blue towel. Oh if she could only be that towel for a morning, caressing every square inch of his perfect body.

Amanda let herself into his bedroom. Bree was saving that for last and it was a shame she had to share the moment with some stranger. Inside there was a king-sized bed with dark blue sheets and a matching cover. A large dresser with two sets of drawers ran along the left side of the room while the right side had a walk-in closet whose doors were mirrors. Amanda was still rambling about something as Bree pictured herself on her back looking at the reflection of Quinn making love to her in the mirror. Someday. It *would* happen. She was sure of it.

The walls of the bedroom had amazing black and white photographs framed perfectly. Landscapes, a spider web, a close-up of some shells on a shore, and other random pictures that only a true artist could make beautiful decorated the room. Some were tiny three-by-fives, others were poster-sized, but they were all breathtaking in their own way. The one that truly captured Bree's emotions was a flower, some sort of orchid, lying on a dirty sidewalk surrounded by trash. She was that flower, waiting for Quinn to pick her up from her life and take care of her.

"Yo, ma'am! I'm doooone!" Amanda called out from the living room. Quinn had given her attention deficit disorder or something. She couldn't focus on any other tasks while her mind thought of him . . . which was way too often.

Bree felt like she was being pulled out of bed at five a.m. on a rainy Saturday morning. Did they have to leave already? She was just getting a feel for the place. She hadn't even gotten to explore his sock drawer, his fridge, or his closet. She took one last look at everything and led Amanda out of the apartment and back up the lot towards her office.

"So, what did you think of it?" she asked.

"I liked it a lot. I don't think I can afford a two-bedroom, but that unit will suit me. I don't count on having any roommates anytime soon." Something was wrong with that sentence. She played back the previous five minutes. The living room, the kitchen, the bathroom, Quinn's bedroom. That was it. Where was the second bedroom?

"That wasn't a two-bedroom, was it?" she asked at the risk of sounding really dumb.

"Uh, no," Amanda said with an attitude. *Fuck you, Amanda. You have no idea what this means.* He shared a bed with Jill! Her new friend shared a bed with him! New friend no more. It was all her way of showing Bree who Quinn really belonged to. Feel free to look at our apartment, she had said. She wanted Bree to find out for herself. That bitch gave her that talk with her own motives in mind, not Bree's. Bree was so devastated that the lease didn't even matter to her anymore. Friends, her ass. The guy walked around at night in his underwear, it's not like he put on a set of footy pajamas before he climbed into bed with her.

"So can we go on with the paperwork? I'd like to move in August first. Is that possible?" *Dammit, not now!* She still had so many questions left. Did Justin know about this? Didn't the two of them go there after they dropped her off last night? What kind of an orgy were they having?

"I promise I have good credit, so if you'll just run my background check on that and let me know this afternoon, that should do it, right?" Amanda was confused. Bree was in a different universe right now, and all she wanted to do was sign a lease.

"Um, yeah. This afternoon. I'll call you and let you know what the status is. Shouldn't be a problem. I'll have the paperwork ready Monday morning if everything goes through, which it sounds like it will. We'll have you in a one-bedroom in Dogwood by August." Bree recited everything from memory, though her mind was still swirling with disappointment and confusion.

22

"Get your ass down here as soon as you can!" was the text Justin woke up to at noon. Two minutes later there was a pounding at his door.

"Just a second," he said, still on his back in bed. Moments later he heard keys jingling and Bree letting herself in.

"Uh, sure, Bree, just barge on in. That's why they gave you a master key, so you could wake up your residents at some ungodly hour—"

"It's noon!" she screamed.

"Shit, what is it?" he sat up.

"They're sleeping together."

"What? Who is?"

"Quinn is sleeping with her!" Her voice was in a complete panic.

"Um yeah, that's what boyfriends and girlfriends do. And you gotta admit, that chick was smoking hot. Did you think he was saving his virginity for you or something?"

"No, you asshole. I mean your fucking girlfriend shares a fucking bed with Quinn! It's a one bedroom apartment."

Justin turned to get out of bed. He sat on the side of his bed, legs to the floor with apparently the last remains of an erection. Why was it that every time she was in the middle of an emotional crisis, something had to come along and turn her on? Nervous, turned on, in pain, turned on, frantic, turned on. That was pretty much the last sixteen hours of her life.

"Huh," he said, closing his eyes to think.

"Huh? That's all you've got? Are you that big of a caveman that you can't generate a response beyond that? Use your words, Justin. *Use your words*." She said the last part in a mocking baby voice.

"Calm the hell down, first of all," he said. "There's no need to go crazy right away. How many conclusions have you jumped to already with this guy?" He had a point, but she wasn't ready to ease up on him yet.

"Does Quinn know you're with Jill?"

"Yes, he saw us at the pool and I've picked her up a few times."

"But you've never been in their place?" she asked, extending her hands with the rhetoric.

"No, now that you mention it. Last night after we dropped you off she drove down and dropped her guitar off, and then we went back to my place." Justin caught Bree's eyes wandering down to between his legs. Neither said a thing.

"So don't you care that your girlfriend is sleeping with the hottest guy in the world?"

"Whoa, whoa, whoa. When I first did her on the rooftop I thought they were together."

"*Did* her? Nice." Even though she complained about his vernacular, it still turned her on. He could do her with that piece he woke up with. Someone needed to.

"Second, she's not my girlfriend. We haven't had the state of the union talk yet. It's only been a few times. I'm attracted to her singing and most of her body, but I barely know her outside of the bedroom."

"You apparently don't know anything about her bedroom because she shares one! Did you get any kind of back story on why they moved here? It was for his business or something, and her music stuff, right?"

"Music *stuff*?" He was happy to nitpick back at her terminology. "She should be signing with a record label. Have you not heard her?"

"Yes, I get it. She's talented and you're hopping on board while you can still afford the stock. The point is, you're not the only one she's sleeping with," Bree said, trying to make her point clear and arouse some sort of concern in Justin.

"So you were okay with me sleeping with her if she was Quinn's girlfriend and he didn't know it, but you're not okay with me sleeping with her if she's not Quinn's girlfriend but they share a bed?"

"Yes! And I can't believe you're okay with it. Do you not value an honest relationship?"

"Value an honest relationship? You wanted to break theirs apart when you thought they had one. We did everything in our power to sabotage them, all for your benefit, and now you're talking to me about an honest relationship? Bree, what the hell is wrong with you? You've wiped everything out of your way for this one guy just based on his looks."

"You don't know what it's based on!" Both of their voices were back to that familiarly loud tone. "You think it's easy being me? I haven't gotten laid in forever. Everyone I hang out with is more attractive than me. You fuck with my heart every time you get drunk." Justin broke eye contact and put his head down. "And in a few hours I'm going to have the mouth of a thirteen-year-old." She was out of tears but still somehow crying. She crumbled to the floor with her head in her hands and leaned against his bed.

"I'm sorry." He sat down next to her and rubbed her back. Again, her urges stirred as the rest of her mourned what her pathetic life had become.

"I give up," she said. She wasn't sure what she was giving up. She didn't have anything to give up. She didn't mean it, it just felt like the right thing to say. Justin had apologized for something, so their fight was over. It felt good to have someone other than herself feel sorry for her for once. He leaned next to her and put his arm around her. It was so warm on her cold skin. She could just push him down and straddle him right there. He was almost naked anyway, he wouldn't have stopped her. That would show Jill. Quinn would find out and get jealous. She could make sure Mark knew about it too, just for good measure. She decided that she would make her move as soon as she counted down from ten.

Ten, nine, eight . . . She leaned her leg up against his to feel more warmth. *Seven, six, five, four* . . . she lifted her right hand. She would lead with it. *Three, two—*

"You really did well last night at the show." Abort! Her heart was pounding through her chest at the close call.

"Thanks," she sniffled. "It felt pretty fun." Could they go back to silence now so she could resume her countdown?

"I mean, you had a lot of rookie mistakes, but everybody does that when they start out."

Mistakes? She thought it was flawless. People laughed the whole time. She was funnier than a lot of the guys there who had been doing it for a few years. What was left to improve on? She knew how to shut him up. She didn't have any more pride to lose, so why not go for it? One orgasm could cure her of this craziness. *Three, two, one* . . .

"And Jill, she really blows me away every time she sings." Nothing kills a girl's confidence like a guy mentioning some-one else's name. "Hey, are you breathing really hard or something?" Oops. Time to scoot away. Lunch hour was running out, so she got up and left Justin without ever answering.

The rest of the afternoon was uneventful. Bree spent most of it fondling her teeth for one last time. By three she was desperate for anything to happen, even a visit from Stalker Ted. However, as the final minutes of the unauthorized shortened workday wound down, she started to feel anxiety, as the reality of having braces put on started to get to her.

She was shaking by the time she pulled in to the parking lot of the orthodontist. On top of that, it was another scorching day, which caused her to sweat. The coolness of the waiting room helped somewhat, but part of her wanted to run out and get her money back. *No. You're never going to attract anyone with this sad excuse for a smile. You deserve this, you hideous beast.*

23

Upon arriving home, Bree ran from her car to her apartment like she had a secret in her mouth. She made sure no one saw her and the mouthful of metal that was causing more than mild discomfort. Once inside, she stood in front of her mirror and finally cracked her lips. Were everyone's braces this messy and crooked? Did they always hurt so bad? How did the young teenagers deal with this pain? The whole process was so humiliating. The young assistants, who were probably her age if not younger, did most of the work while patronizing her every few minutes. "You're going to have such a wonderful smile." When? She'd be nearing her twenty-eighth birthday by the time they came off, *practically thirty*!

Moments later she heard a knock on her door. It had to be Justin.

"Go away," she said.

"Open up, Bree. I want to talk to you before I head to work."

"I don't feel like it. Come back tomorrow." Justin obeyed, and she didn't hear from him the rest of the weekend. She spent Friday and Saturday night on her rooftop trying to craft more jokes. She wasn't exactly sure she would have the courage to perform them on Thursday, but at least it was something to do. By early Sunday morning, she had filled an entire notebook. A lot of it was just free-writing, but at least it was something. *Quinn was flattered*, she thought. Blacking out and telling him that she loved him was definitely a crazy strategy, but what else had gotten any positive feedback? She was competing against Prentiss *and* Jill and had no idea how deep his relationship was with either. Most relationships fall apart at that age, why not wait it out?

She glanced down at her phone and considered calling her mother. When was the last time they had talked? She scrolled through her outgoing calls and then remembered dialing someone on Thursday night. Was it Mark? *Oh no.* She had. What had she said to him? She had a pretty good idea, but maybe it was fixable.

On Sunday around noon she entered her tranquil office and dug Mark's number back up. She put it in her cellphone and decided she would apologize/explain/play dumb when she called him later that afternoon. It always felt weird being in the office on an off day. She looked at her office phone and saw the voicemail light blinking. It couldn't hurt to hear what she could have to face Monday morning anyway. She dialed in the code and listened.

"Uh yeah, this is Amanda. Just checking to see about my status for the lease." Oops.

"Hello, it's Amanda again. Still waiting. It's five o'clock now so I was hoping to know if I get the place or not." Shit.

The third voicemail had a different tone, "Okay, so did I not get the place? You could at least tell me! I have near perfect credit and a great debt to income ratio. Whatever, I'll find somewhere else." Well, that wasn't good. Oh well, one lease wasn't going to make or break her or the complex. She hadn't even remembered to submit the request.

By Sunday night she was debating on whether to call Justin. He hadn't done anything wrong, but technically her life was much worse than his, and he was doing nothing to help. She still had Mark's number as well. He was probably sitting on a riverbed somewhere, writing more poems that would melt anyone's heart. Mark or Justin, Mark or Justin? Quinn. Why couldn't she be in a just-calling-to-say-what's-up relationship with him? Finally she climbed up to the roof, scrolled down to Mark's number, and waited for him to answer.

"Hello?" He sounded confused. Probably from the new number calling him.

"Mark, it's Bree," Would he even remember she called Thursday night?

"Oh, hello again," he said. Yep.

"I just wanted to apologize for calling so late the other night. I was uh, a bit tipsy, I guess."

"Oh, no problem. It was nice to hear from you anyhow. Sorry I couldn't hang out." Oh yeah, that's why she called. She knew that Mark knew what hanging out meant. Everyone knew what hanging out meant. Even her mother probably knew what hanging out meant. Gross!

"Well, it's good to hear from you." It was? She lay down on the blanket and rested the phone on her head. A warm breeze blew as the sun's final rays disappeared over the western horizon. "Are you going to perform again on Thursday?"

"I'm not sure. I just got my braces put on today and I'm kind of in a lot of pain."

"Oh, it'll go away. I had braces a few years ago. The first few days are the most painful and then it's nothing. Sure they'll hurt when you get 'em tightened every few months, but it's really cool to see how your teeth move. Eighty percent of it happens in the first couple months." That was comforting. He was better than her doctor. For the first time she felt good about her decision.

"Thanks, Mark. What are you working on for Thursday?" Maybe it was the breeze, or the fact that Mark was the first and only communication she had had with anyone all weekend, but something was warming her up.

"Oh, I'm trying to nail this metaphor down." Metaphor, metaphor. She scrambled through a mental list of terms from years ago in school. Was that the one that used *like* or *as* to make a comparison? No, that was a simile. "Did you want to hear it?"

"Sure, I love metaphors," she said.

"Well, it's not ready for poetry form yet, but it's about this flower that no one seems to notice. It's surrounded by a bunch of other things that get in its way." *Like the picture!* These guys had both captured the metaphor that was her.

"You mean like garbage or a rough urban setting?" she asked, thinking of the photograph that Quinn must have made thinking of her.

"No, like a bunch of other flowers or weeds. Maybe even some prettier flowers." Sad but true. "Actually, I don't like the whole thing. It sounds too whiney."

"Oh," she said. Whatever connection she had with his poetry was being crumpled up over the phone.

"What about your jokes? That was funny when you ripped on Justin last week," he said with a little laugh.

"Oh, you'll have to wait and see." Bree knew her material wouldn't work over the phone. She had learned that from Justin trying to test stuff out.

"I can't wait to see you," he said. Wait, what? Was that a flirty compliment? She could do nothing but laugh. Hello heart-beat again. She almost invited him over right then, but no. *Self-control, self-control. You still look like a monster-mouth, she thought. He doesn't want to see that.*

"Can you read me some of your poems?" she asked meekly.

"Well, I don't know." He was bluffing. Bree could tell he was dying to share, so she called him on it.

"If you don't want to, that's fine. I'll read some lyrics to a Britney album or something."

"No, don't do that!" he laughed. "Let me dig up some stuff I haven't read in while."

He began to read poem after poem. His voice and tone were sincere and often so serious that she found herself stirred with whatever emotion he was trying to evoke. There were poems about nature, poems about loneliness, and silly poems from his earliest work that made her laugh. He spun her emotions like a movie. Ups and downs teased her tears, and she was glad he couldn't see what effect they were having on her. She could only whisper her praise as to not completely let him win her over. Her phone was starting to die but she didn't want to let him go.

"Wow Mark, you are amazing," she said.

"Thanks. I'm glad they were able to be heard. I don't know why I write them all, but I guess if it can make someone like you happy, it's worth it." Cheesy, but effective.

"I'll see you Thursday?"

"Of course," Mark said with the enthusiasm of a little puppy dog.

"You better not laugh at me," she joked.

"Why wouldn't I laugh at you? You were hilarious last week."

"No, I mean at my braces."

"Oh, of course. I mean, no. I wouldn't laugh at you that way."

"Okay good, see you then."

"Bye," he said. It was over. Maybe they were both dorks, going by the way that conversation abruptly ended. She looked down at her phone and saw that they had been talking for just over an hour. The stars were much brighter, and the moon was making its way to the top of the sky.

Bree set her warm phone next to her and rolled to her back to gaze up at everything. Despite the clear image of the Big Dipper, she was thinking about Mark. He's been there all along. Simple. Sweet. Shit, a poet. Girls would kill for a poet, and he had the nerve to perform his publicly. Not to mention he was a DJ and made his own money. She flipped back through her notebook and reflected on all of the material she had written about being single. Could she replace it with boyfriend jokes? She ran her index finger over her braces. They had already been poking underneath her lips. No one would want to kiss her in those. She thought back to a boy in high school she had kissed at a ninth grade dance. He had braces and she didn't seem to mind. She also remembered the time he went up to talk to her and had a piece of corn stuck in them from lunch. She would *not* let that happen.

One happy night. She would give herself that. A rare night of sleep with a smile on her face would follow.

24

On Monday morning Bree's first thought was not about Quinn. She woke up thinking about Mark, and then thought about how she wasn't thinking about Quinn. And then she was back to thinking about Quinn. As she opened her eyes and came to, her mouth changed everything to pain. They hadn't warned her about the suffering that went along with braces. Again, how did these young kids deal with it? She made some toast, but could barely get it down, because chewing sent more suffering through what felt like her entire skull. She'd go hungry.

She was proud of herself for being over five minutes early and actually remembering to lock the door. As she entered she heard a vehicle pull up nearby. Sigh. It was George.

She hurried into her office chair, booted up the computer and spilled some paperwork onto her desk.

"Got a minute?" George walked in. "Of course you do. It's not like you're busy with work."

"Excuse me?" He didn't have a right to barge in and talk to her that way first thing Monday morning.

"Amanda Hark. Does that name mean anything to you?" Bree paused and looked up at the ceiling for the answer. "Of course it doesn't, she only wanted to sign a one-year lease! But could you call her back Friday? No, she had to email

Corporate for an answer over the weekend. We told her we would've been happy to have her, but she had already found somewhere else. So guess what? *You're* going to find somewhere else. Clean your shit out, you're fired."

Her stomach dropped. "But you can't. I live here. I just spent all my money on my braces!" Her mouth throbbed with pain, tears welled in her eyes, but George stood there stone-faced with his arms folded.

"You get a few more weeks in your apartment and a small severance. I'll be running the office this week until we get someone else. Hell, we could get a monkey from the zoo to run this place better than you did." Bree logged out of the system, grabbed the few belongings she had there, put her head down, and walked out as George was trying to ask her where certain things were. He opened the door to chase after her. "Where are the closing procedures listed?"

"Where's my severance check?" she yelled back.

"In the mail," he said.

"It's under the desk calendar," she called back. It wasn't. She had no idea what the closing procedure list even was. It sounded familiar but she never used it.

Wide awake, finished crying, fully dressed and made-up, all before eight fifteen with nothing to do but fret about the future. She got until the end of August, and who knows how much for a severance. That would take her to August, but then what? She felt around her top row of braces. It was quickly becoming a bad habit. They were to blame. Her entire life savings and a preoccupied mind on Friday had gotten her into this situation. What was she going to do for money? Where would she move? She looked over at the bottle of rum.

No. Not now. She wasn't going anywhere today. It hurt to eat, yet her stomach was growling. It would make the pain from her mouth, stomach, and firing go away for a while. The digital clock on the oven went from sixteen to seventeen after. *Get a hold of yourself, Bree. It's not the end of the world.* She needed to talk to Justin, but he wouldn't be up for hours. Lazy bum. He made his living with jokes, cards, and lucky football bets. Bree thought of all of the expenses she would have to eliminate. Cable TV, internet, her rare splurges on her hair, clothes, shoes, and, most of all, drinking.

This could be a blessing. She didn't want to work behind that stupid desk the rest of her life anyway, although she had had dreams of being promoted to the corporate level once Stevens Chicago Properties took over the three other buildings. She sat on her couch with nothing to do and let the clock tick another fifteen minutes. Justin could get up early this once.

Still in her work outfit, she made her way down to Justin's apartment. She rapped on his door politely, hoping not to garner any attention from her residents; well, they weren't really *her* residents anymore, so they could fuck off. Justin answered the door after a minute or so. He had on an old pair of red gym shorts that hung to his knees. Bree observed that he must have just shaved his chest, because it lacked any of the thin hair she noticed at the pool. This made his abs almost bulge in perfect form. He could rival Quinn on a good day when it came to six packs. It wasn't fair. Did these guys even work out? She saw Justin's steady diet of carbs and beer, yet he always seemed to be in shape. She wondered if Quinn was that gifted too, or if he actually worked for it. Better yet, was Prentiss that way? Of course she was. God gave her everything just as he seemed to with everyone else. Could she even get a straight set of choppers? No. How about parents who would provide her with braces as a kid? Nope, not even that. Justin led her in without even saying hello. As he walked to the couch, Bree noticed a fresh set of scratches down his back. It made her feel jealous. Everyone was getting laid too, apparently. That's what the beautiful people did. Ugly people like her got to wear braces and get fired while the beautiful slept in after a long night of incredible sex.

Bree remained standing to keep herself well above Justin, who had sunken down further into the couch.

"What is it?" he finally asked, rubbing his head.

"I just got fired."

"For what?" He was instantly awake. A toilet flushed from his bathroom.

"Oh, I'm sorry. I didn't know you had company." She couldn't see her, but heard his bathroom door open and his bedroom door close.

"It's not a big deal," he said. Apparently her fingernails were.

"Well, how about you swing by whenever you're free," she said with a sarcastic sweetness before storming out. It was ridiculous. Her wanting Quinn had somehow earned Justin a girlfriend. She stomped up the stairs and back into her apartment, even angrier than before. "No, rum!" she yelled to the bottle as if it was hitting on her. Instead, she changed into a pair of blue shorts and an old t-shirt from a 5K she had run in college. Exercise used to make her feel better. There was a jogging trail a few blocks away that always had people on it. She used to laugh at those people and wonder what they were running from. Now she would silently join. A pair of overpriced and underused cross-training shoes completed the outfit, and she made her way back out of the apartment.

"Bree!" Ted called out.

"What?" She was no longer legally obligated to be nice to him.

"Why is that man in the office instead of you?"

"I got fired, Ted. I really don't feel like talking about it."

"But you can't be fired. I have so many ideas and requests on how to make things better around here."

"You do?"

"Yeah. I made a list of thirty-seven things to change."

"Thirty-seven huh? Wow, that's a lot. You know who I bet would love to hear them? George. He's going to be there all day and probably tomorrow. Why don't you see if you can get that list up to a hundred, and then go over them one by one with George. He would really like that. He loves hearing ways to improve the complex."

"He does?"

"Oh yeah, Teddy. You should definitely meet up with him as much as possible today and tomorrow. Otherwise, he won't know how to make things better."

"I will, Bree. Can you go in with me?"

"I'd love to, Ted, but he knows that since I used to work here, my opinion might be swayed. So the best thing to do is not tell him that you talked to me at all. Otherwise he might not listen. Got it?"

Ted smiled, and Bree could tell more and more ideas were filling his head. "Yeah, I'm going to start with how the pool needs a waterslide!"

"Good thinking, Ted. Don't take no for an answer!"

"What's that mean?"

"Well, you're the customer and the customer is always right. So if he tells you no, keep talking to him until he agrees with you." She said goodbye and walked away as Ted became overwhelmed at his new duty. "Have fun with him, fucker," she said under her breath.

She was almost to the trail when she heard someone else calling her name. "Bree, wait up!" It was Jill. "Hey, we almost match." Jill had on a pair of blue shorts as well and a white faded retro tee that made her boobs look bigger and hugged her sides.

"That was fast," Bree said. Justin must've been too tired to get it up in the morning. She bit her tongue.

"What was fast?" Jill said.

"You got ready pretty quickly is all I meant."

"What do you mean? I've been up and dressed since six. Justin wasn't feeling well last night so I went home early." *Well, I'll be damned. That whore.*

"Is that so?" Bree said. Her mind was exploding with this new information. Who needed to know what? Finally she was a step ahead of something, so she decided to hold onto her secret. It would help later on.

The two began walking at a quick stride. "You're not going to do that power walk shit with the arm-swing, are you?" Jill said.

"No, I hate that!" Bree laughed. Easy, small talk first. She could get to the bottom of a few things while burning calories. The morning could be salvaged.

"Oh, let me see your teeth," Jill said. Before Bree could decide if that offended her, she was pulling her lips back to Jill's gaze.

"Oh, you can barely see 'em," she said. "The top row especial-ly."

"Thanks," Bree said. "They hurt like hell, especially when I try and eat. The top row are actually glow in the dark, but they couldn't do that on the bottom. Those have to have the regular metal."

"I think it's kinda sexy. Do guys like them?"

"What? No. I mean, I haven't really talked to any guys yet. I kind of hibernated this weekend."

"So are you using today as a recovery or what?"

"I got canned. My boss from corporate is a dick. They gave me rent until the end of August and some check for a mystery amount is coming in the mail, but yeah. I'm unemployed right now."

"What? That's such bullshit!"

"I know. But I'm going to try and make the best of it. The hard part is I just spent all my savings on my mouth." Bree stopped walking. She had to face the reality that her days of living somewhat comfortably were over at the end of the summer. It was a familiar grief; she'd grown up with it as she dreaded heading back to school every year. She would try and make the most of every summer, but no matter what she did, it always ended, and her life would swell with responsibility and work come September.

"Well, I understand that. My gig here fell through a week after we moved down here. I was supposed to get my own place once Quinn got settled in, and three months later I'm still there."

What did she mean by *there*? In his bed? On his couch? Platonically? Sexually? Friends with benefits? Was it like her and Justin? She hoped not. They both had ample chances. Did she know Jill well enough to come out and ask her?

"Yeah, he must hate that," Bree said.

"Oh he's taken advantage!" Jill laughed. What the fuck did that mean? Taken advantage of her cooking or her body?

"So does Prentiss come over a lot?"

"Ha, that clueless bitch?" Clueless about what? The first serious conversation she had with Jill led her to believe that she and Quinn were just friends. But now she seemed to be implying something different.

"Why is she clueless?" Bree said.

"Because she's blonde," Jill laughed again. She was the one who was clueless. Justin wasn't sick last night. Was she trying to tell Bree that she slept with Quinn even though she knew how close Bree and Justin were? No. She wouldn't be that dumb. Labeling Jill's relationship with Justin would be the key.

"So, if you don't mind me asking," Bree said stopping to tie her shoe. "You and Justin's relationship? Is there one? Do you like him? Can I help in any way?"

"Oh, it's open for now. We click on a few levels so we're seeing how it goes, but I'm certainly not his girlfriend right now." She could almost hear Justin saying the same thing word for word when she asked him who the other girl was in his bed.

"Oh, that's good." *See, this is why it's best to have these talks after five or so drinks. No one's afraid to ask or answer anything.* She changed the subject to job-hunting after figuring she had pried enough for one morning. She didn't want to scare away her new friend already.

"Jill, you honestly should have an album out right now. Your songs are so amazing."

"Thanks, but it takes a lot more than songs to get anything out. I don't have the money to record. Then it's like, who do I give it to? There are thousands of other singers and guitar players out there. I can't just walk into a radio station and sign a record deal, you know?"

"Well, where else are you playing?"

"Occasionally I'll get a wedding that Quinn is photographing, but those don't pay as well as you'd think. They end up blowing their budget on photography!" she laughed with a bit of frustration. "He actually gives them a discount if they book me. Plus, I just do the beginning of receptions. They use full bands or DJs for the most part."

DJs, huh? She pondered sharing her late-night talk with Mark. Thinking back to the lines he had read her softened her into a smile.

"Well, Bree, I think you should keep trying the comedy business. If Justin can make money, you can too, right?"

"Well, I'm not going to take his job . . . yet," she said smiling. "I don't know. I really have no idea how the business works. Justin said most comics are on the road all the time, and that he's lucky to be able to perform at the same place."

"The road might be fun," Jill said.

"Especially since I'll be homeless in a matter of weeks," she said.

"See? You're funny!" Jill said, building her up. "How many other female comics are there at the club?"

"None that I know of. We'll see if it goes as well this Thursday," Bree said.

"Well, you got the first one out of the way, the second one should be cake."

"Is that how it works?"

"That's how it works in music," Jill said. "My first live performance was at a mall. It was a disaster of feedback and bad acoustics. Teenage boys mocked me from a distance and girls were saying how they couldn't dance to my sad songs."

"Really? When was this?"

"I was eleven." No wonder she was so good. The two continued to walk before they finally turned around and headed for home. They chatted about high school and college and gave their opinions on what most guys' problems were. As they returned to the area, Bree spotted George trying to urge Ted away from his front door. Day one of her new life wasn't so bad.

25

Bree returned from a rare midweek trip to her mother's on Wednesday. It was more of a trial run than a visit. She had debated moving back in with her mother, but by the first evening couldn't take it. Her mother's neighborhood was quiet and noisy at the same time. There were sirens, neighbors, cars without mufflers, telemarketer calls, and an incredibly loud television thanks to her mother's shaky hearing, but there was nothing going on. Instead it felt like a time warp, because she hadn't been there during her mother's weekly routine in years. She couldn't bring guys back to her mother's place, and, though they didn't fight, she had no inclination to return to the nest.

She had ignored Justin's texts asking where she was, but figured she should probably make amends with him before the next open mic. She decided to show up unannounced to perhaps catch him with someone else again.

"Where were you?" he asked, answering the door.

"Oh nice, you're clothed for once." Damn.

"Sit down," he said with a little authority. She couldn't wait to turn the tables on him.

"So . . . Exactly how many girls are you sleeping with right now?"

"At this moment, none. I'm talking to you."

Ah, a joke. He *was* guilty. He always joked when he was trying to get out of something.

"Who was she? And you can cut the bullshit. I haven't told Jill."

"Look, Jill and I are in an open relationship right now."

"Well, are you close enough to figure out her sleeping situation?"

"She's not banging Quinn."

"How do you know?"

"Because if she was, why would she be hooking up with me?"

"Well, you're hooking up with her, yet just the other night you had someone else over here. Has your back scabbed up yet?" He blushed because he knew exactly what she was talking about. "You probably have to let that heal before Jill gets another shot, huh?"

"I've been sick," he said, trying to keep a straight face.

"Already using the sick excuse on her? Wow, what are you going to do next week? Can't keep going to the well on that one. Do you have some relatives that can die? Maybe an allergic reaction to something? Keep in mind that you're going to put me in the middle of this. I happen to like her. It's nice to finally have a female friend who won't fart on me."

"That only happened once!"

"She's still my friend. And you're my friend. And everybody's fucking everybody except me."

"Hey, I'm always game for a three-way!"

"Stop it, you know what I mean."

"You're jealous?"

"No!" She looked down to the floor and lowered her voice. "Yes."

"Look, you're only after what you can't have. I guarantee it. Think of that time we almost hooked up in college. Was I single then?"

"No."

"There you go. Look, I had this thing for you most of the time when you were with Brad." This was either news or bullshit.

"I was hotter back then."

"No, you were just thinner." She punched him on the arm. Half joking, but half because he was right.

"I'm kidding, I'm kidding," he said.

"No, you're right. I've lost my looks."

"No you haven't. You just hide them now. Remember that day when you had the thigh-highs on? That was hot."

"But that's not me. It's trashy to have to rely on slutty clothes to get guys."

"Do the guys want you or the clothes?"

"What guys?"

"Hypothetically. Listen. You know when you go to a dance club and there's some chick there with stupid hair and an even more ridiculous outfit? She'll have like a streak of blonde and a top that shows off her stomach. Or maybe like a complete open back with one of those shirts that looks like a napkin?"

"Yeah. There's one every time."

"She's never the best looking girl there, but she always gets the most opportunities because she's noticeable. It doesn't mean she's actually a slut. For all we know she could just be out for a good time. Sure she'll get in your car with you and make you pick up tacos at three in the morning even though the drive-thru line is out into the street, but that's not a guarantee she's going to have sex with you."

"This is getting pretty specific," she said.

"Well, I may have picked that girl up a time or six."

"And she's not a slut?"

"No. Her friend who talked her into wearing that outfit usually is, but she's actually almost always a prude. But do you ladies know that? No. You criticize her for wearing something you would never have the balls to wear. You sit around and make fun of the way her hair is styled. You bitch and bitch and then watch her walk away with a stud like me at the end of the night."

"So what are you trying to tell me? I need to a get a streak of blonde in my hair and tie a napkin on my tits?"

"That would be hot, but no. You just need to own whatever look you're trying to pull off. For example, you have braces now. I think they're pretty damn cute. Before, guys probably didn't like your teeth."

"I'm glad you're not sparing my feelings or anything, jeez."

"Quit your whining. As I was saying, before, you were ashamed of your teeth. You didn't smile. You tried to hide them."

"Wouldn't you?"

"Just listen, Bree. Now, you're unique. Those braces can be your blonde streak. They can be your crazy shirt. You're that girl over there with the braces. How many people have metal pierced on themselves already? It's not a turnoff. This isn't fourth grade anymore. Take what you have and *own it*."

Own it. Could she do that? She imagined herself at a bar and hearing some woman yelling, "That chick with the braces just stole my man!" If glasses were hot now, why not braces? They had destroyed her savings account, but what an investment.

Though his compliments were saturated with a few cracks, she was really enjoying the courage that Justin was giving her.

"But what about, you know, the rest of me?" she pinched part of the side of her stomach and pulled it away from her ribs. Maybe Justin would touch her.

"Let me feel." Justin looked up like a doctor avoiding eye contact and touched around her midsection. *Ah, sweet, sweet human contact.* Other than a hug from her mother, it had been awhile. It tickled a little, but also stirred her. There was that heart race again. Maybe she could get him aroused just to mess with his heart for once. That was connected to his heart, right? She put her arms around him like they were about to slow dance. Her wrist rested on his tight bicep. He got quiet and looked into her eyes, unsure of what to do. Something like this usually only happened when they were both hammered. It wasn't even noon yet and her body was screaming for him. He leaned down and pressed his forehead against hers. It was warm and a bit oily. His arms weren't around her; instead, his hands were on her hips, thumbs resting high while his hands stretched down her sides toward the top of her thighs. Jill, the mystery girl, Mark, and even Quinn left her mind. She leaned into him. How was he not aroused? She was ready to pounce. Instead she kissed him on the mouth. His opened up and he was reciprocating. It was so quiet. She could hear everything. Every little noise.

There was no soundtrack other than their breathing. Then he pulled back.

He cleared his throat and said, "Bree, I can't right now."

"I know, you've got others. Your plate is full. It would mess up our friendship, blah blah blah." Eye contact was done.

"No, seriously. I just rubbed one out like five minutes before you got here." This was the guy she was falling for?

"God, Justin!"

"What, I'm sorry! How was I supposed to know we were going to have . . . a moment?"

"A moment? A moment? That's what I am. A moment." She was so embarrassed that she had let her guard down. It was like she had lost all the leverage, power, and dignity that she'd had in the friendship. Her only move was to lash out at him and make him feel like he had done something terribly wrong. "You know what, I can't compete with Jill, or the girl you fucked the other night, or apparently even your right hand now. See you at the fucking show!"

As she walked back to her apartment, she realized that even though they were just kissing, both of them knew it was going to result in sex and neither thought otherwise. She could've played dumb and said they were just making out, but why lie? She would have had him, been on top of him, grinding herself on him all morning if he hadn't been such a fucking ape five minutes before she got there.

When she got home she grabbed one of the final two beers that had been sitting in the corner of the fridge forever, along with her notebook, and went to her bedroom. However, not one joke came from what just happened. How could she write about it? Instead she added another line or two about her braces and then ripped on herself for getting fired. A fresh four minutes would be ready for Thursday night. She cracked the beer open and sipped. It was so skunky she could barely choke down the first sip. She walked over to the bathroom sink, poured it out, and watched as the foam covered the drain. The stale beer gave her thoughts of her childhood and her dad yelling at sports on the television.

26

Through the power of texting Bree and Justin were able to resume communication. She told him that she needed a ride and he obliged. "Where's Jill?" she asked instead of saying hello.

"She's driving herself tonight," Justin said. "She was running a little late."

Bree thought about getting some advice about her set, but instead stared out the window the entire drive to the club. Justin turned the radio up and blared some new alternative rock band he was way too proud of.

They were the first ones to the club with only a half-hour before show time.

"Where the hell is everyone?" Justin asked, glad to be able to vent about something. Bree didn't answer; instead she went inside to the dark bar area and looked over her set. She really hadn't practiced much at all this week. She couldn't decide whether to try new jokes or the ones that worked from the previous week. The ones from last week were already fading. She tried to recall all of her braces jokes and then realized she'd need to change the wording of the setups since she already had the braces. What was wrong with her this week? Maybe the show would be canceled.

A few minutes later Mark found her in the darkness. "Hey you," he said, pulling up a bar stool next to her. "What's wrong?"

"Oh. I don't feel ready for tonight. This is going to be bad," she admitted.

"I'm sure you'll do fine. Remember how much better you were than most of the guys last week?"

"Yeah, but I've just had a lot on my mind this week. I lost my job and everything that I thought was going to work isn't working."

"What can I do to make it better?" he asked, leaning on his hand.

She let herself be a sucker for his charm. "Every poem you read makes it better." She felt lame saying it, but it was true.

"Any requests?" he asked, flipping through his pages of ink.

"What was that one about the fire and the red?" she asked. It was one of the few specific ones she remembered.

"Oh, that one? Hm, it's kinda done with."

"Don't make me beg," she said playfully.

"Okay, but it's about my past, and I really don't even think about that one much anymore." Bree peeked outside where the patio was filling up. There seemed to be a youthful vibe in the crowd tonight, and the bartender was already scrambling to get drinks to the tables. The rest of the performers came in as Justin went over the show's format for the night. Bree was scheduled to follow Mark, and once again Jill was the last to perform.

The air felt perfect as Bree headed back out to the patio. She took a seat on the other side of the bar so she could be near the stage but hidden from most of the crowd until it was time for her to perform. It may have been the slightly cooler air, or perhaps the drinks were a little stronger, but the crowd was definitely into it. Justin debuted two new jokes that absolutely killed. Bree was glad she didn't have to follow him. The first three comics did okay, but the crowd was starting to get frisky. A few heckles had already come, though Bree couldn't see from who. One sounded like an old man, but the other two were from a drunk girl.

As Mark took the stage, the applause seemed a lot louder for him than usual. He had the benefit of following the other guitarist who was "still learning," as Justin put it nicely. He introduced his first poem and read it, making sure to glance up here and there. One time he even looked all the way over at Bree, who was pretending she was the only one there. She thought back about the long talk they had on the phone. Mark was so . . . cute. Yes, Quinn was god-like and hot, and Justin was—well, Justin was sexy in his own way, but Mark was cute. She thought about how, when they messed around, *she* would be the one in charge. She would ask him if he *liked that* and he would be so awestruck he would only be able to nod his head yes. She would make him speechless with pleasure and then rock his world. She would melt his heart and drain it out through his pen until she became the subject of every one of his poems.

As if on cue he glanced over one more time to finish with his poem called "Red." His words produced beautiful imagery of the trees in the fall and the nostalgia that goes with each season as it changes. Midway through, he took a long pause and almost stumbled through the second half of it, like he was suffering through the emotions that this *red* caused. Bree dismissed it as him trying to add some passion for her benefit. Maybe he was thinking back to their long talk the other night as well. She would make it all better for him tonight. Instead of talking to him on the phone from the rooftop, she'd have him there between her legs. Her heart started to shoot these devilish thoughts through her bloodstream right as Mark finished the poem and quickly left the stage.

"That was about me," she heard a female voice say in an intentionally loud voice. *She wished.*

"Coming to the stage next…" Justin paused, looking over at Bree. She suddenly jumped up. "…is a good friend of mine who made her debut last week. Please welcome the very funny Bree Andrews!"

Blank. The stage lights were so bright. They reminded her of the first time she got pulled over as a teenager. The cop's flashlight was so bright she couldn't even think. Now the pressure seemed even higher as she struggled to find her first words.

"So, um. I just got braces last week," she said to no laughter. "I was the oldest person in the waiting room." *Shit, how did this joke go?* Last week everything rolled off her tongue and hit hard. She stammered her way through all of her braces material to only a few chuckles. She could hear the same female voice chattering from the back of the patio.

"Let's see, there was something else I wanted to talk about." Ugh. She sounded like all of those terrible comics she had heard eating it so many times, unprepared and struggling through transitions between jokes. With the last bit of light, she was able to see a young redhead in the back. She was the one with too many drinks in her to stay quiet. She had the face of a doll with lips that complimented her hair perfectly. Beautiful and bratty, Bree sensed danger immediately.

"Should've tried poetry!" the young girl yelled out.

"Should've tried puberty," Bree snapped back to her first real laughs of the night. *Fuck my act, this bitch is going down.*

"You're the one still wearing braces," she heckled back.

"Yeah, and I still give better head than you!" A previously untapped compartment of Bree's brain was taking over. She didn't know where the words were coming from and there was absolutely no way she was going to filter them. Before the redhead could respond, she dug in a little further: "Aw, too scared to take the stage yourself but need all the attention because Daddy never hugged you? Didn't get a bicycle on your tenth birthday so you had your third step-mom teach you how to dress like a tramp and yell at people who have bigger dreams than you?" The crowd had transformed into a taping of *Maury*.

"Fuck you!" the girl yelled.

"Yeah, I don't have all night to wait in line," Bree said to a roaring crowd. She thought about dropping the mic, but instead just flipped it to Justin as he came back on stage.

"Bree Andrews, everyone!" he said as the crowd continue their applause.

"Holy shit, Bree, that was awesome!" Jill said, kneeling next to her back at her seat.

Even with the tremendous applause, she felt that she had failed. She remembered Justin saying that hecklers don't want to heckle a good comic. She had been bombing up there before that girl gave her an excuse to change the subject. She continued to fume and decided against getting a drink for the first time in her adult life. She wanted to fight, and rum wouldn't keep her out of the back of a police car.

Jill eventually closed out the show, continuing its vibe with a very upbeat, almost angry song. How great it must be to just be able to sing and play, Bree thought. Singers never got heckled. Justin's strategy of putting Jill last was definitely paying off. No one was leaving the show early since she had become a weekly spectacle. As the show ended, people were still seated at their tables ordering more drinks. Bree stood up to see where her nemesis for the night was.

Some background music began playing at a light volume. The sun had gone down and the patio house lights hadn't been turned back on just yet. Only the spotlight from the stage lit the crowd. Suddenly it went dark for a moment, and then the patio lights gradually grew brighter. She turned away, trying not to be too obvious. There she was. There was Mark sitting right next to her. It all came together instantly. Mark, his poem "Red," and the redheaded girl who said that it was about her. She just *had* to request that one. The girl and her friends stood up. They were so . . . skinny. Such tiny waists, even smaller than Prentiss's size two or zero or whatever the hell that mutant frame fit into. Their shorts were so, so minuscule. Tiny shorts, tiny belts, tiny baby-doll tees with little designs that directed attention to their tiny but present boobs. The redhead was almost as tall as Bree and surrounded by some slightly shorter girls, but none of the four could've weighed even a hundred pounds. *What the hell, Mark?* Her visions of rocking his world turned into fears of crushing him under her frame. Who were these girls, and how could they be so obnoxious if they weren't even drinking? Everything she thought about Mark disappeared.

Jill walked over, sipping a cocktail from a straw. "Those two used to be a thing, I guess," she said. She put her hand on Bree's shoulder and directed her away from staring.

"She's like a little girl," Bree said. "Why would he be with her?"

"He's a little boy, Bree. Dude just turned twenty a few weeks ago. You weren't here that week."

"What? He's *twenty*? I'm a child molester!"

"You hooked up with him?"

"No. I haven't touched him, but I was going to. I mean, I used to want to."

"Shot time!" Justin barged in with three double-shots of something clear with a lemon slice on each glass.

"I can't. I don't want to risk punching someone," Bree said, hinting with a nod.

"Ha, you better not. Those chicks are still minors. Sooo, bottoms up?"

Bree ignored the other two as they went through the ritual of clanking their glasses together, touching the table top with the bottom of each shot and then slamming down the clear liquid. Justin was overdramatic and dancing around on one foot as he reeled from the shot. Jill set her empty glass down with a gasp. Bree drank hers calmly like it was water, still eyeing Mark and his teeny boppers.

"Let it go, Bree," Justin said, pulling out chairs at a table for them. It still had a few bottles from whatever group had been there during the show. The extra seat of the four next to Bree suddenly got pulled out. Before Bree could react, Quinn was sitting right next to her as if he had been there all along. Turns out he had.

"Wow there, Tiger, that was quite a display you put on up there. Bravo," Quinn said as if the two were best buddies. Bree's brain had a Pavlov's dog sex-response at the slightest thought of Quinn. Him saying something to her sent her sexual imagination into overdrive. She let his words echo in her head in a different context. She had just dismounted him as he told her the same thing: *Wow there, Tiger. That was some display you put on up there. Bravo.* If he would just give her one chance to have sex with him. *C'mon,* she imagined begging him. *You know we'll both feel so good doing it. What's the problem?* When could she have that conversation with him? Under what context, during what miracle of the universe could she even get him in the right situation to bring that up?

"Let's do another shot," she said. That was a start. Justin signaled his bartender buddy and waved four fingers. Within moments he was setting the glasses down on the metal patio table.

"Oh, not tonight," Quinn said, to Bree's disappointment.

"Quinn hardly-never-ever-barely-rarely drinks," Jill said, already showing signs of intoxication of her own. *Dammit.*

"More for me then," said Bree, giving up on anything she had planned for the night. This time she slammed both shots before Justin and Jill could even reach for their glasses. Justin's eyebrows were up to his hairline, and Jill was doubled over laughing.

"I'm going to be a mess, aren't I?" Bree said meekly. She cowered against the back of her seat, realizing her mistake. Why get drunk around a guy who doesn't drink? She noticed Jill and Justin shooting quick glances at each other. They were up to something. Justin picked up his shot, nodded to Jill who did the same, and then they downed them in a creepily synchronized way as if they had rehearsed. As they finished they both stood up.

"Quinn, we're going to take off. Can you make sure she gets home okay?" Justin was forgiven. Yesterday morning didn't even happen. Jill was her new other best friend. Mark and his underage ex-girlfriend were in a different universe. For now it was Quinn, Bree, and a perfect amount of alcohol in her hormone-saturated bloodstream.

27

Maybe it was the three shots; yes, it was definitely the three shots that gave Bree the courage to grab Quinn's arms as he walked her back to his car. She knew the vehicle well and almost dragged him there the way a dog drags its owner out the door for a walk. The internal struggle of voices battled in her head. In one corner, a voice told her to make the most of the contact and lean her head against him until he was almost carrying her back to the car. The oppositional voice told her, *Be cool. Don't ruin this in the first thirty seconds.* Quinn let out a long exhale. What did it mean? Was he nervous too? Impossible. He was probably mad at Jill for leaving him to babysit the drunk while she ran off with Justin. She tried to interpret even the slightest bit of his body language. Was he walking faster to get this over with? No, he was taking his time. Was he plotting and planning? What if Prentiss showed up out of nowhere? Nowhere, ha. She's the type that would descend from a cloud, preceded by doves to make everyone aware of her presence. When they got to his car, he clicked his key to unlock it and opened her passenger side door with one smooth motion. Not Brad, not Justin—none of her dates had ever opened her door for her. She was falling in love with him with each action that he took. His car was spotless except for a few camera cases in the backseat. It smelled of a fresh scent she had never smelled before. She would remember it for the rest of her life.

"Are you buckled in?" he asked as he started the ignition.

"Yep." Bree was no longer in her own body at this point. She was an onlooker cheering her flesh on, like a mom watching her son play his first soccer game. *Just don't mess up.* She was buckled in. He could wreck the car for all she cared. She pictured Quinn at the side of her hospital bed, waking her up from a coma with a kiss. As she came to, he would be pleading for God to just give him one more chance to love her. She would open her eyes to a hospital room full of his flowers and his smile. *Goodbye, hospital gown!* The nurses would all be so jealous of her as Quinn spent day and night by her bedside. He would feed her, teach her to walk again, and be there as she finally took steps on her own, only to have him bend down on one knee and propose.

Suddenly the instrumental dance beat that was playing in the rear speakers was interrupted by a phone call that rang through his system.

"What's up, Quinn?" The relief that it was a male caller penetrated Bree's soul. She couldn't have handled hearing him talk to Prentiss and pretend she wasn't there.

"Hey, John. You come through with everything?"

"Yep. Guns *and* boat." Oh shit, is he a bad boy too? She was ready to start undressing right there in the front seat. He wouldn't care if she unbuckled her seatbelt to remove some clothes, would he?

"I'm still not sure about this," he said. Great, more questions. It was around this moment that Bree admitted to herself that, despite being in his apartment and going through his file, she still knew absolutely nothing about Quinn.

"Ah, c'mon. You can at least come with us. You don't have to do anything. Have some fun."

Bree wished Quinn would just leave the fun up to her, though it was intriguing hearing him interact with someone else. He chatted a little more, laughed at an inside joke, and then politely excused himself to end the call.

"Sorry 'bout that." He looked over to Bree at a stoplight.

"That's okay," she said.

"My buddy wants me to head up to Wisconsin to go duck hunting with him." The truth was so far from what she was expecting she had no idea how to feel.

"Do you hunt a lot?" Any conversation was good conversation. It was like stage time. The more it happened, the less of a big deal it would seem, and she could improve on just being normal. She pictured a day where Quinn showing up at her door wouldn't be the greatest thing to ever happen in the universe. Nope, it still was and always would be.

"No, not really at all. I head up there later next weekend, though, just to get away." Get away from what? From who? Prentiss? Was this okay with her? There were other women in Wisconsin. Some of them had to be attractive. It had colleges and sororities. Dammit, he was going to move back there before she even got a chance. What would be her excuse to just happen to move into whatever area he returned to? Fuck it, she'd become a librarian. They had those everywhere, right? She'd get the naughty glasses and everything. He seemed like a reader.

"Do you read a lot, Quinn?" Of all the questions that needed to be answered, that's the one she fires off?

"I do—how did you know?"

Flatter him or lucky guess, flatter him or lucky guess? "I don't know. You just seem . . ." *Amazing, sexy, god-like, heroic, for the love of all that's sacred pull over and do me now!* "You just seem like a reader. You know, laid back and whatnot."

"I am. I'm extremely laid back." *Laid.* "I try not to get too worked up about anything these days, so yes, a book is often the center of my evening." She pondered whether librarian glasses came without a prescription, and how she could get a pair.

"What do you read?" Bree was starting to calm a bit. She could at least speak a normal sentence without over-thinking it. She hoped that her shirt would smell like his car from now on.

"Oh, everything really. A lot of nonfiction. I keep up to date on the latest technology for photography. Magazines here and there. I still like a good classic novel, too. Fitzgerald and Dickens are my favorites. Some of their better books I've read three or four times."

Why in the hell didn't I read all of those books in college? Stupid young me could've had a killer conversation right now.

The phone rang again. This time it wasn't John. Bree's heart shot up into her throat.

"Hey," said a familiar voice.

"What's up?" Quinn asked, scratching his right temple as if to shield his face from Bree.

"Did she find her own place yet?" She was bitter. Bree could sense her breathing heavily over the phone. It echoed into every speaker in the car. The angst of another woman in love with Quinn pounded against Bree's ears, which were growing warmer by the second. Bree stayed quiet because she was dying to know the answer. Apparently the whole one-bedroom ordeal wasn't flying with Quinn's girlfriend at all.

"Nope. Still looking," Quinn said, as if he'd answered her a thousand times already.

"Wait, am I on speaker phone in your car?"

"Yep," he said back, as if to hint he wasn't alone.

"Oh, hi, Jill," said the voice, injecting as much sarcasm as it could.

You're up, liquor! "I'm not Jill," Bree replied in a friendly tone, despite what she actually wanted to say.

"Who the hell are you?" Friendly time was over. "It's just Bree. God, we met the other day." Quinn shot a look of panic over at Bree. What was the big deal? After seeing Bree in a bikini, the same bikini plus a few sizes, she had no reason to worry about her competition.

"Unless you were up in Milwaukee and I somehow magically forgot Quinn being home and introducing me to someone— wait, Quinn, who does she think I am?"

"Look, Brenda, I'm just giving a ride home to a drunk friend who needed a lift. Can I just call you back tomorrow?" Instead of an answer there was a click. Before Bree could apologize or say anything, the phone rang again.

"I wasn't done talking, Quinn!"

"Then why did you hang up on me?" What dimension was this girl from that she could talk to Quinn like that *and* have the nerve to hang up on him? Quinn remained calm and kept a smile on his face without showing any concern at all.

"We're talking tomorrow, Quinn!" she yelled before hanging up again. Bree's eyes were bulging in shock. What had just happened? If that wasn't Prentiss, who the hell was it?

"Sorry about that. You're probably confused, huh?"

"A little. Sorry, I thought it was Prentiss, your girlfriend."

"Nope. That was Brenda." How long was the waiting list for this guy? "She's someone from back home who—well, it's a long story."

"An ex-girlfriend?" Bree said trying to drain the mystery from the whole incident.

"More of a friend who was a girl, but never really a girlfriend. Do you get what I mean?"

Sure, she was in love with him like any other sane girl, but couldn't have him, so she became insane just like Bree. She wanted to hate the girl, but feared turning into her years down the road.

"So is she trying to move here and live with you, then?"

"No, not with me. I mean, at times she's been a really good friend, but once I decided to move here she got a little nutty; and then, of course, she's jealous of Jill." Now she was getting somewhere. She continued to tiptoe for each question, but could tell he was becoming more and more uncomfortable. They were almost home and she had attempts of her own to make. Plus she had to pee.

"Yeah, of course, are you two kinda cramped?"

"No, not at all." That's not what she wanted to hear. "I don't mind being close to Jill." *How close?* How close? He had to be aware she was sleeping with Justin, right? Time to give him a little nudge.

"Well, you get some nights to yourself, right?" *Or does Prentiss fill in?*

"Yeah, Jill will pass out anywhere. The kitchen, the floor, the couch, and even once in the bathtub." That was the answer she had been waiting for. Well, not the answer, but at least the information. They shared a bed. Probably. It was a big bed, but still . . . But what about Prentiss?

"Quinn, I don't mean to pry, but—" Bree said timidly. She giggled to mask how awkward she felt asking. How could she phrase this? "Does Prentiss get jealous of Jill?" Quinn turned into the complex. There weren't many open spots. Maybe he was driving her all the way down to his building! Nope, he found one.

"Oh, she doesn't know there's anything to be jealous about," he answered as if that just summed up everything in a package—as nice as his—with a pretty bow on top. Was he a player? *No, don't be a player.* He turned the car off.

"There's not?"

"No, Jill and I aren't romantic in any way." Bree sighed and they both started to get out. Right as she shut her door, she could have sworn she heard him say, "Anymore."

Bree tried to rewind the last few seconds. Yes, she was sure he heard him say "Anymore." She also reminded herself the talk Jill had had with her about their past. The stories definitely conflicted. One of them was lying. Quinn was staring straight up into the sky. "Wow," he said. "With the moon not up, you can see a few of the constellations. I think the stars are so good at putting everything in perspective. When you think about how far away everything is," he paused. He was using that sweet sexy tone again as if he was doing a voice-over on his own movie. A sea of female moviegoers would be on the edge of their seats in anticipation of his next word. "It just makes problems seem so insignificant compared to the distance of each star." Melting.

"Well, if you want a better view, I know of a place."

"That's okay, I don't feel like heading anywhere else tonight."
He started to dismiss her.

"No, it's on our roof. It's perfect up there. I go up there all
the time to look at stars and planets." *Sound like you have a
similar interest!* "And comets and stuff." *Yes, genius, and stuff.
Stuff* ranks up there with meteors and the rings of Saturn.

"Cool, let's see it," he said. She paused an extra moment just
to stare at him. She had to take him in every few minutes.
She could gaze at any part of his body for long periods of
time if that was ever allowed. From her superficial likes and
turn-ons to her primal instinct that said "Mate this!" she was
drawn to him worse than ever. Keeping her courage from
earlier, she grabbed his hand again and led him up the stairs
to the top floor. She could've saved some time by using the
elevator for most of the way, but that would've decreased
the amount of time she had an excuse to hold his hand. Her
pulse had already quickened, and the steps felt like an es-
calator. She dared her thumb to caress the top of his hand.
Perhaps he would reciprocate. She could take it from there;
she just needed one little sign, one little hint. Take an inch
from her and she'd give him the world.

Finally they got to the rooftop. Bree's heart was pounding
more from Quinn than the flights of steps. It was a good
excuse to breathe heavily, though.

He let go of her hand and stepped away in wonder. There
were absolutely no clouds in the sky and the distant Chicago
city lights seemed more faint than usual for some reason.

"Wow, this is great. I should bring my telescope up here," he said. *Yes, bring everything! Bring your telescope along with that sweet ass any time you want!* It was all falling into place. Bree's performance tonight was a distant memory. Unemployment? No concern. Everything was in the right place. No sirens, just crickets and tree frogs peeping in the background.

Then it was over.

"Is someone crying?" she heard Quinn ask. Right away she knew who it was and what it was about. They both looked to the far corner of the roof to see Justin with his hands on his hips. Jill's hands were in her face.

Son.

Of.

A.

Bitch.

28

Back in Justin's apartment, Bree was berating him as expected.

"I wanted to be honest with her," he said.

"First of all, that's my fucking rooftop, okay? You don't get to use it anymore. I should've never let you up there in the first place. Second, did you have to be honest right then? Do you know what a connection I was making with Quinn tonight?"

"A connection? You had been with him for fifteen minutes." Was that it? It felt like an entire evening in her mind. They had talked about so much. She had seen him interact with other people on the phone. She even found a new enemy from up north.

"It was something, Justin. I was going to spend the rest of the night up there with him under the stars."

Justin started laughing. "What movie are you living in? Do you think you're the only woman he's talking to? And technically you're not even *talking to* him."

"I am so!"

"Okay then, what's his phone number?" Bree rattled it off. "Oh, I forgot you computer-stalked him for that one."

"Shut up, I did not."

"Oh, so he finally gave you his number?"

"That's not the point," she said, knowing she had lost this argument. "What did you say to Jill?"

"I told her that I liked hanging out with her, but we weren't exclusive."

"You're a bastard. Why can't you be exclusive with her?"

"She sleeps in the same bed as him, Bree!" Justin yelled.

Bree had never wanted to hit him so bad. "Was I not trying to point this out to you before? Why in the hell does that all of a sudden matter? The real truth is you've been fucking someone else. I don't know who that was in your bathroom the other morning, but it wasn't Jill. So figure out which of those two you want. Make up your fucking mind already!"

"I don't want either of them," he said, turning away.

"Figures," Bree said, sitting down on the couch. Justin paced back and sat beside her.

"I want you," he said softly.

"Oh no, not now. How dare you openly sleep with two other women in the same week and then tell me that you want me?"

"Oh, so you were lying yesterday morning? You kissed me!" Justin said reeling.

"Yeah, well, it was a mistake," she said, getting up and leaving. Quinn was so close to being hers.

The following morning, Bree found herself waking up early on her own, as if she still had to get to work and the alarm was still part of her life. Normally Friday would be her favorite day, but now it was the furthest moment from Thursday. The weekend was now her enemy. Quinn would be working at a wedding or out on a date with one of the hundred girls in front of her on his waiting list if Prentiss wasn't available.

She considered heading out for another walk, maybe even a jog, but she didn't want to chance running into Jill. She guessed that Jill probably cried herself to sleep in Quinn's arms, her tear-soaked cheeks against his muscular chest. What she wouldn't give just to lay on him. She would drift to sleep as his chest rose and sank. Then as he awoke she would touch him here or there with her ear pressed up against his heart to see if she could hike his pulse.

A text interrupted her fantasy. It was Mark. *Hey, sorry about last night. Can I explain over coffee later this morning?*

"What's to explain?" she wrote back. That's the best she could come up with. Mark blew his chance when he invited Romper Room to their show. After a few back and forths she agreed to meet him at a little café a few blocks away. *If he orders a hot chocolate, I'm calling his mother to pick him up.*

A bell rang as she entered the door of the retro-feeling café. Without even trying to find him, she went straight to the counter to order. The baristas were both busy as she glanced around to find him. He was cowering behind a laptop in the far right corner. The smell of coffee was overpowering and through the clatter he didn't seem to notice her. It was so warm she felt like her clothes were choking her.

"Large mocha," she said when they took her order.

"Name?"

"Bree," she said loudly, hoping Mark would finally notice her standing there and begin his series of apologies. No dice yet.

"Okay, miss, you can have a seat and we'll bring it out to you."

"I'll wait here, that's okay." Still nothing from Mark. What blog was he digesting? What status updates was he commenting on? Why wasn't he noticing her? She had actually fit into an older pair of jeans (which she was now starting to sweat in after the long walk) and a tight t-shirt. *She looked good.* The rest of the café was nothing but old people and hipsters, and it was evident that neither of those demographics had put nearly as much thought into their outfits.

As they finished her coffee and transaction she glanced back over at Mark one more time. He looked up and smiled and then returned to his computer. Her insecurities got the best of her. Was there something wrong with the outfit? He had seen her there the whole time and not moved a muscle. Quinn would've gotten up and carried her to the table while balancing her hot coffee on his head *because that's what a gentleman does.*

"Hi, Bree," he said, finally showing at least a little bit of interest in her. It must have been her waist. Compared to those jailbait bitches, she was a hog.

"Hey," she said in a cold tone. It felt like he invited her there just to show that he wasn't interested. It reminded her of how she used to break up with guys in one of the little "in the meantime" relationships years ago. They both knew it was coming. She always did it in a safe public venue that she wouldn't miss if it turned into a scene and she could never show her face there again. But how could Mark be dumping her? They weren't even a thing. Little did he know her confidence was swelling from the night of hand-holding with Quinn. She pictured Quinn at a different nearby coffee shop setting Prentiss down lightly. "It's not you, it's me," he would tell her as tears streaked down her face. She would be cold and shivering from being so skinny, but Quinn wouldn't care because he'd be thinking of his new love. "I just need a real woman who I can connect with."

"So I guess I owe you—" Mark interrupted her thoughts.

"An apology?" she said with her new attitude.

"An explanation. I don't think I did anything wrong, but obviously I knew the person who did."

"Person? More like child," Bree said, and then looked out the window as if something more interesting was going on.

"Are you going to let me explain or not?"

"I'm listening," she said, folding her arms.

"Well, that girl, um," he couldn't think of the right words. "She's still in love with me."

"Nobody likes a bragger." She was in full smartass mode.

"We dated like four months ago—er, that's when I ended it. We dated for four months and then stopped and four months has passed."

Bree started mimicking like she was jotting the facts down like a newspaper reporter on a small imaginary notebook. "And what about the rest of the training bra gang? Did you dance with them at prom, too?" She took a sip of her drink. It burnt her tongue which was about to get even looser. "Why are you telling me all this? Your poetry might be impressive to your little teeny boppers, but I'm an adult." Ouch. That one even felt mean to her. Her words froze him. His emotions were a full glass that would spill if moved even the slightest bit. They sat in silence for another minute or so while she pretended she was still unfazed.

"I like you," he said, finally breaking the silence. "I didn't know they were going to show up." He seemed so much more boyish than the guy who owned his own DJ business or could woo a crowd with the words in his notebook. Was he going to cry now? His brown eyes looked into hers and finally took some control back.

"I may be a little young and maybe not as cool as those other guys you hang out with all the time…" *Yep, all the time!* "But I'm old enough to know when I have a connection with someone. We all have a past and I've done my best to put mine behind me. And when I see you, all I can help about thinking of is what a great future we would have." And with that he folded up his laptop, shoved it in his bag and got up. She sat motionless as he turned to walk away. He set a white sheet of paper, double-folded, on the table in front of her. She heard the bell ring as he exited before carefully unfolding it.

Dreaming the Chase

29

Mistook the nod for an approval

Mistook the look for a real smile

Felt the pain at this moment

It will sting a little while

A step towards you is how it started

Saying what I had to say

I thought you might have felt the same way

but feared you might also step away

Perhaps we'll drift away to nothing

Like the wind carrying away a beach's sand

You never got to really know me

I never got to hold your hand

I wanted so much for that one chance

Though I never knew what to do

Mistook the nod for an approval

Though I really already knew

So he *wasn't* out late with those girls? He was writing about her. She thought about running out to see if there was a chance he was still in the lot. She didn't know how to feel, how to think. No one had ever written a poem about her. She read it again and found a tear crawling down her right cheek, then her left. Two people were laughing at the other end of the café, but Bree was oblivious to her surroundings. She felt oblivious to everything. If Mark felt this way about her, what was Quinn feeling?

She took her phone out of her purse and texted Justin. *"A walk in thirty minutes?"* She had a pretty good idea his situation was getting to be as messy as hers.

"Please come over, I'm not up for a walk" finally popped up on her phone as she finished her drink. The café had grown even stuffier. With no windows nearby, it could've been winter outside. She felt hidden and safe from everything for another minute, and then finally got up to leave. As she opened the door, the sun shone brightly in her face and she was back to the now. She paused a bit to let her eyes adjust. So how did she feel about everything? Mark was nice, and just over twenty-four hours ago he would've done, but still—that moment with Quinn. There were a lot of moments. The chat at the club, the ride home, and the walk up the stairs had all been the most romantic moments of her life. She couldn't help but smile as she started the walk home. Her smile was

countered with a shot of pain from the braces, reminding her they were still there.

Half of her felt like everything was going to work out. Mark liked her, and Quinn just needed to break things off with Prentiss and get a restraining order for that girl he was on the phone with. She had options though; deep down she knew Mark was a distant second. At least one of them could save her from another lonely night on the roof. Still, a little voice reminded her of the kiss with Justin. How whimsical her heart had become. She pictured that same kiss with Mark, and then with Quinn. She fought through the pain of her braces and smiled even more deeply, thinking about all three of them fighting over her. Poor little Mark wouldn't stand a chance. She pictured him trying to fight off Justin by swinging his notebook at him. Justin would put up a mildly good attempt to take on Quinn, but in the end Quinn would grab her and hold her against his chest like King Kong and that pretty lady he climbed up the building with. Hmm, she would need a red dress to complete the scene.

When she finally got to Justin's apartment, the door was cracked open. She stuck her head in. "Hello?"

"Back here," he said from his bedroom. Oh great. Not another attempt. Thank goodness she had these other boys, or her hormones would probably let Justin get away with anything right now. He better not try anything today—though she secretly hoped he would. The second best feeling to saying yes was being able to say no.

She stepped over some dirty socks on the way back to his room. His lights were off and his closed curtains only allowed for a bit of the early afternoon sun to come through.

"Holy shit, you look terrible!" she said. Justin was curled up on his bed, teeth chattering, with sweat on his forehead.

"I don't know what's wrong with me. Just a fever or something."

"Are you hungover?"

"No, I was fine until about two this morning, and then I just started to feel hot, then cold, then back and forth." Bree picked up the bedspread that was bunched up in the far corner of his room and pulled it over his soaked sheet.

"Let me get you some water. Do you have any tea left?"

"Water's fine. Look, if you see Jill, will you tell her I'm sorry?"

"For what? Actually I don't want to know. I probably already know. Were you guys finally honest with each other?"

"Yes," he said in almost a whisper.

"Wait, how honest? You're not taking me down on this one, are you?"

"No Bree, just tell her I'm sorry and that I'm a little under the weather right now."

"Got it. That's if I run into her. Anything else?"

"Actually there is. And you can't say no because I've already kinda got it approved."

"Oh great, what?" She really didn't want any more surprises.

"You're hosting this weekend's shows at the club. The manager was cool with it, and I think you know the basics. You only have to do a few minutes to warm the crowd up. Brad Brewer is there all weekend, so there's no middle act. He does close to an hour and a half on his own."

"Who?"

"It's this guy from L.A. that's got a little heat behind him. He's been on a few of the late shows in the past few months and has an hour special debuting this fall. In fact, that's pretty much your intro for him."

"I'm not ready for a real show," she pleaded.

"Why? What's the difference between tonight and last night?"

"About two hundred crowd members! Plus, my act wasn't any good last night."

"Had you practiced at all during the week?" Justin said in a fatherly tone.

"Well, no, but my jokes stink."

"They worked well the first week. Besides, if you can make a small crowd laugh, a big crowd is no problem. Hell, you've seen me kill it in front of crowds for no reason other than they're excited to be there." She closed her eyes and tried to picture a full room staring back at her. Could she really do this?

"Besides, it pays two hundred bucks for the four shows. Oh, and last time I worked with Brad he threw me a little extra. He's a really cool guy to work with. In fact, tell him I'm sorry, too. Wish I could be there."

Wow, this could happen. What would the crowd think? What would Quinn think? If she was famous, he would have to love her. Mark would fall further in love with her. He was in love, right? Close enough. "Justin, I have a question." She had a lot of questions, but as she watched him shiver in a pile of bed sheets, now was not the time to bust his balls about whatever he said to Jill.

"Yeah?" he asked. He seemed to be slipping back into a nap.

"What should I wear?"

30

The ride home from the mall was exhausting. Her air conditioning had decided that this would be the perfect weekend to take off. The trip itself was a success, but not without hours of searching. She found a blue summer dress that was nearly perfect in all three of her "fitting categories." It was cut low—but not low-low, actually medium low. She could adjust it to produce as little or as much cleavage as she wanted right before taking the stage. The second category was overall tightness. This was the hardest quality to decide on and find because she actually had to try each dress on to see how well it hugged her hips and butt. She would deliberate for minutes and minutes about whether a dress was acceptable or not. Several times she became dizzy spinning in the mirrors, and her neck hurt from looking back at certain angles. She wondered if other gals endured this much pain for one outfit. If so, she had a new bit to joke about. The final requirement was the one she always let herself be a little more aggressive on: length. At one point she had walked a black dress up to the cashier whose length would've stolen the show, but she didn't want to establish that kind of reputation on her first night as professional comedian. The blue dress was still fairly short, but covered enough thigh to give off the illusion that she had some definition above her knees. The black heels at home would do the rest.

She texted Justin at a stoplight but never heard back from him. His absence was the reason she got the gig, but he happened to be the one person she needed there the most. It wasn't so much for moral support as for all of the questions she had. She hadn't even done a show indoors yet. What if someone else heckled her? How would she know how long to perform? Who was Brad Brewer, and what if he hated her for screwing up his show?

She got to the club over an hour and a half before show time. The manager, Jeff, was telling the bartenders what still needed to be stocked in the bar. He gave her a confused look as she walked in.

"You here early enough?" he asked.

"Am I?" she asked, stopping and already feeling exposed in her blue dress. His eyes were feasting on her and she felt like a small child. She had just adjusted her boobs to "mild" after getting out of her car and looking at them in the distorted reflection of the window. It could've been her dress length. She could feel it climbing its way up her thighs. She rubbed the side of her hip to make sure she had indeed remembered to wear panties; there had been an incident in college during which she'd partied too much before going out and overlooked that very important piece of her wardrobe.

"Yes," he said, shaking his head as if she was the dumbest person on earth. She looked outside to the patio. It was still closed, but the tables were set up differently than their Thursday night formation. There seemed to be more of them. She wanted to cower outside and get away from the servers who were busy lighting candles and setting out drink menus in the bar area. She walked to the other side of the bar near the showroom entrance and peeked in. It was dead silent and dark. A neon sign that said *Laugh, Dammit!* glowed in the far corner and gave everything an orange hue. She turned back to the bar area and decided that it would be best to see how long she could wait outside under one of the patio umbrellas. If she started sweating, she would head back in. The first door was locked, so without checking to see if anyone had noticed her failed budge, she stepped over to the second. Locked as well.

"What are you doing?" Jeff asked, looking up from a beer cooler behind the bar.

"I was going to wait out there," she said, pulling up a stool to the indoor bar.

"Not there either," he said, pushing two glasses into the suds. Where the hell did comics sit then? She remembered Justin always hanging out there during the shows she attended. The blood rushed to her face. She felt like an intruder in a place in which she was supposed to be working. Servers were staring at her, Jeff seemed to be going out of his way to be rude, and she wasn't even close to the hardest part of the night.

"Follow me," he said, acting as if he was bothered. He led her back into the show room. The candles were slowly being lit by a doorman who looked like he could've still been in high school. As she approached the front of the room and the stage, she realized she had never even sat that close. Even on the slow nights she would plant herself in the back row away from the crowd. She was already sweating, and she hoped her armpits wouldn't dampen the blue material just beneath them. She pulled the two straps up on her shoulders as her heels stayed muffled against the ultra-thin carpet. She followed him to the corner of the room and through a swinging door into the kitchen area. A few of the line cooks looked up from their prepping and right at her chest. She tried to ignore them as Jeff finally took her to a small room that shared a wall with the back of the stage.

"Here's our green room." It was white with black signatures all over the walls from previous comics. "Make yourself at home. If you need a drink, just tell Rick behind the bar," he said on his way out. She stood alone. The mirror on the wall lied to her and told her that her dress was plenty long enough. She looked at her reflection, which was partially blocked by all of the old comedian bumper stickers that plagued the mirror. The signatures on the wall were all unique, but she only recognized a few. Where was Justin's? She had all night to find it. The newer wall messages seemed to all thank "Jeff and the Gang" for a wonderful week, while the older ones were directed at a guy named Pete who must have left several years ago. She wondered if there was a direct correlation between the size of the signature and the comic's ego.

A small television set faced her from the corner. Its cable box was a model that she thought had been endangered for a decade. The remote's buttons were larger than usual and all of the numbers had worn off. The ceiling was stained yellow from the cigarette smoke that still lingered in the room. A half-filled ashtray sat on the small coffee table next to a Playboy from when Carmen Electra was still doing covers. Bree opened her purse and took out her phone. 6:41. She still had an hour and nineteen minutes to do nothing but stress out about her set. She closed her eyes and mentally went through each bit over and over as a good part of an hour passed. She found her courage and headed back out to the bar area to get a bottle of water.

People. There were people everywhere. Every single stool at the bar was filled: couples on dates holding hands, groups of married folks, even a bachelorette party of seven all wearing obnoxious t-shirts and using penis straws with their drinks. Bree could only smile as she thought about the fact that these women were the complete opposite of her right now. She envied that they had each other, one was getting married, they were having fun without worrying about performing, and that they each had a drink in hand. She was envious of everything except their waistlines; those they could keep. But was hers bulging in this dress, which seemed to grow smaller by the minute?

She walked up and leaned against the bar.

"You're Bree, right?" He must have been Rick. He was an older man, married, with really hairy arms, but he was at least treating her like a human being.

"Yep, just filling in for Justin tonight."

"Well," he said, "I don't want to sound like a dirty old man, even though I am, but you're as beautiful as he said you were." She liked Rick. He was instantly fatherly, even with that comment. She thought about her own parents and what they would say if they knew their daughter had lost her job and was now turning to performing as a means of income. Rick got her the coldest bottle of water he could find and made small talk between taking orders from the patrons.

Bree was looking back towards the entrance to the long line at the box office when she saw a tall man excuse himself through the crowd. He was carrying a large coffee, wearing a jacket for some reason, and gliding between the high-top tables between sips.

"Rick, my man!" he yelled. It had to be Brad Brewer.

"Double B!" Rick called back before shaking a mix. "You're going to want to chat with him ahead of time, darling," Rick nodded to her. She followed him through the showroom doors and to the back of the room, struggling to catch up in her heels. He just seemed so comfortable and familiar with every step that he took. His introduction—that's what she was supposed to get from him, right? When she caught up to him in the kitchen he was discussing what level of spiciness he wanted on his buffalo wings with the head chef. Coffee and buffalo wings? Right before a show? That would've destroyed her. He finished his order and dropped a large duffle bag on the floor of the green room. It seemed to make the small quarters even more cramped.

"Well, hi," he said, removing his sunglasses. His eyes were no longer blue, but gray. His face was a worn late thirties that only a man could get away with. His raspy voice suggested a history of smoking, though he didn't reach for the ash tray.

"Hi, I'm Bree. I'm filling in for Justin and I'm really nervous."

"No shit? How long have you been in the game?" The game? He must have meant comedy. Should she lie or be honest?

"Well, this is uh, kinda my first paid gig."

"Cool, don't fuck up," he laughed. Was that a joke? What if she did?

"What's your introduction?" she asked, getting out her pen and a small note card she found on the floor. Before he could answer, his phone rang, and he ended up in a call that involved an open week in his schedule mid-October. It was almost eight o'clock and she still had to make her way through the kitchen to the showroom. His call finally concluded after an obscene reference about a waitress in Detroit. Bree looked at him with her pen wagging like the tail of a puppy.

"Oh, just say Late Night Show and a half-hour special on Comedy Central this fall."

Wait, what? So he's been on those? Couldn't he write it down for her? She was so jealous of how relaxed he was. He sprawled out on the couch as if it was his own bedroom and let out a sigh.

"Look, just relax. They're all drunk. The opening comic always sucks, so they don't expect much from you." *The first guy was always Justin.* "Just do a few bits to warm them up for me and we'll have a good time." His head was tilted back but she could see him eyeing her legs.

"Got it," she said and then scooted through the kitchen to the corner of the showroom. There was a small pathway between the doors to the stage. Right before the house lights shut off, she noticed how overdressed she was. The crowd was a mass of sports jerseys, t-shirts, and even tank tops. What was his intro again? Her first joke? What was the bachelorette party yelling about off to the side?

"Excuse me!" a waitress behind her said, holding a tray of a dozen or so drinks. The last few tables were seated and the lights went down. Where was her path to the stage? The cheesy introduction music, which seemed to be an outdated rip-off of the Rocky Theme, blared as the crowd cheered with anticipation. *Stop thinking, just perform.*

She opened her eyes and stared into the crowd. Her mouth was working on its own, welcoming everyone to the show. She heard herself echoing the introductory remarks that Justin always made and started to settle into her set. Right after she finished a pretty solid piece about her braces, a man yelled out, "Nice ass!" from the back of the room.

"Sir, if you could stop talking to your boyfriend . . ." she said to a roar of laughter. Then it was the bachelorette party's turn to chime in.

"It's Megan's bachelorette party!" they screamed, and then wooed. She had recalled Justin bitching about how these groups always seem to ruin comedy shows by trying to focus the show's attention on them alone.

"That's great, congrats, Megan," she said nicely. "Let me guess, the bachelor is at a comedy club on the other side of town tonight, right?" Laughter. "Yep, him and his boys catching some laughs on his last big night out. Strip club? No, thank you. Who needs boobs when you've got the arts!" Her rant was killing. She looked up and saw a flashlight waving in the back of the room. It was time for the dismount.

"Okay, are you guys ready for your headliner tonight?" It was an abrupt end to her set, but she wanted to quit while she was ahead. They cheered as she stared up to remember his intro. "You've seen him on television late at night—err, on the Late Night Show and you've seen him on his own Comedy Central Special—" What was his name? *Shit, not now, brain!* "Please welcome," there it was, "Brad Brewer!" She put the microphone back into the stand and made her way stage left, the side from which she had begun. Where was he? Suddenly the crowd burst into laughter and she looked back to see Brad standing behind the mic already. He held his hand out to shake so she took a step back towards the middle of the small stage. He grabbed her hand and held it up like she was the new heavyweight champion of the world. Whatever this little bit was, it was getting cheers and laughs, but she couldn't help but feel how high up her dress was on her thighs. She smiled and looked up at him, hoping to make eye contact so he would let her go. Cameras flashed and the bachelorette girls were screaming like it was a concert. Finally, he released her and she hustled her way to the corner of the room. She wanted to cower back in the green room, but was curious as to what he would say about her.

"Keep it going for Bree Andrews. It's her first paid gig, everyone." *Thanks for outing me.* "Most openers wait for a round of applause after their set, but not this girl. Fuck that, she's got a drink waiting for her." Were they laughing *at* her or *with* him? True, she had forgotten to smoothly end her set and transition into the announcements she was supposed to deliver, but at least they laughed. It was a win in her mind. She finally relaxed at the only empty table in the back of the room and watched Brad turn the rowdy crowd into one that was eating out of the palm of his hand. He was just so casual and smooth up there. He would lean against the back wall, play with the mic stand with his free hand, and make eye contact with anyone he wanted to in the crowd. The eyes of the bachelorette party were all entranced by his expressions and they all seemed to be longing for his next few words for the entire set. This guy owned them. And after watching him control a room full of drunks with such power, he owned Bree too. Part of her wanted him, while an even bigger part of her wanted to be like him.

"When will I be this good?" she whispered to herself.

31

The second show went as well as she could've asked, and, other than a few stumbles on the announcements, she was feeling really good about herself as the last of the crowd exited the club. Brad ducked out before she could even say goodnight, and, other than the bartender, everyone else was counting money and cleaning up. Bree was about to order a shot at the bar, but Rick disappeared back to the kitchen. It was just her alone at the bar. Where was everyone? Moments ago she had just taken the stage to close the show out and get one last round of applause, now all of those people were on their way home. They were happy and in love. She was single and absolutely crashing from her first performance high. Justin never warned her about this. Is this why all of those famous comedians were on drugs, she wondered? Just then a girl popped her head back into the club. She was drop-dead beautiful with long straight dark hair and a tan that matched.

"Is Brad still here?" she asked, holding a camera in her right hand.

"Sorry, he left a few minutes ago, I think." The girl frowned and left. No compliment for her? Not even a "Hey, you were good too" or anything like that? The whore just wanted a picture and a shot with the headliner? Bree leaned back in her barstool and crossed her legs. Her skirt rode way up on her thighs but there was no one there to notice. She pulled out her phone and started a text. *"What's up?"* was all she could come up with for Quinn. Erased. She could do better. She stalled and sent one to Justin, asking him how he was feeling.

No response. She thought about sending something to Mark. Not yet. She wasn't in the mood to dissect and attempt to interpret any more of his encryptions.

"You have GOT to come to my shows tomorrow. I'm filling in for Justin!" she fired away to Quinn's phone. She didn't let herself pause between key strokes because she knew her brain would tell her to stop and think. It was sent.

"Bree, can I talk with you a second before you head out?" It was Jeff.

"Sure," she said, looking anywhere for some positive feedback.

"For tomorrow, I need you to do the announcements before you bring Brad up to the stage. We've got to promote the next two weeks of shows. Also, don't forget to mention that they need to tip the wait staff. I know you don't have that much solid material yet, so maybe this could help fill some time. The crowd isn't exactly warmed up in those four or five minutes you're doing before bringing Brad up. Also, check around the crowd to see if there are any birthdays or shit like that to mention. Oh, and for God's sakes, move the mic stand off to the side after you take the mic out of it."

She deflated. So many things she had done wrong were all trumping any chance of validation for the night. It was her first real gig, and all he could do was tell her how bad she did. Her face started to turn red and, as Rick brought the bar lights back up to full strength, she was struggling to hide her emotion.

"Did I do anything right?" she asked, looking down.

"Yeah, nice legs," Jeff said and then headed back to the kitchen.

By the time she got to her car, the tears were more than ready to streak down her cheeks. She turned the key to start her car as her phone vibrated on the passenger seat. *"We will try and make it. I'll ask Quinn: P."*

Was that an emoticon for a tongue sticking out from Quinn, or was it a P for Prentiss? She texted Jill to find out. *"Do you want to come to one of my shows tomorrow night?"*

"I just don't think I can at this point," Jill texted back. What was wrong with these people? Why did everyone have to be so fucking mysterious? She can't because of a gig or because of Justin? What the hell is so hard about being straightforward?

"Oh, do you have a gig?" she wrote back.

"Wish I did. Another thing you have over me." Guess I can write her off.

"Thank you so much for the poem," she started a text to Mark. *"I'm still nodding at you."* Ha. It was her chance to mind-fuck someone. She started home, reflecting on all of the things Jeff had said she needed to change for tomorrow. *Toughen up, it's showbiz. You just earned a hundred bucks for being on stage for only a few minutes. Bring your best stuff tomorrow and maybe it'll open some doors.*

When she got home she took the long route past Justin's apartment. Usually she could hear his television blaring even if he was already asleep. Nothing.

"You have no idea what you mean to me," Mark texted back to her. Heads up! Wow. Oops. No. It was too much. Yes, it felt good to be wanted. It felt really good. It would've felt even better if it was Quinn talking to her like that, though. Knowing that Mark felt that way about her almost turned her off at the same time. She thought about their talk at the café. It wouldn't have been possible to meet with him for a drink at a bar because of his age. She thought about what sex with him would be like. His torso was much skinnier than Quinn's or even Justin's. Could he even grow hair on his chest yet? And the sex itself. A minute? Minute and a half at best? She knew men were not at their best at that age. She imagined herself lying awake, naked and unsatisfied while Mark curled up next to her, sucking his thumb like a baby. He just didn't feel like a real man to her all of a sudden. He was a boy, and a cute boy, and a boy who could write well and woo her with words, but *just* a boy.

Her mother's words echoed just then: "Your problem is that you only want what you can't have." She had been telling her that since her first dance in high school. It was accurate, but she still wanted to prove her mother wrong.

"What are you doing tomorrow night?" Mark texted. Wow, he didn't even wait for her to reply to the last one.

"I have two shows. I'm filling in for Justin at the club." There. Ball was in his court. He could come watch if he wanted. She was just an innocent girl working from the stage.

"Wow, I'll be there!" he texted back. *"Do you need a ride?"* She knew that he knew if she didn't have to drive, she would get drunk and make another bad decision. As tempting as that was, she didn't want to jeopardize her young comedy career already. She needed the money and the opportunity to do this again in the future.

"No, thanks," she wrote back and then did something she hadn't done in years. She turned her phone completely off. She crept back down Justin's hallway, paused by his door, and knocked with just one knuckle as lightly as she could. There was a slight hint of television noise from the other side of it. She waited a moment and, just before giving up and heading to bed, the door opened slowly. She could barely see him inside. "Come in," he mumbled.

"Are you feeling any better?" she whispered before stepping in.

"A little," he said. She followed him to the couch. The television was the only thing that lit the room. He was watching a replay of a Rose Bowl from a few years ago. "I won three grand from this game," he said, still sounding ill. "How did the shows go?"

"Pretty well," she said, unsure if this visit was going to be brief or if he actually wanted to know. "Jeff told me the hundred things I did wrong, but I got along with Brad pretty well."

"Good," Justin said slowly. Each sentence seemed to be painful. "He's going to be really famous soon. I'm so pissed that I can't work with him. I've been looking forward to this week for a long time."

"Yeah, the people there seemed to already know who he is," she said. Wow, she was going to know someone famous. It made her even more nervous for tomorrow. It wasn't just about her sets anymore; it was about trying to impress Brad Brewer. More pressure.

"Well, he's trying to land a pilot in L.A. this fall. If that goes through, this will be his last tour for a while. CBS and ABC are looking at him."

"Holy shit, I had no idea!" she said in a volume that ruined the quiet moment. Justin seemed to be more interested in a football game he already knew the result of. "Well, can I get you anything?" she asked.

"Nah, I'll be okay." She really was concerned about her friend. Or was it just his advice she needed now? She needed to know what happened with Jill. Now wasn't the time to ask. She waited and followed his eyes as the game cut to a commercial. Justin leaned back into the corner of his couch and started coughing, sweating, and shivering all at the same time. She got up and found an old blanket from his hallway closet. When she came back, he was sprawled out, leaving her nowhere to sit. She covered him with the blanket and kissed him on the forehead. He gave her a slight smile without opening his eyes. Poor guy. She had no idea she had taken the one week of work he had been looking forward to all summer.

As she entered her own apartment, she felt like she was a completely different, more accomplished person than the one who left it hours ago. Sleep was easier with her phone off.

32

She didn't wake up until almost noon on Saturday. It was the latest she had slept in in years. Was she morphing into a comic already? She hurried to the mall and, using her credit card and her newly acquired courage, chose a dress that she was terrified of just a day before. It was black, strapless and tight. She pulled it off the rack and didn't let her feet stop until she was swiping the plastic at the register. *Go for it, bitch.* Who cared? Mark wouldn't think she was fat in it. Quinn wasn't going to leave Prentiss for her the way she was. She recalled the long talk with Justin about how, if the girls at the bar were talking about another girl's outfit, the guys were definitely noticing it too. Even Jeff had complimented her appearance. This dress could neutralize his asshole-ness with one look. She got it home, tried it on, and felt really good in it. Her thighs seemed to give some definition in the front and, with her boobs peeking out up top, who would worry about that spot just above the backs of her knees? Damn, she felt hot. She killed the rest of the afternoon rehearsing her set and getting some color in a tanning bed with a free coupon from her junk mail.

"Holy shit."

"Wow!"

"Can I bang you on the bar when everyone else leaves?"

These were the first three things spoken to her at the club that night, the latter coming from her new buddy Rick. "I mean, nice smile!" he said.

"That's a new one," she flirted back with him. It may have been all in her head, but her teeth did seem to be moving already. She had embraced her identity of being the girl with braces *on* stage, now she needed to be comfortable about it off stage.

She hurried back to the green room as to not draw any attention from the early birds at the show. It was quiet back there, apart from the cooks yelling about this and that. It was weird that no one had texted or called all day. She had focused on herself all afternoon and no one had interrupted—her phone was still off!

She held the power button, almost shaking with anticipation. Booting . . . booting . . .

Text messages galore. The first were from Mark.

"*Which show can I come to?*"

"*Well?*"

"*I guess you went to bed.*"

"*See you tonight?*"

"*Are you ignoring me?*"

Oops. No surprises there. She quickly texted back, *"Sorry, my phone was off all night!"*

Before she could even explain any further, Mark responded with *"I'm here!"* At the show? Already? Did he come alone? Would he be front row? Next.

"Hey—we'll be there tonight. Any chance you can get us tickets to the first show? I think it's sold out." Mark Schmark—Quinn was coming! *Us?* Who cared, even with his doll-baby at his side he would still get to see her perform. With this thrilling rush came an avalanche of insecurity. Was the dress too much? Was she going to be funny? She felt like her jokes alone weren't doing that great unless some asshole gave her a reason to snap back. All of her best sets, her biggest laughs stemmed from someone who was asking for it. She had to get him tickets. Showtime was less than an hour away, but there was still a chance.

"I'll get your tickets . . . sorry, had my phone off!" she thumbed back into her phone. "Jeff!" she yelled to the kitchen. He was talking with a server about wrapping silverware. He shot back a glance as she leaned against the open frame of the door, pushing her left boob up towards her chin. His eyes shot down and up like they were nodding to her and he did his best to keep an angry glare at her.

"What?" he snapped back.

"I'll wait until you're done, sorry," she said, and then retreated into the green room. Within moments he was staring back down at her chest from above. She had him in check now, too. She leaned back and sank into the couch.

"Is there any way you can get my friend Quinn and his girl-friend into the first show?"

"Sure," he said. "There's usually a few who don't pick up their tickets, so I'll put them at the top of the waiting list. Be sure they're here fifteen minutes before show time, though."

"Be here by twenty till and they're yours!" she texted back. She reread the text from Quinn over and over. It filled her heart and made her feel butterflies just seeing his name on her phone. *He* texted *her*. That means he saw what she wrote, thought about her, thought about her some more, and wanted to see her again. He practically wanted her the way she wanted him, right? Should she have worn the thigh-highs? No. Being on stage they would've been too close to making her a complete stripper.

"On our way!" Quinn texted back. An exclamation point! He had taken the time to hit shift and find the correct punctuation to display his excitement to see her. She bet that he didn't give Prentiss an exclamation point when he told her what time he would be picking her up. Calm, stay calm.

The next message was from Justin. *"Thanks for checking on me last night. I'm starting to feel better today. We should probably talk about some things that happened the other day. Jill's pretty upset."* She didn't have a response for this.

"We need to talk" was the final message, and it was from Jill just three hours ago. She had a million guesses to this, some friendly, most not. What could Jill be mad at her for? How could Jill, who seemed to be sharing not just a bedroom but possibly a bed with Quinn of all people, be jealous of her?

Wow, this turning the phone off for a long period of time move was exciting. She thought back to the days of college when she didn't have a computer in her room and had to go to the lab to check her emails. Some days it would be empty, but on others there would be a half-dozen friendly emails waiting for her to respond. Being unavailable had its advantages.

She looked over her set list one last time and then strode her way through the kitchen. The entire line of cooks followed her with their eyes. She could feel their perverted stares. Part of her liked it. *You whore.* She turned back and smiled with her braces shining back and acknowledging that she knew they were looking. Maybe she'd try the wings later on.

She pranced her way past a server and popped into the bar where Rick was swamped with orders. The ticket line was unbelievably long as people who made reservations were eager to get into the showroom. No sign of Quinn. The crowd parted as the tall, now familiar figure of Brad comfortably excused himself through everyone. Rick dropped everything and handed Brad another cup of coffee as if he was just showing up for another day at the office. So relaxed, so smooth, and wow, pretty sexy tonight. His scruff was a perfect length. He was dressed up in a dark gray suit and tie with a white shirt. He didn't seem to notice her, and, without breaking his stride, he disappeared into the kitchen. She stood in a daze for a moment. Something about the way he big-timed himself through the crowd and the trail of people who stood pointing and smiling. She sensed that they were intimidated and yet in awe. So he was kind of famous? Of course this made him ten times hotter. *Play it cool.* She imagined flipping through the channels one night with a group of girls at her place and Brad Brewer's special playing on Comedy Central. "Been there, did that," she would say as they would all beg for details. *Who are these fictional friends who are just hanging out at your apartment? Shut up, brain.* Okay, maybe she would just make Justin jealous. She forced herself to count to twenty and then headed back to the green room to schmooze with Brad.

"What's up?" he asked. Somehow he was the only person to just look her in the face and then back at his phone.

"Hey," she said, unsure of his mood. She pretended to look at her set list again. "Brad, how do you do so much material and not even jot down a set beforehand?"

He laughed a little. "Because it's the same shit I've been doing forever. Some of it's kind of new, but a few of these bits are close to ten years old."

"Really? So none of it's true?" She didn't care if she sounded like a dumb rookie. Any conversation was good conversation. She wanted to make him feel important, even when hundreds of people were already doing that for him.

"C'mon. You really think I went to all of those neighborhoods I was making fun of? They're just stereotypes I'm playing on. I insert different areas and highway names to the jokes depending on whatever city I'm in."

She was well aware of this trick already. Justin had pulled the curtain back on so many comics that she didn't fall for any of their gimmicks. So why was she pulling this act?

"Well, I'd like to pick your brain more but I'd better just worry about my five minutes."

"No problem." She was hoping he would insist that she ask more questions, but he was clearly busy with a game on his phone. She stared at his face. So focused, so much character. It was definitely made for television. He became hotter by the second. She was getting turned on and was supposed to perform in a matter of minutes. She left the green room quietly and got a bottle of water to take on stage with her. It was getting close to show time and there was no sign of Quinn and Prentiss. Maybe they were already seated in the dark showroom. She decided to hide in the doorway and wait until it was her time to get on stage. *Stay aloof.*

33

Bree quickly learned why most comics say the first show Saturday is their favorite. Everything she said got more laughs than she had ever experienced. They were with her from the moment she grabbed the microphone and set the mic stand at the back of the stage. There were whistles and friendly yelps at her outfit, but she expected it. Her only mistake was that she left her bottle of water on the stool, which gave Brad his first two minutes of material.

"That's it woman! If we're going to make this relationship work, you're going to have to clean up after yourself!" The crowd was already his. She shrugged back from the corner of the room, beaming with pride that he was joking about the two of them being in a relationship. She knew every girl in there wondered if he was serious. What would Mark think? What would Quinn think? Brad settled into his act and she went back into the green room.

A message on her phone read *"Thanks for getting us on the waitlist. We're way late, but we got them."* How late? Did Quinn miss her whole set? And the friendly banter with Brad? Famous Brad? Dammit, how was she ever going to come off as someone who could be in Quinn's league if he couldn't see her in her element with her famous friend who was joking—or was he—about a relationship?

She went out to the patio and thought about all that had happened there. Its bar was closed and she thought it would be best to just sit and organize her thoughts for the rest of the night. Within minutes she saw Mark's familiar face spot her. Sweet and cute, but not who she wanted right now. The novelty of his written words was wearing off.

"Hey, that was awesome!" he said, going in for a hug. She tried to reciprocate, but then he kissed her on the cheek and, as if by reflex, she jerked back. "Jeez, sorry," he said.

"Oh, it's okay. I just…" She just nothing. She didn't know what to say. She had shown her hand and she may as well have kicked him in the balls. "Thanks for coming out and supporting me," she said, trying to be friendly and recover from the awkward moment. "Who all did you bring?"

"Oh, it's just me tonight," he said. Not earning any cool points on that response. He should've brought one of his teen lovers; that would've probably turned her on, since her mind and heart were messed up these days. "What time does your second show end? I was just going to hang out at the bar until then." And do what? Not drink because you're only twenty? What was the correct term for cock-block when it was the other way around and the girl was going to miss her chance? Hm, possible topic for a new joke, she thought. She'd try it out some Thursday night and hope Mark didn't realize it was about him.

"Oh, you don't have to do that. How about I just text you when I'm all done? You don't want to hang out here all night."

"Oh," *He was getting the hint.* "Well, I'll stay until I get bored." *No he wasn't.* He was still clueless. What had she done that had given him so much hope in the first place?

"I'd better get back in there," she said and started to turn away.

"One more hug," he said and grabbed her. He held her close as she found herself rolling her eyes to the sky. He was strong and sturdy, just not in a manly way. Mark ended up heading back into the showroom before she even moved. Once again she was alone outside. As the patio grew darker, the lights in the bar seemed brighter. The windows worked as a one-way mirror, allowing her to see inside but no one was able to catch a glimpse of her. Just then, the showroom doors opened, and a tall blonde in heels that made her tower above one of the bouncers headed around the bar to the restroom. Prentiss turned Rick's head to the point of him dropping a bottle.

"Sweet lord almighty!" she read his lips through the window. *At least we're not wearing the same fucking dress.* Prentiss must have been the reason Quinn was late. She had on a green dress that hugged—no, that wasn't the right word because she was too thin—outlined her disgustingly slim body. She was a silhouette of perfection, and Bree now hated her for it. After she disappeared into the restroom, Bree re-entered the bar.

"Rick!" she called. He looked up like he had just been caught stealing from the collective tip jar. "Do me a favor and give that bitch a double-shot of Cuervo. I'll pay for it later." She sure would.

"Roger that," Rick said and had it waiting behind the bar. He could tell what Bree was up to, but didn't know why. She darted back out to the patio and watched from a distance. Rick played dumb as she watched him explain to Prentiss that she had a free shot. Prentiss paused a long time but then picked it up, tapped the bottom of the glass to the bar, and downed it like a champ. Even her *I-just-did-a-nasty-shot* face was beautiful. Bree watched as Rick tried to offer her another. She politely declined and headed back into the showroom, perfect ass and all.

As the first show came to an end, Brad was still killing it. He got a standing ovation as Bree finally returned to the stage, shook his hand and closed out the show, reminding everyone there was one more show tonight so, if they could all finish their drinks in a timely fashion, it would help the club out. She hated sounding bossy, but those were the instructions that Jeff had given her.

She wanted to head out to the bar to accept praise from everyone there, but wasn't sure what to do. Brad would be signing autographs and selling his funny t-shirts, and she knew not to get in his way. Justin had told her before how headliners need to talk with the crowd afterwards. He had learned that lesson the hard way when a headliner nearly ripped his head off for getting in the way of a sale once. She wondered how the tequila was sitting with Prentiss. For all she knew, it could've backfired. Some women got horny from tequila. Some liked to fight. Some passed out. Bree herself often did all three.

She hesitated and then went back to the green room. *Be unavailable,* she told herself. Especially when it came to Mark. He was nice, but . . . She knew he wanted her. The thought turned her on, but then off because she knew he would be too much of a puppy dog to commit to. Then she thought about Quinn some more. Of course there was also Brad-fucking-Brewer who could be an A-list celebrity at this point next year. She took her heels off and lay down on the couch. Her daydreaming almost turned into real dreaming as she closed her eyes and relaxed for a few more minutes.

"Oh the things I could do to you." Eyes open, Brad standing over her. She looked down and realized her dress had ridden halfway up her ass when she turned onto her side.

"Do 'em," she heard herself say over her beating heart.

"See, that's the problem with the late show," Brad said. "We still have to work and then yeah, you're coming with me." Was he serious? 'Cause she was. She had heard Justin talk about "slump-busters" that he would have sex with when he got desperate after a long drought, but Brad was someone she would give herself to under almost any circumstance, especially these days. She sat up.

"Wow, napping on the casting couch, huh?" she laughed.

"You'd fit right in in Los Angeles," he laughed back.

"It would be more exciting than here," she said. "I just got fired from my day job."

"You're working a day job? Well, shit, how are you going to get better at comedy when you're tied down?"

"Maybe I like being tied down." He wanted to play ball, so why not go with it?

"You're good at this," he said and turned away for a moment. "Do you not have dates?"

"I haven't had a date in a long-ass time," Bree confessed.

"No, not *dates* like let's go to Outback, pretend we have a connection, and then fuck on a futon. I mean like dates as in shows. Do you not have a schedule?"

"No, of course not. I just started."

"Perfect. I've got another eighteen weeks of this shit over the next five or six months. Want to open for me?"

"Like tour with you?"

"Uh huh."

"Wait, how much will I make in this deal?"

"Shit, I don't know. Anywhere from three to five hundred a week. You'll have to get yourself to some of the gigs on your own, but for the better venues I can usually get you a flight." She was ready to fuck his brains out right then and there.

"Deal."

34

Right before the second show, Jeff walked up to her with three napkins. Each had handwriting on them. "Ditch your set and just announce these birthdays in the crowd, please."

"Wait, what?" Bree said. "Ditch my set?"

"Yeah, instead of your jokes, mention each of these three birthdays. You can tease the people a little or riff or whatever the hell you do, just make them feel special. One's forty, one's thirty-seven, and one just turned twenty-one. All three are women." Bree was still confused. She had seen Justin do a few birthday announcements but he never had to ditch his set. "Look, these birthday parties bring in big groups and we don't have time for you to go over five minutes because Brad's sets are so long."

"Got it." Part of her was relieved because she was better at just banter with the crowd. Still, she envied the fact that Brad got to show the people he was funny with all of his stories and material while she was just a clown announcing birthdays.

There wasn't a whole lot to joke about with the thirty-seven year old. The forty-year-old was a bit rowdy so she said, "Happy birthday, you don't look a day over fifty!" which got a huge laugh. The twenty-one-year-old was an easier bit. "Let me guess, it's your first legal drink. Well, don't have too many. You don't want to get drunk for the first time and lose your virginity." She got a monstrous laugh and kept going. "Who are you with tonight? A bunch of friends?"

"And my parents!" the girl yelled out. An even bigger laugh roared through the crowd.

"And that's why it's believable that you're still a virgin," Bree said calmly, reaching back to get the mic stand and then placing the mic back to its starting position for Brad. She kept an oblivious look on her face, as if she could make slams like that all that time and it was no big deal to her. She caught Brad laughing in the corner by the door. He nodded and, after a few announcements, she brought him on stage.

Within moments his laughs were even bigger than the ones she got. She headed back out to the bar where Rick was wiping up between rounds.

"Some guy was looking for you right before the show," he said.

"Younger looking? Probably carrying around a notebook?"

"No, not him. This guy was built. Real handsome fellow."

"Quinn?" she asked. Had they come back? "Was he with a skinny, super-model-looking bitch? That girl you gave the big shot to?"

"Didn't get his name. He's in the showroom now. He wasn't with no super-model either. I haven't seen that girl since the shot."

Moments later Quinn appeared from the showroom doors. "Hey, that was great!" He walked right through her modest shrug and gave her a big hug. She felt like a tiny doll with his arms wrapped around her. She pressed her chest against the top of his abs and squeezed back to the point where it became awkwardly meaningful.

"That's the one!" Rick called out before turning back to a new string of drink order tickets.

Bree knew the hug was coming to an end, but quickly inhaled the cologne on his neck. Whatever it was, it blended perfectly with his natural scent. His light blue shirt had the softest fabric and her hands scanned the muscles that flexed in his back. She was tempted to wrap her legs around him and climb him like a tree, but knew it wasn't the time or place.

"You stayed for another show?" He finally released her.

"Well, we missed your whole set the first time because we were running late, so I felt bad." *He doesn't want to mention Prentiss. Is she still in the showroom?* "My lady friend was getting a little too tipsy, which is weird because she only had two or three during the show. I dropped her off at her place, which is nearby, and then headed back to catch your set."

Fireworks ignited in Bree's head. Red, yellow, and orange explosions streamed down from her ears where these perfect words registered and streamed down to her heart, which was beating right through her noticeable cleavage. She took a deep breath and a little voice told her to calm down and make the most of it.

"Well, I owe you one. You didn't have to come back here just to see little ol' me," she said. *Little ol' me? Who says that? I'm not little or old. Show some game, Breezy!* "I'll make it up to you on Wednesday night."

"What's on Wednesday?" he asked. "Another show?" What was Wednesday? She was taking him out. She was taking him anywhere. She had to think of something that didn't sound like a date, but would definitely feel like a date. He wasn't single so she couldn't use the word *dinner*, but she had to make some sort of move out of this. Were four days enough for him to dump Prentiss and finally see that she was perfect for him?

"Wednesday is my whatever night," she said. Here come the improvisational skills once again. "I run some errands, take care of this and that and it usually involves food." Well played.

"I like food," Quinn said matter-of-factly.

"Yep, you get the privilege—no, the honor—of being part of my Whatever Wednesday." How many sit-ups could she fit in between now and then? If she started tonight and did five hundred per night . . .

"Cool, just text me what time," he said. "By the way, how did you get my number?"

Bree's entire body seemed to be pulling her to the ground. He had never given it to her formally but she was texting him like they were best buds. "Oh, you know." She had no answer.

He paused an extra moment, still waiting, but her tongue was frozen.

"Well, I better head out. Gotta take care of the lush!" No! Where was he going? Couldn't he stay and talk at the bar for the rest of Brad's set? Maybe have a few drinks? Maybe need a ride home? Maybe have her ride him home?

"Oh, yeah. The ol' ball and chain," Bree tried to joke back. There was no use pretending Prentiss didn't exist. Quinn didn't laugh. Oops.

He pulled his keys out of his pocket and swung them into his palm. Another hug would've felt like sex. Nope. "I guess I'll see you Wednesday," he said, sounding deflated. He turned and walked away as Bree opened her arms behind him. Had she offended him? Did she already screw up Wednesday days ahead of time and, by the way, what the hell was she going to do to "make it up to him" anyway?

She had over another hour to dwell on it while Brad continued to crush another audience. To get her mind off of it she crept back into the showroom and observed. Within a few minutes she was completely in awe of the way Brad would set up a joke and then deliver a plethora of punch-lines that all hit their target. Every single set of eyes were focused on him in anticipation of what was coming next. After every topic he would get an applause break, which gave him a chance to sip from his beer and wipe the sweat from his forehead with a small towel he placed on the stool.

Topic after topic: religion, sex, past relationships, everyday struggles, he continued to hypnotize the entire audience.

How was Brad not famous? Maybe he already was and she was just out of the loop. She retreated to the green room and pulled out her phone to run a quick Google search on him. Wow. Fighting her slow connection from being back in the green room, she learned of multiple major-network appearances, guest starring roles on shows she had heard of, and even a small role in a movie from a few years ago. His webpage alone had over a hundred thousand hits. There were pictures of Brad with famous actors, athletes, and on various studio sets. This guy was the real deal. No wonder Justin was so disappointed that he couldn't work. She was glad she didn't know all this ahead of time; she would've been an even bigger spaz.

The show ended with yet another standing ovation for Brad as Bree proudly closed the show out. Fans stayed and chatted with Brad for the good part of an hour. Many of them bought t-shirts from him at twenty bucks a pop. Others stayed and chatted or had him sign an autograph. One of the more attractive women even pulled her shirt down and had him put his signature on her left breast. She yelled with excitement as her friends all took pictures on their phones. At last the crowd cleared out as Bree waited patiently at the bar. Even with her dress she was invisible in a room that also contained Brad Brewer.

"Looks like we're done," he said, looking over.

"Yep," Bree said, hoping to continue their talk about her new career and only source of income.

"Let's take care of business," Jeff said with a towel in his hand behind the bar. Brad followed him back to the office. Bree was coming down from all of the excitement and her body was suddenly fatigued. She was drained. The emotions from the shows, Quinn, and now Brad had rendered too many heartbeats for one night, but she couldn't go home yet. She watched the clock past midnight as Rick killed all but a few of the bar lights.

"Rick, how long does it usually take to get paid?" she asked.

"Oh, the pay isn't the tough part. It's the chatting afterwards. Jeff always chats up the headliners. Did you not take care of business while he was on stage?"

"Take care of business?"

"Get paid."

"Oh. No. I didn't even think about it."

"Typical rookie mistake. Yep, you're not doin' it for the money yet, just the thrills, right? Well, now you gotta wait your turn. Shouldn't be but another twenty'r thirty minutes."

Thirty-eight exactly. Her dress was uncomfortable, her shoes were uncomfortable, her back hurt from sitting in the barstool for so long. Finally Brad came out, still laughing about whatever he and Jeff were talking about for so long.

"Still here?" he said. *Uh, yeah! Remember that whole giving me a career thing we agreed on?*

"Shouldn't we talk about our business deal?" she said, trying not to sound mad.

"Among other things." Well, yeah, that too.

"Bree, get your ass back here. I'm not staying here all night," Jeff said. Asshole! It was his fault they were still there in the first place. The servers had already cleaned up, balanced their tabs, and smoked their last cigarettes on the patio. Even Rick was headed out the door.

"Wait for me," she said to Brad and then hurried back to the office. That's right. She, the rookie comic, was telling the great Brad Brewer to wait on her.

Jeff was already babbling something in a negative tone as they entered the office. It had the tone of an excuse. "Look, I'm not gonna bullshit you. Justin makes fifty a show, sometimes more when he has to compensate for the other comics. You did, what, five minutes per show? I can give you a hundred bucks for your trouble."

"A hundred?" She had spent that in clothing already.

"Yeah, you got a problem with that? 'Cause I can calculate with minimum wage exactly how much you should make for a measly twenty minutes of work and use that." He was so blunt staring her right in the eyes that wanted to tear up. She was too tired to argue.

"A hundred is great," she said, defeated. He handed her five twenties. She started to put them in her purse.

"Count 'em! Always count your money when a manager gives it to you. If there's only eighty in there and you don't notice until you get home, you're shit out of luck."

"Yessir," she said, feeling like a child. She counted the money and almost ran out of the office before emotion could give Jeff any satisfaction. She saw the door at the exit closed and Brad was gone. She hurried out to the parking lot where only a few cars remained. He was parked way in the back, so she did her best to catch up with him in her heels.

"Brad!"

"Hey, was wondering if he was going to talk your ear off too."

"More like bite my head off and fuck me over a hundred dollars."

"Yeah, that's showbiz. Sure you want to be a part of it?"

"Yeah, can we talk about working together?"

"Sure, follow me to the hotel."

"Um. Okay."

35

Though Brad seemed to be drinking all night, his driving certainly didn't suggest it. She followed his rented BMW's flawless path back to the hotel. *Oh my god, the front desk is going to think I'm a hooker.* She adjusted her dress one last time and followed him into the automatic doors without talking.

Her conscience was pummeling her with decisions, but after the night she had she was tired of thinking. The little devil on her shoulder casually kicked back and told her how to feel as Brad—still quiet—hit the number five button in the elevator. *Right now Quinn is fucking Prentiss so hard it would've woken you up in your lonely bed. Justin had his chance and seems to be with Jill. You don't want to lose her as a friend, do you? For Justin? I didn't think so. Mark? He's probably breastfeeding from his mother's bosom and pondering whether tomorrow's sonnet should be Petrarchan or Shakespearean. When was the last time you got any? When was the last time you got any from a celebrity? Do you have any idea how famous this guy is? How about how famous he's going to be very soon? You've made worse decisions! It's showbiz and you need a job! Play a little hard to get and then do whatever you want. It's in a hotel so it doesn't count. He's not going to fall in love with you and ruin everything. He's offering you a job that could lead to possible fame of your own. Any idea of what kind of crowd he hangs with? Do you want to be part of that crowd, or would you miss lying on a rooftop every Friday night for the rest of your life? Then you can grow up and be a single old lady like your mother! No? Well, then do your thing.*

"Okay, this shouldn't take long," Brad said, leading her down the hall. He pulled out his keycard and unlocked room five fifty-five. What wouldn't take long? The foreplay?

He dropped his bag on the ground and she followed him in, unsure where to sit. There were no lights on, just the television. The room was chilled from the loud air-conditioner blowing under the window. On the desk there was a notebook-sized calendar with various notes jotted down towards the end of each week. He sat at the desk as she stood next to him.

"Okay, well, next week I'm in Kansas City. Then it's west to Denver." He flipped the page into the next month. "Things are mostly out west through August and then back over to the east and south for September. I'm pretty sure the clubs already have openers booked through those weeks, but I'll have my manager call and clear out everything after August for you."

"I'm moving at the end of August," she said.

"Well, don't waste too much money on rent if you're going to be touring with me. Your folks still around?"

"My mom lives on the south side," she said.

"Good. Dump all your shit there and learn to live out of a suitcase."

"Really?"

"Really," he said standing up. "Want to have sex now?"

This guy didn't mess around. Here's your career, now put out.

"Is that a good idea?" It was. She just didn't want to seem too easy.

"I know what you're thinking. This will mess with our professional relationship that, by the way, we haven't established yet. Here's the catch. This is a one-time thing. Instead of having all this sexual tension from wondering what if for weeks at a time, let's just get it out of the way and move on. Oh, first, write your number down so I can get you the tour info later on next week."

He was so casual. She didn't even have to answer him. He had correctly assumed the yes and then added a minor second instruction. She couldn't make eye contact. The television was airing the highlights of another Cubs loss. The bullpen had blown another save opportunity.

"Man, they suck," Brad said, taking his shirt off. He was no Quinn, but he was still lean and muscular enough for her raging hormones.

Bree jotted down her cell number in his calendar and then clicked off the television. The room went dark and she felt him breathing on the back of her neck. The air-conditioner kicked off a moment later. Complete silence except for his breath and her heart. He had to hear it. Moments later she was naked and on her back. *Finally*. Five minutes went by. Once! More time passed as she felt months of frustration grinding out of her. Twice! Holy shit, he wasn't done yet. She had never been with a man over twenty-five, let alone late thirties. He just kept going. She felt her sweat touch his and tried to catch her breath. He was diligent, focused and steady. A scream escaped her over what must have been a half hour later as she felt herself orgasm a third time.

For the record, she had established the employment *before* the sex. She was okay with that.

There was no shame in her walk as she left the room some time later. She looked to the east and saw just a touch of blue sky starting to creep into the horizon. A few birds were already chirping and she recalled these walks in college. Sometimes it was just a late party, but often it was truly a degrading experience because of the other people who were sharing it. She recalled once seeing three girls walking out of a dorm all at once. Had they all been with the same guy or did they date a bunch of roommates? She was classier somehow.

If anything, the world seemed clearer and she was able to focus on something besides sex, although she relived that— moment was definitely not the right word—experience? Brad Brewer. People would know who that was. Damn, why didn't she have any female friends to brag about this to? The work. Had she really just committed the last half of the year to touring? She wasn't a comic. She was an apartment manager who needed to spend a Saturday morning updating her resumé. What about health insurance? What about a new apartment? What about Quinn? She had arranged a date with Quinn—it would count as a date in her mind at least— and had no idea what to do for it. What had she told him, Wacky Wednesday? Whatever Wednesday? Yeah, that was it.

She smiled the entire drive home. She let out little laughs to herself as she recapped the night. *Score.* That's how Justin would look at it if she had the nerve to tell him.

Her smile continued as she climbed the stairs to her floor, turned the key, and collapsed on her bed after taking off her dress a second time in only a few hours.

36

Bree was able to resist texting Quinn about Wednesday until exactly five minutes after noon on Monday. She had spent Sunday in a vigorous workout of sit-ups on her living room floor. She tried again on Monday but was so sore she could barely sit up in bed. She had to wait exactly four minutes before he replied that five thirty would indeed work. Normally she would never venture anywhere during rush hour traffic, but being stuck in her car with Quinn would only lead to a longer night. Every moment with him was a blessing, so the more traffic the better. Maybe they could even survive a mini-crisis together? She imagined the next time Prentiss was around and how she and Quinn would have all of these new inside jokes that Prentiss would only wonder about. Prentiss would fume and steam that Quinn could only laugh at what Bree would say while ignoring his girlfriend. Prentiss would throw her arms in the air and stomp away, mad, while Quinn wouldn't even notice. Yep, traffic was going to be thick.

Her credit card bill talked her out of making another purchase. Be casual, relax. Having all of this time off was not good for her. She spent the afternoon trying on her outfits and timing how long she would need to get ready. She measured how far down each shirt came to her waist and her cleavage. Did she want to show any navel? Too trashy for a Wednesday. She needed a shirt that would just hang off of her chest to give the illusion that it was bigger and her waist was smaller. Yes, that's why she couldn't tuck anything in. She knew a tight shirt wouldn't work in Wednesday's heat. Worrying about pit stains would be too much. She dug and dug through her closet until she finally found something with potential. It was a dark gray top with small straps. The fabric was thin but not transparent. She put it on sans bra to see how it fit. Perfect. Why did nipples have to ruin everything? A bra would be necessary, but she would have to find the "special no top strappy one" as her old roommate used to call it. Deeper into her closet she rummaged until finally locating it. Pants? Black capri pants would work. With everything on she felt good enough. Not great, but good enough. A simple heel would help her with eye contact once they were walking.

She took out her comedy notebook and flipped to some blank pages in the middle. She wrote "goals" at the top and started a list. *Sex. Getting to know each other. More sex. Dump Prentiss. Make him want me. And get him to say, "Let's do this again" and really mean it.*

Her bedroom floor was a wreck of clothes she had tried on and sorted through. Her kitchen, bathroom, and living room had all somehow transformed into not just messy, but dirty piles of this and that. She setup a playlist which she named "Clean it bitch" and got to work. The symbolism was overwhelming. Hours were spent scrubbing, changing, throwing out, and eliminating everything that was holding her down. As she finished the bathroom she found herself reflecting in the newly clean mirror. The spots were gone from its surface and she paused to have a look at her teeth. Were they already moving? They were! She smiled a fake smile and held it until her cheeks hurt. She felt more attractive. The braces were becoming part of her new identity. Her teeth and new career were lining up. She was going to learn to feel sexy somehow, and she knew the perfect person to practice on.

"You still alive?" she texted Justin after finishing the final touches in the living room. She put on a tank top and one of her best bras. Yeah, she was going fuck with his head before he could even get mad at her.

"Yep," he sent back after a few minutes. Knowing Justin, he probably waited those few minutes just to make a point. She knew he got the text right away but didn't want to seem like a puppy dog fetching a stick, so he waited. Three minutes, nice try.

"Well, get up here, I cleaned for once." He didn't text back. She waited. Now she was the puppy. Where was he? Why was he ignoring her? She went back to the bathroom mirror and messed with her hair. A knock on the door let her know she was still in control.

Justin looked different. It had only been a few days but he looked, well, pretty rough. He hadn't shaved his face. The half beard wasn't bad around the corners of his mouth and his cheeks, but the part that crept down his neck was a definite turnoff. She opened with a crack only a Chicago girl could make: "Nice neck beard."

"Hello to you too, smartass," he said, still not smiling. Was he honestly mad? What was wrong? Did he already know about the tour with Brad? Jeff probably told him the night it happened. She was thankful that wouldn't be the only club she would be working from now on. Certainly the other club managers had to be more respectful.

Justin sat down on the couch like he was about to hear how many months he had to live from a doctor. "How was your weekend with Brad?"

"It went really well."

"Good." He didn't mean it. She could tell he was already jealous. Did he know about the "after-party" as well? Justin had a pretty good read on her most of the time.

"He gave me some weeks with him this fall." Justin's lips disappeared in his expression. He was trying to hold it in.

"And what did you give him in return?" That bastard! He was right, but that bastard! She may as well fess up.

"For your information," she smiled, hoping it would lighten the mood, "I agreed to the work first."

"Uh huh," Justin said, looking down to his folded hands. "Well, then I guess I'll be pretty lonely this fall."

"You have Jill, stupid," she reminded him.

"Wow, you're really out of the loop I guess. Maybe all that star fucking has made you forget about your friends."

She stood up as Justin sank back into the couch. He knew he had gone too far. "What the fuck did I do to you? I covered you while you were sick and you come here to call me a whore? What the fuck, Justin?"

He stayed calm. "Jill and I aren't a thing anymore. I told her."

"Told her what?"

"That I'm in love with you," he said.

"*In love* with me? You're ridiculous. We almost have sex once and you're suddenly *in love* with me? That's not fair. You're wrong."

"Great, so you're mad at me for it. I dump a really nice girl who I have a decent connection with and put my whole heart on the table—"

"Your whole heart on the table? You had years and years to have feelings for me and you never did. Now because I've got a chance with a guy you know that I would be happy with, you suddenly feel attracted to me? I don't buy it. You'll be over me and messing around with whoever as soon as I reciprocate whatever supposed feelings you have. Then I'm left with nothing."

"Fine. I guess you're some road comic now with no time for sensitivity or love. It's not like I was there helping you with Quinn all summer. It's not like I was your best—no, only— friend for who knows how long. How dare I want you? Sorry I'm not Quinn, or Mark, or Brad. This whole summer has been one big drunken dating game for you. And who was the only one there to help? Me! Who led you to this new career of yours? Who knows you better than any of those guys? Me! Who were you ready to have sex with, sober and before noon? Fuckin' me! So don't act all fucking shocked when I feel something towards you. I crushed Jill when I told her. In fact, she'll probably write a fucking platinum album that I'll get to hear on the radio for the rest of my life, dedicated to making sure I never forget that I chose you over her. Good luck on your tour!" He didn't slam the door behind him. He just left it open. She waited for him to get to the end of the hall before closing it.

Oops.

Justin was wrong. He didn't love her. How could he? He had all that time to love her. He only wanted her because there were other guys involved. She felt good about herself for Justin being attracted to her. Then she felt bad for feeling good about herself.

Quinn would make it better. Wednesday was coming.

37

It started at the cologne counter—and it never really let up.

"Miss, may I interest you in something that will make your man irresistible?" A young, or was she older, blonde with layers of perfectly applied makeup was holding a bottle near Quinn's wrist before Bree could even answer.

"Spray me," laughed Quinn. The woman took her wrist and rubbed it into Quinn's muscular forearm. There had never been such an aggressive sample sprayer. The woman babbled about the new sport edition she had just doused him with and was going on and on as part of Bree marveled at how it felt for someone to call Quinn "hers," while the rest of her grew furious with her hands-on approach. Bree wished she could sprout claws and tear this bitch off of his arm.

"Let me smell and see if that blends with your natural pheromones." Bree was frozen in horror as the woman pulled his entire arm towards her nose. She closed her eyes and inhaled, even letting her nose make contact with the hairless underside of his forearm. She guided his elbow on her left breast, paused and said, "Yeah . . . that works." She opened her eyes to a glare of hatred. Finally, Quinn's arm was released as he put his hand into his pocket, unsure what to do next.

She adjusted her name tag, which had been turned sideways by the contact of Quinn's arm, and politely stared at Bree as if she had done nothing wrong but try and make a sale.

"Are we done here?" Bree finally said, still flabbergasted.

"Oh, he's not your boyfriend. I can tell. Otherwise you'd be insisting on getting this eight ounce bottle for him, huh darling?" *You fucking whore.*

"Yeah, we're done here," Bree said. She knew it was either leave or shove that eight ounce bottle up that woman's ass. Getting arrested wasn't on the agenda for Whatever Wednesday and the night had just begun.

"Sales tactics, huh," Quinn grunted as they walked away.

"Is that what that was? A sales tactic? She just nasal-fucked you in public," Bree said, trying to keep her cool.

"Whoa. It's a cougar thing. You know how they are these days," Quinn said, trying to dismiss the whole incident. The woman was way too young to even be considered a cougar, but Bree found his defining her as one as somewhat of a consolation. She took a few deep breathes and thought about how they would look back at this moment and laugh about it someday. She could even write a bit about it for the next open mic. *Nasal-fuck, good stuff.*

"Well, what all are you shopping for tonight?" *Please say underwear, please say underwear.*

"Underwear," he said, straight-faced.

310

Bree gulped, "O-kay." Her voice cracked like a teenage boy's.

"I'm kidding, I'm kidding. You think you're the only comedian here?" She gave him a little punch in the side and laughed. Her knuckles registered nothing but very firm muscle. And wow, he smelled amazing from whatever that shit was.

"I need a new belt, actually." Mind-to-gutter. She thought about how she would love to get to know this belt over the following months. She would undo in it her place, she would undo it in his place, she would undo it in the car, she would undo it late at night in the green room while whatever headliner was up for the late show, she would undo it outside underneath a tree as soon as Stalker Ted passed by safely, she would undo it on her rooftop, she would undo it in a downtown hotel over Valentine's Day, she would undo it on a cruise around the Mediterranean. Yes, she would grow quite familiar with this belt.

"Belts are important," she agreed, completely turned on now. They walked by a Victoria's Secret. Quinn's eyes stayed focused ahead in a daze. Didn't he want to jokingly take her in there? Didn't he want to let her play dress-up? They could play, play, play, joke, joke joke, oops, it just got serious! Nope, he focused ahead.

"There's a men's store at the end of this hallway I get a lot of my clothes at." Bree knew it well. She once followed a guy in there during a busy holiday shopping weekend last year. She pretended she was shopping for a fictional brother and even asked the guy's advice on what he thought between two sweaters. He told her to get them both so she did, just so she could wait in the long line and chat him up for fifteen minutes. The conversation went so well she remembered it feeling like a script until he mentioned his wife and kids were probably waiting for him at the fountain. He wasn't even wearing a ring. Twenty minutes later she was in that same line, which had grown to nearly a twenty-minute wait, to return those same two sweaters. Those pathetic lonely days were in the past.

"What are you in the market for?" *A husband.* What the hell was she going to buy? She was already buried in credit card debt and there was still no word confirming all of that work with Brad.

"Panties," she said. Quinn's head tilted towards her and he almost tripped. "Ha—got you! We're even now," she laughed.

"You're the pro, not me," he admitted. Speaking of, how was she going to let this relationship blossom if she was on the road with Brad so often? Or worse yet, living on the South Side with her mother? Maybe Jill would move out. Maybe Justin would take her in for Bree's sake and leave Quinn's one-bedroom for Bree to handle.

"Oops, just a second." Quinn pulled his phone out and answered. "Yeah . . . At the mall, you need anything? Nope . . . Yep . . . I don't know, just a couple hours. Tomorrow sounds good. Okay, bye . . . okay . . . Got it . . . Okay, bye."

Bree's mind dissected that snippet immediately. No doubt it was Prentiss. First positive: he didn't say "I love you" at the end. If fact, he seemed annoyed and eager to get off of the phone. Second plus: he didn't mention he was out with Bree. That made it seem secretive, wrong, and dare she say, *dirty*? She would be fine with him cheating on Prentiss for a while at the start, but eventually he'd have to let her go. She didn't know how she felt about him saying "just a couple hours." She replayed it in her mind and decided it was a negative. It came off like: "I'll be in your arms soon, just a couple more hours until we can be together again. I'm just doing my Dreamy Community Service that I owe the universe for being so gorgeous."

"Hungry?" Yes, but she didn't want to eat in front of him again. Last time she attempted that she ended up choking on cheese and nearly killing herself. Then again, the ending wasn't bad.

"Kinda, but not for a whole meal," she lied. She had barely eaten all day.

"Giant cookie? We can split it." Aw, they were going to share something! They waited in line in the food court as random people walked by. Bree watched as every female within range stared at Quinn. He was a magnet for their eyes. Oblivious, he stood waiting calmly . . . or perhaps aware and just used to the attention.

"Fuck, this dude is hot!" a short teenage girl dressed like a hooker said as she walked by. She couldn't have been but fourteen and reeked of daddy issues just in the way she overdid her eyeliner. Her dyed blonde hair showed nearly two weeks of black roots and her pants barely fit around her slightly exposed stomach. Bree couldn't bite her tongue any longer.

"Hot Topic is back that way, little girl."

Quinn laughed and put his arm around Bree for a moment. "Relax, I'm taken." He was, but not by Bree. The girl stomped off and waited a safe distance until she extended her middle finger.

They finally sat down with their giant cookie at a table among a chaos of more teens and older people. *Do you see me, everyone? Do you see us?* Bree wanted to shout. *I'm with him. Not you, me!* It only got worse. Moments later the girl who had sold them the cookie approached their table. Quinn was tearing a chunk off and about to put it in his mouth when *Michelle*—another name tag—interrupted. "Hey, um, here's a lemonade on the house. Let me know if there's anything else I can get you. I mean *anything*."

"Are you fucking serious?" Bree said with a chocolate chip stuck on the tip of her finger.

"Excuse me, ma'am. I was just trying to be nice. Jealous much?"

Quinn blushed. At least he was finally uncomfortable too. He finally said something, "Could you be nice and get my friend one too, please?"

"Your *friend*? Sure." She smiled at the word for its lack of prefix. This time Bree couldn't hide her emotion.

"Is this normal, Quinn?"

"Is what normal?"

She tipped her head to the side as if to say, "Cut the bullshit."

"Sometimes, I don't know. I'm just having a good day. I promise you, this isn't normal and I doubt that anything else will—" He couldn't even finish the sentence!

A small girl, maybe eight years old, walked up and put both of her hands on the edge of their table. "Will you marry me?" she asked in an adorable voice that sounded like a voiceover for a Christmas cartoon. Bree could do nothing but laugh.

"Like I said, it's been a good day. Well, hello, cutie, what's your name?" he asked. At least this one was innocent.

"Can I tell him my name, mommy?" She turned around and yelled to a woman two tables away. The woman quickly got up and joined her daughter at the side of their table. She was maybe thirty and tan, with brown straight hair that shone as bright as her daughter's. No part of her body resembled that of a mother who was no longer on the prowl. She pulled her tight t-shirt down to her waist and stuck her not-so-humble chest out. Quinn looked up and met her lustful eyes. She took that as her cue to sit down right next to him.

"Ma'am, can you excuse us? My girlfriend and I are in the middle of something important. And as flattering as your daughter's marriage proposal is, I'm taken. Sorry, honey," he said, looking down to the girl sympathetically before giving the woman another serious look to call out her foul play. Bree's heart exploded with joy. Finally! She didn't even have to imagine anymore, at that moment she was indeed his girlfriend. Reality aside, he chose her exclusive company to someone else's. Even if that someone else used her daughter as a secret weapon, he wasn't falling for it.

It continued through the evening. Quinn finally found a belt and the cashier, a redhead just in her twenties, gave him half off of the purchase for no reason. She didn't even say anything about it. She locked eyes with Quinn as long as she could, told him he would look nice in the belt, and then produced a fifty percent off coupon from the register. "Come see me for anything else you need," she said.

"Okay, now you're getting discounts?"

"I buy a lot from that girl. She's always hooking me up with good deals."

"Deals? That was just a straight discount. Remind me to have you do my shopping." She tried to laugh, realizing that her jealousy was apparent.

"It doesn't always work," he said.

"Oh, so she only gives you discounts sometimes?"

"Yeah, when I'm just getting one or two little things."

"She just saved you fifteen bucks on a belt," Bree said. "When doesn't it work?"

"Oh, you know," he said, and then tried to change the subject.

"I don't know," she said. Then she did. She knew exactly when he didn't get his discount. She knew exactly when the whole mall wasn't trying to steal him away.

"It's different when you're out with Prentiss, isn't it?"

"No," he lied. She knew why it was different. Tall skinny blonde with model body, intimidating. Obviously his woman. Shorter, braces girl who wasn't exactly turning any heads was just his friend. With Prentiss around, Quinn was an illusion meant to be stared at from afar. He was something a woman could look at, but not touch. He was an ad in a magazine beside his perfect mate. Next to Bree, he was eligible. He was a nice guy too. He was a realistic shot. He was an obtainable dream.

"I have fun with you," he said. The way he said it made it sound like they had been on so many adventures together. Like they were a team who could conquer anything in their way. He made it sound like they could go home and flip through pages and pages of photos together.

"I like you too," she said. Oops. That wasn't exactly what he had said, but who cared? He knew how she felt about him. She let that secret go a long time ago. "I guess I just have to find a way to fend all these women off of you."

"This usually does the trick," he said, and took her hand in his. She let out an almost orgasmic sigh. No words were coming to her mouth. She could feel her hand pulsing in his. It was warm, but not sweaty. Large, but not overwhelming. How did a man who lifted so many weights have such soft hands? She wanted to ask. She wanted to joke. She wanted to say or do anything to mask the pure bliss she was experiencing. She wanted to do lap after lap around the mall like those old people in the overly bright white shoes on Saturday mornings. She wanted to take a picture of the two of them and finally open a Facebook account. She wanted to tell Justin and Jill to get over whatever was keeping Jill from moving in with Justin. She wanted to rub it in Prentiss's face.

"Can we make one more stop before we head out?" Still no words. She had to nod yes. She stayed by his side, trying to keep the rest of her body focused. Any wrong move would cause him to let go of her hand. The heat in her hand became more intense. It felt like she had a glove on. Sweat was inevitable. She thought of icebergs and penguins and the cold Chicago wind that would freeze her every January on her way up to her lonely apartment. This time Quinn was there waiting for her. For some reason her apartment had a fire going and a shirtless Quinn adding wood to it as she came through the door. *Not helping, not helping!*

"Don't make fun of me, but I still buy CDs." Making fun of him would require speaking, and she still wasn't able to do that while holding hands. As they entered the store, she was relieved to see only men working. Alas, he dropped her hand and started digging through the CDs. Bree found her voice returning but had nothing interesting to say. She let him wander away up and down the aisles, knowing he would come back. She eyed another pair of teenage girls who nudged each other as Quinn got near them. They kept quiet and Bree's pulse refrained from jumping too high. *He's all mine. Girls, cougars, whoever. They can stare all they want, but he's leaving with me.*

Bree decided to pretend she was CD shopping too. She hated to take her eyes off of Quinn even for a moment, but she knew she needed to train herself to act normal around him. Even after all of this time her mind and body were in a different mode while he was around.

And then came the curveball. Staring back at her on a display case of new releases was Brad Brewer's latest release. A shelf of his albums, each with a perfect photograph of his face looking back at her. He was leaning on a bar with a brown bottle in one hand and gazing at her from the cover of every copy. There were dozens in this store alone —how many copies had been made? Was he already famous? People were paying money to hear his comedy anytime they wanted. Somewhere there was a factory producing copy after copy of his act, his album, his face on the cover. His gorgeous face on the cover. Brad was in demand and she had already seen him naked! Bree realized that, for the first time in days, Quinn was not her top priority. She looked around frantically like a mother whose child had wandered off. He was already at the register with yet another flirt. This time it was a man.

"Mm! Did you find everything okay?" he said. "You are a lucky lady. This guy is a knockout," he whispered to Bree as if Quinn couldn't hear him.

"Oh, I know," Bree said, clutching his hand again as soon as he put his wallet back into his pocket. Bree left the store laughing. "Wow, even the dudes are after you tonight!" She looked back one last time at the display case as if she was leaving Brad behind.

The car ride home was rather quiet. Bree was trying to think of the next topic of conversation while Quinn fumbled around trying to get his CD open.

"How's the job hunt?" He asked, finally giving up on the wrapper.

"Well, I'm kinda making a major change here soon," she said as if confessing something dirty. "Brad Brewer wants me to tour with him."

"Wow, that's great. You're going to be famous! That guy is hilarious. He's really taking off, so ride him to the top, I say." He had no idea. Was he patronizing or was he legitimately happy for her? Did he care that she would be gone a lot?

"Yep, we hit the road at the end of the month and go pretty strong through the fall. Most weeks I only have shows three or four nights though, so it's not like I'm going to be a stranger."

"Oh good. I would miss you." He would? Bree set her hand in between them, knowing he would grab it. He didn't. What if she became a big deal like Brad? Would he like her then? Could being away help?

More silence followed. *Time for the end game.* She had less than five minutes before they were home.

"So what's up with Jill and Justin?" Quinn asked.

"I thought you would know."

"Nope," he gave a half laugh. "She said he hurt her feelings and that's all I got out of her. She was crying a little bit the other night." *I'll bet she was. Probably nuzzled right into his bare chest, soaking up his sympathy through each muscular ripple on his torso.* "I told her whatever Justin's problem was, it'll pass. I think he's into someone else."

Shit.

"Could be," Bree said, desperately thinking of a way to change the subject and create a mood where it would be appropriate to grab his hand and eventually rip his clothes off.

"I mean, how's a guy not love Jill? Who the hell could be more artistic, talented, intelligent, and just, you know, all around cooler than her?" *Um, hello!*

"Well, Justin's not known for his decision-making skills."

Quinn was in deep thought. He looked back down to his CD and started digging at the wrapper again. "Maybe I should talk to him about it."

A board of executives immediately filed into Bree's head. Should she agree or disagree? To disagree would mean she actually disagreed with his opinion on something, and maybe he would think they just thought differently and would never work out. To agree would show that she had no thoughts of her own. If Quinn sat down with Justin, Justin might get upset and just spill the beans about Bree's plotting and scheming the entire summer. He'd been so distant lately, and after her "stealing" Justin's dream job, he might say anything to get back at her. At the same time Bree was pretty sure that Justin could be honest and tell Quinn that he wasn't into Jill because he had feelings for Bree. Was Quinn the kind of guy who would back off completely? Or would it help him see what a catch Bree was by raising her stock? How could she make this decision in the next few moments? The board members were all screaming at each other in her head. Finally, one of them stood up and said, "I'll have to think about that. We'll talk about it tomorrow." Boom! Excuse for contact and a full follow up while buying some time to consider the consequences. They would talk tomorrow and then the next day. The day after that would make it a habit. Maybe by then she could remain somewhat calm in his presence and he would grow his appreciation for hers.

"Yeah, I suppose it's none of my business. I just think they'd make a great couple."

"Aw. And you could finally have your place to yourself, right?"

"No, that's not it at all," he said. He didn't see the humor in her semi-joke. "I mean, I just want her to finally be happy."

Less than two minutes until the car ride was over. The entire summer's work and her happiness would all depend on her next set of actions. *Don't screw this up!* She thought about her married friends from college and how they were probably all sick of each other by now. The ten year class reunion would be right around the time she and Quinn would be officially starting their life together. The echoes of that awful day in the cafeteria rushed through her mind. The best friend from high school she never talked to again would be stunned to see her with Quinn at her side. Those lonely nights on the roof, the embarrassment of getting fired, Justin messing with her head—it was all going to disappear.

"You're such a good guy, Quinn," she heard herself say as she put her hand on his. His didn't move to squeeze hers back right away. If his hand wasn't so warm she would have thought he was frozen. He knew what she was doing, but she had no idea how he felt about it. Was he sick of being hit on? Could someone get tired of being so damn desirable? Jill had warned her that every woman Quinn encountered seemed magnetized to him. She just couldn't help herself. No one could. As she squeezed a little harder towards his thumb she could feel his pulse getting faster. This was as good a moment as she was ever going to get. She turned into their lot and decided she would park halfway between their buildings so that either way one would have to walk the other home. The lot was crowded but her headlights finally found an open spot and was about to turn in. Finally, he put his hand around hers and rubbed the top of it with his thumb. Each stroke of it sent joy through her entire body. She was his, he was hers! As she started to turn in with her left hand a tall, blonde figure appeared wearing a short skirt and heels. Prentiss looked like she had just climbed down from a billboard. Instinctively, Quinn's hand cowered away from Bree's and he was out of the car before she even had it in park.

38

"So why didn't you just run her over?" Justin asked, cracking another beer.

"Trust me, the thought was there," Bree laughed. Justin had seen the whole thing and texted Bree about it before she even got to her door. She went straight to his apartment, eager to mend the fence with her misfortune.

"So what was Prentiss's tone when he got out of your car?"

"Oh, she didn't say anything. She didn't have to. Her face was very clear that she was not happy. They're probably fighting right now at his place."

"Nope, he actually left with her," Justin said. "You were walking back and didn't see what happened."

"What else happened?"

"She slammed her door and drove off with him."

"Did he slam his door?"

"I don't think so." Justin took a sip but didn't offer Bree anything.

She wasn't sure whether to sit down or just go back to her place and call it a win for the night. A silence fell in the room. Why couldn't he have just turned his TV on or something? "Have you talked to Jill again? You know, fixed things." Nope, wrong words. That wasn't the right thing to say at all. Anything but that.

"Really? Have I talked to Jill again?"

"Sorry, but we need to talk about some stuff and we're both sober, so . . ."

"Like I said, I told her I wasn't interested in seeing her anymore."

"Why'd you do that? You know you really have feelings for her instead of me. You two would be so much better than us." Bree wasn't sure if that was true since there technically never was an us, but she continued to plead with Justin as if it was her heart on the line. Maybe it wasn't about her after all.

"I guess I'm just a dumb guy," he said. "I've always wanted to be in the spotlight so I find it attractive on girls. First Jill," he sipped again, "then you."

"Me?" Bree played dumb. "I still think this is all just curiosity about that dumb thing that happened that one morning."

"Now see, if it was the other way around and I called it 'that dumb thing,' you'd kill me," he said, looking at his can. He lifted it to his mouth and finished it off.

"I know, but it's just—" but she knew he was right. "It's just that our timing has always been wrong. I have some options right now between my career and love interests."

"Options?" Justin said.

"Yes, options. Believe it or not, I have a life now."

"Options? You think you have options? Let me guess, Brad Brewer is number one. Brad Brewer, who is getting a lot of heat in the comedy world right now—"

"Heat?"

"Yes, heat. God Bree, you don't even know the jargon of your own new profession. That means he's taking off and doing well. His face will be popping up on TV every five seconds soon."

"I know what heat is!" Bree lied. Point for Brad. She thought about the sex. The sex that seemed to make up for the void before it. Hell, this sex made up for the bad sex before the dry spell of no sex. She would have to give him a chance to go for four.

"So yeah, he's famous and, no offense, but you're not the only woman who's throwing herself at him these days."

Ouch! "Well, he already threw himself at me and it felt *pretty fucking good*!" she gave Justin her meanest glare but he didn't stop there.

"And let me guess, Quinn is going to dump the hottest chick I've ever seen to date you while you're out fucking Brad on the road for three months. Yeah, that sounds like a great plan, Bree! All of these men are suddenly into you just out of the blue all because you have two minutes of material which gets sympathy laughter! Guess what, *my crush is over*!"

She smirked. Closed her eyes for a moment. Let the word *over* echo in her mind, and left without shutting his door. Instead of going back to her place, she marched back down the steps. Maybe Justin was lying about Quinn leaving with Prentiss. If she was that mad, she would've left on her own. Bree needed a shoulder to cry on. She needed to finish their wonderful evening together. She needed to hold his hand again. She needed him as a friend too, because Justin was obviously not taking the improvements she'd made very well. She legitimately needed Quinn. The date didn't end right.

The walk to the building was peaceful. She looked up to a cloudy sky that had a bit of a glow from the city lights from afar. She paused. What would she say to him? Would he be waiting for her? Maybe he would be on his way over thinking the same thing. She looked towards the Dogwood building and saw a figure coming towards her. She squinted.

"Quinn?" she called out.

"Yeah!" a voice called back. Her heart raced but something was wrong.

"Hi Bree!" It was Ted. Shit. It was just Stalker Ted making his rounds of nosy for the night. "What are you doing over here tonight? Do you deliver pizzas now?"

"Yes, Ted. I deliver pizzas in my regular clothes and walk around empty handed." Her sarcasm only confused him. "Sorry, I'm kidding. I'm just walking around. You know, getting some air." Wow, why was she so mean to Ted? It wasn't his fault he wasn't Quinn.

"Care if I join you?" He sounded sad. She wanted to keep walking but she still wasn't sure what she was going do or say if Quinn was there. She was suddenly embarrassed by her behavior towards Ted. *I deserve this terrible karma.*

"Okay, Ted. We'll do a lap around the lot, but then I have to take care of some things."

"Bree?"

"Yes, Teddy?"

"Why do the people we like never like us back?"

"Aw, what do you mean, Ted?"

"I asked someone out and she said no."

"Oh, well, it happens to all of us, Ted. Trust me."

"Every time?" Ted said.

"Every time it mattered," she said. "I once asked out my very best friend in high school in front of hundreds of other kids and he said no."

"Wow, mine wasn't that bad," Ted said and then started laughing. She felt a little better as his mood seemed to change.

"Ted. I gotta go talk to Quinn now, okay?"

"He isn't home," said Ted. Justin was right. He did indeed take off with Prentiss. Just then a familiar car pulled up and Jill got out with her guitar. "Hi, Jill!" Ted called out.

From the look of her face, she was unsure how Ted knew who she was.

"Uh, hi." Bree gave her a "save me" look and she obliged. "Bree, you ready to talk now?"

"Yeah." About what?

Ted chuckled to himself again and continued his stroll alone. Jill stood with her guitar case next to her like a friend who always had her back.

"Tell me this, Bree. Did you sleep with Justin? Don't lie, don't give me a reason, just tell—"

"No," Bree said, trying not to get angry. She knew she *would* have, but didn't, and sure as hell wouldn't now. No one but Justin knew that, and surely he wouldn't have a reason to tell her. She was glad things had worked out as they had.

"Then why is he all of a sudden into you so much?"

"Look Jill. Justin's a bit whimsical when it comes to who he's after. He has a hard time connecting feelings with sex. In fact, who he has sex with never even involves feel—" Oops! "I mean, sometimes it does. I mean—"

"You know what? I've done nothing but try and help you all summer and I've even planted some seeds in Quinn's ear about you, and this is the thanks I get?"

"I'm sorry! Look I don't know what I'm saying half the time, but trust me, Justin doesn't have a thing for me. In fact he just yelled at me louder than you just did. In fact, everyone hates me right now, so are you happy?"

"Yeah, I am. And you can forget me ever saying anything nice about you to Quinn ever again. In fact, you'll be lucky if he ever talks to you again. And in case you were wondering about our bedroom situation. Yes. Yes, I have fucked him! As recently as this summer."

Bree's ears insisted it was a lie. "Good, go write a fucking song about it!" She turned and walked back to her apartment. Her entire circle seemed to be turning on her all at once.

She slumped as she walked up the steps to her apartment. Attached to her door was a lease renewal notice. Even if she could afford another few months it wouldn't be worth it. Justin hated her. Jill hated her. Just an hour ago she was holding Quinn's hand and making wedding plans, but after Jill talked to him there was probably nothing she could do. Had he really had sex with his roommate? It was the first mark against him if so.

She stopped at her place to change into some sweats and then took a blanket and her phone to her spot on the rooftop. As she lay on her back, small sprinkles touched her skin every few seconds. She didn't care. The sprinkles picked up. They weren't cold. More and more they fell, until it was suddenly a shower of rain. She put her phone in the pouch of her sweatshirt and continued to see how long she could withstand the pelting drops. Thunder rumbled in the distance. She struggled to keep her eyes open as the drops fell upon her. Her hair dampened and then grew wet. Steam rose from the rooftop around her, submerging her in a surreal fog. She started to get a chill, but part of her started to enjoy it. It was as if the rain was washing any guilt away from her. She hadn't done anything wrong other than love someone and reject someone else's love. That wasn't a sin. Somehow, out of all of this, she would find the right person, the right job, the right place to live. She would know what to do eventually. Her phone gave a quick vibration from an incoming text from a number she didn't recognize.

"Hey—it's Brad. I'll be in town in a few days, lunch?"

Time to get the hell out of this complex and start touring.

39

Several days of solitaire and writing had Bree feeling better. A dramatic life change would work best for problems. She thought about all of those clichéd speeches about going for it in life, achieving goals, following her dreams, finding her own path and blah blah blah. It was time to put that into action. She was done saying no to any opportunity, and whatever mistakes she made, she would have to live with. How could things get any worse? She had Brad in her corner now, and he was more successful than Quinn, Justin, Mark and anyone else she knew put together.

She looked in the mirror one last time before heading out. Since her firing, the weight was starting to come off. A lot of that was lack of appetite from being upset so much. She remembered how many snacks she must have left stashed away in her old office. Oh well, someone else could have them, and the pounds, too.

The restaurant Brad chose was a bit of a drive and slightly out of her price range, but she figured he would buy. She went out and bought a calendar to book all of her dates in, and then filled it with random other decoy items to give it the illusion of something she had always carried with her. She dressed mildly sexy, but just with jeans and heels. A low-cut shirt was reliable for something like lunch. It probably would be just lunch since Brad had explained he was passing through. She kept her texts brief with him so she wouldn't seem clingy or overly excited about touring. She had ended the exchange with *"Looking forward to seeing you"* to which he had replied with *"Me too, it's been too long."* The upper hand was hers. She had thrown out a compliment, he saw it and raised it to imply that he missed her after only a few days. Maybe it was more than just lunch? Just in case, she did a load of laundry so that she could wear her best panties.

Why did her dignity always leave her in the laundry room? She recalled earlier in the summer when she had schemed the not-so-chance meeting with Quinn. She had tried so hard all summer, and last Wednesday it seemed to be coming together, but she hadn't heard from him since. Prentiss must have reminded him over and over how much better looking she was than Bree. She didn't want to quit, but really had no idea what else to try. Maybe laying low a few days would be more effective than whatever plan she could come up with. It's not like Quinn had completely forgotten the evening with her. He remembered holding hands. He knew what he was doing. Just once during all of the sex he was having with Prentiss, the thought of Bree would have to pop up. *He has to wonder, doesn't he?*

Surprisingly relaxed and confident, Bree pulled into the lot, wondering which car was Brad's. Would he wait at the door for her or would he take a table already, like people always seemed to do in the movies? *"I'm here"* she texted to the number. She had not saved it in her phone yet. That was bad luck. She waited another minute and restarted her car so that the AC would kick back on. Finally she programmed the number in under "Brad Brewer" just as a response came.

"I'm at bar, rum and Coke for you?" He knew her drink already. This was definitely going to be more than lunch.

She inspected herself in the rearview mirror one more time and smiled a now much-straighter smile. The doctor had told her that she would eventually learn to make a charming smile. Now was a time to put it to the test. She took the cut of her shirt and lowered it, then raised it up a bit, then lowered it even more. Who cared? He had already seen her naked and she wanted it to happen again. Right then an epiphany hit her. What did Quinn have over Brad? Yes, some abs and arms and an amazing back, but what about everything else? Brad was on the doorstep of stardom and she could be his sidekick. Brad offered her a career and life that was well beyond a mediocre apartment complex of friends who now seemed to hate her. She could move to L.A. She could come back and piss on everyone who had disowned her. She'd cut her mother some slack, but her dad would definitely be on the shit list. Quinn would be begging for her. Once she made it, she could afford a personal trainer, hair extensions, and designers would be paying *her* to wear their clothes. She'd be sure to thank her old boss for firing her in a note that included *PS: fuck off.*

Bree floated into the restaurant as a distinguished looking man opened the door for her. She turned right to the bar and there was Brad.

But it wasn't Brad Brewer. It was her ex-boyfriend from college. He was smiling. She was in shock. He got up to greet her, but she was still motionless. Her heart dropped, then panicked into a racing pulse. No words yet.

"Well, hi, stranger. Wow, you look great, Bree." That voice. It all came rushing back. The smell of the apartment they shared, the shitty music they listened to together, and even his same cologne injected stimuli into her, sending her back several years to a different time that almost seemed like the different life of a different person. The love, the arguments, the friendship, the trips, and just being carefree, it all flooded her brain.

"I," she started to say. She couldn't tell him she was expecting someone else. "Um, yeah, hi."

"Wow, you look beautiful, and did you get braces? What made you finally do it? I always liked your smile how it was . . ." On and on he went about how great she looked. She took a moment to inspect the changes in the man she used to think she was going to marry. He seemed taller somehow, as if he had hit a second puberty for another inch or two. His hair was still full and black. He was bigger but not fatter, just thicker in the shoulders. He hugged her, still trying to catch her up on the last few years all at once. She could smell his skin and it made her tingle, first in the good way that pheromones subconsciously do, but then she remembered the bitter way it ended. She hated herself more than him at that time. Were things so bad? They were young and stupid. They woke up at eleven most days and worked multiple part time jobs at places where the bosses were usually high. They did fun things on a whim. They had sex outside all the time. He was good at that. By a couple months into the relationship he knew every button to push on her body. She almost wished that he could've written an instruction manual for her to share with any men in the future, although Brad Brewer seemed to already have read it. Their embrace ended and he soaked her in one more time, stealing an extra glance at her cleavage. *This wasn't for you,* she wanted to tell him.

"Well, what have you been up to?" *To tell him or not to tell him.* Brad was the kind of person still connected with everyone. If she was going to tell him about the comedy, it would spread within days to all of her classmates, college friends, and other shitheads Brad still kept up with. She surely wasn't going to tell him about getting fired.

"Oh you know, just living the dream," she nearly mumbled.

"Yeah, me too. I started my own company after the last stock market crash and have done really well in the recovery of it all. Good timing, dumb luck, whatever you want to call it, things are really good now." *Ah yes, typical Brad. Give him a bullshit answer to a question he didn't care about in the first place and then let him ramble on for ten more minutes.* He went on about his business and even offered to start an account for her if she needed. The funny thing was he didn't mention a relationship. No wedding ring on his finger and, besides, if he was happily with someone, he wouldn't be texting ex-girlfriends out of the blue to have lunch with them. Bree continued to nod along with the occasional *Jeez* or *Wow, that's good*, but the whole time she was thinking about how bad she needed to hear from the other Brad. The real Brad. The Brad of her future, not her past. Finally something significant came out of his mouth: "So, I heard you're not working property anymore."

"How'd you know that?" she asked.

"Well, I had to track you down and your mother gave me your work number. Or your old work number, I guess. She wouldn't give me your cell. What'd I ever do to her?"

"Oh, don't worry about it. Yeah, I've moved on."

"Oh yeah? What's next?"

"*Pending*" was not a successful sounding answer. "The arts," she said hoping that being vague would let him start talking about himself again.

"What kind?" Nope.

"Comedy. Stand-up, you know. Tell some jokes, get some laughs, whatever."

"No way. I don't believe you!" he said. Of course he didn't. There's no way he could comprehend her life being more interesting than his.

"Yeah, I'm kind of waiting on an important call, so if I have to step away for a moment . . . You know, showbiz." She knew there was no chance that call was going to come during lunch, but it gave her a sense of power over the white-collared clone her ex-boyfriend's professional life had become.

"Look at you," he said first, in that patronizing joking way. Then he said it again looking straight into her eyes. "Look at you, so beautiful. I should've never given up on us." A stirring went into Bree's heart. Compliments were compliments, and she wasn't used to them. Was this the result of being desperate all summer? Every guy who talked to her she fell in love with? Quinn was one thing, but she recalled even Mark mattering for a moment just because of some romantic poems. She had to get herself under control. She wasn't used to being called beautiful. She wasn't used to guys being interested in her. It was so much easier when she could pursue and fail miserably. It sucked, but it was easier. Though she had to admit to herself that the old attraction, the old spark as they say, was more than flickering. She caught herself with dirty thoughts and wondered if Brad had a hotel room nearby where they could get a few drinks and he could put that "Manual to Having Sex with Bree, Version 2.0" to good use. She looked down and noticed that her drink was almost empty. That wasn't going to help. Before she could stop him Brad signaled for a refill. She knew that he knew what he was doing. *Now* it was going to be more than lunch. The manual had a preface about how to get her to bed, too. No matter how mad she would get at him, somehow she always found herself naked and forgiving during that what now seemed not-so-distant past. *It wouldn't count today since I've already been with him. Sleeping with someone I thought I was going to marry isn't slutty.*

"So where are you living these days, Brad?" It was the first time she had said his name to him in years. It felt weird saying it to a different Brad from a few days ago.

"Right now? I'm in a transition to moving back to the area. Office space is more affordable and I'm going to be expanding in the next few years. I just need a couple guys under me to take care of the smaller stuff. It's a risk, but I think I can pull it off. What about you?"

"Well, I'm moving out of my apartment at the end of the month and I have no idea where I'm going." Stupid rum. "If I'm going to tour a lot, it wouldn't make any sense to pay hundreds of dollars for an empty apartment, you know?"

"If?" he asked.

"Well, yeah. Thus the important phone call. I can't exactly tell you what it's about, but it's a really great opportunity if it happens." *Just spill everything, you idiot!*

"Seriously? You're going to be famous or on TV or something? Did you have an audition?"

"No, but it's a lot of work if it comes through. I'll let you know when I find out."

"Well, if you need a place to crash for however long, I've got a finished basement. Would that be weird?"

Hell yes, it would be weird! "No," she said, sucking her drink through her straw at a much faster pace. "I can't afford a lot, but it might work." She couldn't even look him in the eye as she answered. How could he just casually spring that on her? His feelings towards her were definite, but hers were a twisted mess, as usual. She pieced the scenario together in her head. Four days on the road with Brad Brewer. They'd have sex maybe once or twice, she'd come home Monday from a week of shows—and do *this* Brad when he got home from his office that night if she felt like it. She could head straight down to her "lair" and write jokes about her new exciting life while Quinn got Prentiss out of his system and she took one step closer to becoming a star with straight teeth. She could see how Quinn liked it knowing she was living with someone of the opposite gender.

"No, it wouldn't be weird," he paused and looked away just so he could engage her eyes again when he turned back, "or no, you don't need it?"

"Well, it would be weird, but I think we could handle it."
*Anything else, rum? Want to talk to him about parenting a
child as well?* "Money between friends can cause trouble."

"Oh, don't worry about it. A couple hundred bucks would
do. Especially if you're only going to be around a few days a
week." This was making sense. It was either that or her mother's place. Cats. A phone that still rang from telemarketers all
hours of the day. Limited comforts, like basic cable and weak
air conditioning. Christmas music the day after Halloween.
Her aunts visiting constantly. Not having a place to have sex
with guys. Yep, her mother's place was not a good option.

"Shouldn't we, like, think about this? I mean, it's not like
we're just two old chums," she said, finally being the first
to admit the idea was a bit crazy. "We should talk about it
more."

"Yeah, that's what we're doing. Look, no pressure. If you
want to move in I'm not going to take that as a sign that you
want to get back together. I'll be honest, just in this time
that we've spent here today I'm remembering the way I used
to feel about you, Bree. I'm curious about what would happen because I think we're both two different people now.
No pressure, but if you ever wanted to give us another shot.
Well, . . ." Oh wow. There it was again. A swooning came over
her because someone was sharing their feelings with her. She
tried to fight it. *If Stalker Ted came onto you like this, would
you hook up with him, too?* She scolded herself, but it wasn't
working. She just wanted to be with someone. Was Quinn
ever going to feel the same? Was he even the man that she
thought he was? She knew Jill would always be in the picture. Hell, she'd be part of the wedding party. How could she
marry Quinn and have wedding pictures that included a girl

he had previously slept with? That might not have even been true. She thought about how jealous she was of Quinn living with a girl. Maybe she could do the same to him. That's what Jill had implied earlier in the summer. Moving in with an ex was definitely a way to play the game of love with a challenge like him.

Brad told her about the house and a little more about his business, but she was already sold. He agreed to take her by to see if she wanted to move in. Justin would shit if he knew what was going on, but then again, she probably needed a solid break from him, too. If nothing else, some space. How would she even share the news about this?

Brad paid for lunch with a fifty and she followed his Audi to a nice neighborhood just far enough away from the busy streets, but not too far away from everywhere she needed to get to. It wasn't perfect, but it was no longer Stevens Chicago Properties.

"I didn't know you were *building* a house," she said, not even hiding her amazement.

"Yeah, it's all but finished. I just figured I'd go for it. Like I said, business is going well." He led her down through his empty fortress of fresh white walls, hardwood floors, and plush carpets. The basement alone was much bigger than anything she had lived in before.

"See, I built it along this hill so the basement has its own door. Just don't be sneaking any young men in and out of here," he laughed. Funny he should mention that. She had already envisioned Quinn pulling his jeans up and skipping into the yard as Brad barged in on her without knocking.

"You know me, all right!" she laughed back nervously. "Is three hundred enough?"

"More than enough, babe." He hadn't called her that since before the fight that ultimately broke them up. Did he do it on purpose? The word echoed and caused another time warp in her mind and heart. What was he doing? What was she doing? He knew it caught her off guard, but in a good way. He took a step closer and put his arms around her. She felt something against her waist. It was her phone.

"I gotta answer this," she said, snapping out of the moment.

"Of course," he said stepping back.

"Oh, hi, Brad *Brewer*."

40

Dear Quinn,

I guess I can't really ask where you've been the last few weeks because I know the phone works two ways. I hope that Wednesday night didn't get you into too much trouble. I had fun, though it's exhausting fending so many women (and one guy) off all night. I could go into details about how you make me feel, but you already know. You've heard them. You've heard them from everyone you encounter, I was no different. I know that you can have anyone you want and that I'm not even among your top choices, but that's okay. It wasn't meant to be at this point.

Tell Jill I'm sorry for whatever I did or said to her. If you see Justin, well, I have no idea what to say to him. By the time you read this, I'll have already moved to a new home. I have a friend who's leasing out a basement to me while I'm on the road with Brad. I have no idea how it's going to go, but at this point in my life it seems like the best option. I need to get away from this place. I need to tear my heart away from you. You've had it since that day you walked into the leasing office and we shared an umbrella. There are some things I just need to work on as a person as I evaluate my emotions and figure out what direction to take my life.

I would've liked to talk to you about all this, but you're like a drug to me. I can't allow myself "one last hurrah" with you because it will only hurt more. Also, I want to apologize for infringing on your current relationship and any other tension I may have caused with the people who you care about. So anyway, I'll be on the road pretty steadily for the rest of the year, hopefully getting better at my new career and meeting the right people. I don't know when or if we'll see each other again, but I wish you nothing but the best. I think I've already told you this, but I was in a drunken state before, so it may have come off as insincere.—I love you, Bree

Quinn stood by the pod of mailboxes near his building and reread the entire letter. His car was still idling as Jill pulled up in hers. "Where's Prentiss? We're supposed to have our big talk about the apartment situation, aren't we?"

"We broke up this morning," said Quinn.

Book Two

Coming later in 2014

1

The showroom at Chuck's Comedy Club was nearly empty as the last few crowd members made their way out; some in costume, most not. Justin reflected back on the previous Halloweens of his twenties. He had hooked up with a sexy nurse one year, a schoolgirl the next. One time it was just a girl who wore her underwear to a party and called herself Victoria's Secret. Halloween parties were the one occasion he was perfectly fine arriving at alone because he knew he'd have company on his way home. This year it was different. The late show had ended and he hadn't really been in the loop about any gatherings. Sometimes people from the show would invite him to wherever they were headed, but not tonight. It took him awhile just to recall the last time he had actually been to a party. Weeks? Maybe months?

The comedy club seemed more quelled than usual, and the staff was in a rush to get out. Justin sat sipping the last few ounces of a warm beer and scrolling through his phone. He thumbed through the past text conversations with this random girl or that, all the while daring himself to review the last few interactions with Bree for the hundredth time. It was beyond a game of chess. It was a war of who could wait longer and seem less interested in each other's lives. He waited a full week after Quinn was nice enough to show him the letter she sent during the summer. After much consideration, he texted a simple question mark to her. Two days later she returned the same symbol of punctuation. Weeks went by as neither one would put aside pride long enough to see how the other was doing. Justin had a pretty good idea, though.

Brad's website kept an up-to-date schedule of the shows on his tour. As his opener, Bree was performing in the best comedy clubs from Seattle to Philadelphia with even some upcoming shows scheduled in New York City. Halloween night ended no differently than the other nights of the past two months; he went to his bedroom alone and slammed his laptop shut before trying to fall asleep, knowing that Bree had now had sex with Brad in all four American time zones.

The following Thursday he was surprised to see Jill at open mic night.

"Where have you been?" He approached her as if her absence had nothing to do with him. He hoped she would play along. It seemed like weeks (maybe it was) since he had had a real conversation with someone he respected. The few pseu-do-dates from the internet felt like role-playing and went nowhere.

"I went back home for a little while. Had to get some equip-ment and visit my old voice coach," she said. Justin started to place an order to the bartender when she continued.

"Did a lot of writing too. I missed having something to write about." Uh oh, he thought. He pictured an album cover of hers with his face on a dartboard.

"That's cool. Anything new tonight?"

"Maybe," she said looking away, uninterested in continuing the conversation. She began digging through her guitar case, and, unable to find what she was looking for, headed back out to her car.

"Great talkin' to ya," Justin said once she was out of range. Just then Jeff, the manager, signaled Justin back to his office. "I'll be right there," he said.

Jeff was quiet on the walk back and finally broke the silence with "Wasn't that that Jill chick you used to see?"

"Yep, she's back with new songs. Hopefully it'll help raise our numbers back up."

"About that," Jeff started. He sat and leaned back in his office chair, crossed then uncrossed his legs while keeping perfect eye contact with Justin. "We're probably going to make this the last Thursday open mic. The club's weekend numbers have been picking up, so as the weather gets colder and baseball season ends, we're going to have a normal Thursday night show with the professionals."

"Oh, that's cool. I was getting tired of these amateurs bombing every week anyway. I'd rather work with the pros, too."

"Well, here's where it gets hairy . . ." Justin's heart sunk into his stomach. Jeff's eyes glanced up to the clock away from Justin. "We're gonna try some different openers for the next few months. I mean, we'll still give you a week here or there, let's say mid-February, but for now, they want to stop using you as the house emcee."

"They?" Justin asked. He was trying to stay calm but his last bit of self-worth was disappearing.

"You know, the owners, their friends, patrons. A lot of the comment cards are people saying they're ready to hear from some of the other local talent or even some guys from out of town. Plus we always paid you a little more, and with numbers down this summer, it just made sense. Look, why don't you hit the road yourself? Certainly you'd like some different audiences, right?"

"Are you going to book me somewhere?"

"You know I'm not a booker outside of this club. I can recommend you to a few clubs around the Midwest, but you gotta hustle your way into it like everyone else."

Justin instantly thought of Bree and how she slept her way to a tour of sold-out shows around the country. She was probably making the same amount of money as most middle-acts, and here he was being let go from a $50 a show gig that paid most of his bills.

Jeff got out his calendar and flipped through the next few months. "I've got February open. Valentine's Day weekend is always solid. You want that week?"

This was the conflict of showbiz. He had basically just been fired from a job, but would be allowed to come back in over three months when they could use him again if he wanted. His prideful instincts said to turn it down, but he knew better. "I'll take it," he said.

"Can you still host tonight, buddy?"

"How about you let someone else take a shot? I'm going to sit this one out." He caught his voice about to crack with emotion. He had never been fired before. True, there wasn't much to get fired from, but this felt so personal.

"I understand," said Jeff as Justin walked out of the office.

Justin kept his head down as he walked back out into the bar. The showroom was being seated slowly as the crowd was thin yet another week. It wasn't his fault no one came to amateur night. Hell, he didn't even like the show most weeks. He grabbed his coat off of the corner bar stool and put it on as he walked to the exit. Still staring at the ground he pushed open the door into a blustering wind.

"Where are you going?" Jill asked.

"Home," he said, still keeping his eyes on his feet. He pulled out from his front row parking spot and went through the familiar routine of walking up the steps alone. At exactly 8:00 he sat on his sunken couch and pictured Bree taking the stage to a sold-out crowd in Washington D.C. He hated himself for knowing her schedule, and now he hated himself even more for not having one of his own.

He had canceled his cable TV to save money awhile back, and it was too cold and windy to go up on the roof. He hadn't been up there in so long, it would just feel weird anyway. The wind blew harder, and some of the trees scraped up against his outside windows. Noises echoed through the hallway. Someone was banging something against a wall for some reason. By nine, Justin was sure he would be spending the entire evening awake and upset. What was that noise? Still frustrated and unable to find anything to watch on his two channels, he walked out into the hallway to figure out who was causing the disturbance. He listened a little closer. Those were heels. Someone was walking up and down the stairs in heels. The trips were infrequent, maybe every twenty minutes or so, but still. What kind of woman, other than a prostitute or stripper, does that much stair-climbing in heels when the elevator worked just fine? She's gotta be hot!

Justin threw on a large t-shirt and straightened his hair in the mirror. He then opted for a much smaller t-shirt to make his shoulders and arms look bigger. He lifted the front of the shirt to his nose and inhaled. "Clean enough," he said. He grabbed his keys and casually strolled down towards the steps just as the clicking got closer.

"Oh hi," he said pretending to be surprised.

"Well, hello," she said, already flirting back to him. Now he actually was surprised. She was dressed in what had to be the most expensive sweatpants and sweatshirt produced. It was some European brand he had never heard of, but the bright pink color and obviously smooth fabric hugged every part of her trim body. She was carrying a large box of picture frames with photos Justin was dying to see. He caught glimpses of college parties and perfect smiles in the thin frames that were about to spill from the box.

"Can I help you with those?" he asked. He started to take the box from her before she could even answer.

"What a gentleman," she said. "I'm moving in upstairs."

"No one else to help you?"

"Well, there was. My friend Kim was here a bit ago, but her feet were hurting." The heels.

"Why aren't you taking the elevator?" Justin said.

"They told us not to use it to move in because it can overheat if it goes up and down too many times. Is that not true?"

Justin's mind dipped its toe into the gutter. Should he make a joke about overheating and going up and down? Too soon. "Wow, the staff here. Sorry, I've never heard that, but that's Stevens Chicago Properties for you."

"Oh, trust me, I know," she said laughing. "It took me months just to get a lease here. I've been trying since summer."

Adrenaline poured into his arms as he now effortlessly lifted the box to his chest. He followed her up the flight of stairs, knowing exactly where she was headed to. There was only one empty unit on the floor above him. As she got to the door, he was nearly shaking. He hadn't been inside in months. Would it still smell the same? Did they change the carpet both he and Bree had spilled drinks on so many times? What would the place look like without her? There would be no bottle of rum on top of the fridge. No tipped-over pile of magazines next to some old sweatpants. They arrived at the door as she reached into her pocket for her key.

"It's in here somewhere," she said. Justin didn't mind the wait. He let himself stare at her. Her sleeve was rolled up to just below her elbow but still hugging her slender forearm.

She pulled her keys out as they fell to the floor. Don't stare at her ass, don't stare at her ass! It was perfect.

"I'm Justin by the way. I live downstairs."

"Oh, I'm sorry. I'm Amanda. Amanda Hark."

"Your name sounds familiar," he said but he couldn't remember why.

Made in the USA
San Bernardino, CA
19 April 2015